Home Front 1914–1918

Home Front

1914–1918

How Britain Survived the Great War

by IAN F.W. BECKETT

the national archives

First published in 2006 by
The National Archives
Kew, Richmond
Surrey, TW9 4DU, UK

www.nationalarchives.gov.uk

The National Archives (TNA) was formed
when the Public Record Office (PRO)
and Historical Manuscripts Commission (HMC)
combined in April 2003

A catalogue card for this book is available
from the British Library

ISBN 1 903365 81 3
978 1 903365 81 6

Jacket design, page design and typesetting by
Ken Wilson | point 918

Printed in the UK by
CPI Bath Press

Contents

ONE   War's Beginnings   7

TWO   Men at Work   17

THREE   Working Girls   65

FOUR   Life Goes On   107

FIVE   Enemies Within   145

SIX   Enemies Without   177

SEVEN   War's End   197

EPILOGUE   The First 'World' War   205

Chronology   216

Further Reading   219

Index   220

Author's acknowledgements

Quotations from documents in the care of the Imperial War Museum appear by permission of the Trustees of the Imperial War Museum and of the following copyright holders of papers located there: Mrs Christine Bland, D.P. White and the copyright holder for the Hollister Mss.

I also wish to acknowledge the tremendous assistance I have received from the staff of the National Archives, particularly Sheila Knight, who initiated the project, Alfred Symons, who arranged for the copying of the documents, and Jenny Speller, who undertook the picture research. At the Imperial War Museum, I received invaluable assistance from Rod Suddaby and Simon Robbins of the Department of Documents. None of the above, of course, bears any responsibility for errors in the text.

IAN F.W. BECKETT

PICTURE ACKNOWLEDGEMENTS

BRIDGEMAN ART LIBRARY p. 162
BRITISH LIBRARY p. 50
BURRELL COLLECTION / GLASGOW CITY COUNCIL p. 45
CHRISTIE'S IMAGES pp. 94, 163,
GETTY IMAGES / HULTON ARCHIVE pp. 9, 119, 120, 127
HAMMERSMITH AND FULHAM ARCHIVES AND LOCAL HISTORY CENTRE pp. 20–21, 30 (top), 39, 65, 139
HULTON DEUTSCH COLLECTION/CORBIS pp. 54–5,
ILN (Illustrated London News) p. 141
IMPERIAL WAR MUSEUM, London endpapers (royal visit to wartime clothing factory) Q30782, Q30783; p.7 Q27724; p. 10 Q53305; pp. 11–12 Q53298; p. 15 IWM 2987; p. 17 Q20031; p. 18 Q20051; p. 19 Q110144; p. 22 Q20099; pp. 28–9 Q30558–9; p. 30 (bottom) Q27740; p. 41 Q30873; p. 44 Q110142; p. 61 Q109783; p. 68 Q31089; p. 73 110BB1033; p. 74 Q30863; p.82 Q2453; p.87 Q31032; p.89 Q53310; p. 91 Q30832; p. 92 Q31065; p. 95 (right) Q33173; p. 99 Q96380; p. 107 Q96386; p. 109 IWM PST10996; p. 113 Album 148; p. 116 IWM PST4470; p. 118 Q31162; p. 122 Q96383; p. 123 Q30519; p. 124 Q30494; p. 128 Album 163; p. 131 IWM PST10115; p. 151 HU52451; p. 164 Q31030; p. 166 Q103334; p. 175 IWM PST10385; p. 177 Q53622; p. 179 Q53476; p. 194 Q30550; p. 197 Q30609.

The National Archives gratefully acknowledges the cooperation of the Imperial War Museum, whose collections cover all aspects of conflict involving Britain and the Commonwealth since the start of the 20th century. These rich resources are available online to search, browse and buy at www.iwmcollections.org.uk.
LONDON BOROUGH OF NEWHAM p. 34
THE NATIONAL ARCHIVES p. 14 ADM1/8388/228; p. 24 MUN5/165/1124/41; p. 25 MUN4/1084; p. 36 MUN5/297; p. 58 MUN5/165/1124/42; p. 75 MAF59/3; p. 80 (top) MAF59/3, (bottom) COPY1/526; p. 81 MUN4/1085; p.83 MUN/297; p.85 EXT1/315/2; p. 88 MUN5/297; p. 90 MUN5/165/1124/48; p. 95 (left) HO45/11382; p. 108 HO45/18971; p. 112 MUN4/671; p. 114 MUN4/671; pp. 148–9; p. 184 MH8/9; p. 186 AIR1/569/16/15/142; p. 192 AIR1/7/6/98; p. 200 WORK21/74; p. 205 & 214–15 WORK21/74; p. 207 CO23/281; p. 208–9 ZPER34; p. 211–12 WORK21/74
PEOPLE'S HISTORY MUSEUM, MANCHESTER p. 157
POPPERFOTO pp. 70, 145, 169, 199
RONALD GRANT ARCHIVE pp. 134, 136, 137, 171, 174
TOPFOTO pp. 67, 77, 147, 202

ONE

—

War's
Beginnings

Once the Great War – the First World War – was imminent in the summer of 1914, there was a readiness, and even an eagerness, to accept its challenge. Or at least that is what later generations thought. It was commonplace in the 1920s to stress the war's inevitability. Caroline Playne's *The Pre-War Mind in Britain* for example, published in 1928, spoke of the general mood as one of infectious mental contagion, which 'swept down the mindless, expectant, half-frightened, wondering crowds, and … swept down progressives, earnest people, intelligent people as well'. In fact, the contribution of the popular mood to the actual events in July 1914 was limited. For one thing, the public had little time in which to react to events. There was no long-building tension, no sense of inevitability. The public had little influence on decisions taken, and war, when it did come, was the result of diplomatic steps (or diplomatic failures) and conclusions reached by relatively small coteries of leaders.

Caught by surprise

On 28 June 1914, the heir to the Austro-Hungarian Empire, Archduke Franz Ferdinand, had been assassinated in Sarajevo, in Bosnia-Herzegovina. Austria-Hungary blamed Serbia, its regional competitor. There was no noticeable sense of impending foreign crisis in the British press, however, until 29 July, attention having been fixed on the continuing Irish Home Rule problem. The Foreign Office was equally taken by surprise. Winston Churchill, then the First Lord of the Admiralty, wrote later that it was only on 24 July, when news arrived of the Austro-Hungarian ultimatum to the Serbian government, that the Cabinet became fully aware of the developing situation in Europe. The Cabinet meeting had actually been called to discuss Ireland, but, as Churchill graphically described it, 'the parishes of Fermanagh and Tyrone faded back into the mists and squalls of Ireland, and a strange light began to fall and grow upon the map of Europe'. As late as 31 July the Prime Minister, Herbert Asquith, had told the Archbishop of Canterbury that Britain would not intervene in any European war; but, as Churchill wrote in a note passed to the Chancellor, David Lloyd George, on 1 August, ' the march of events will be dominating'.

The final crisis unfolded over the bank holiday weekend. With Russia mobilizing in defence of Serbia, Germany – Austria-Hungary's ally – had declared war on Russia and its 'Triple Entente' ally France. German forces invaded Luxembourg on 2 August and demanded passage through neutral Belgium. The news of the German ultimatum reached London on the morning of bank holiday Monday, 3 August.

There had been little sympathy in Britain for Serbia to this point. In Manchester, for example, the opposition to intervention on the part of

A big news day. Crowds assemble in Parliament Square, London, around noon of 4 August 1914, the day Britain entered the war.

New arrivals. Bewildered
Belgian refugees in
transit, outside Hudson's
Furniture Repository
near Victoria Station,
London, September 1914.

the *Manchester Guardian* reflected the fears of the local influential business community about the economic consequences of involvement. As the newspaper's editor C.P. Scott noted, 'We care as little for Belgrade as Belgrade does for Manchester.' The Manchester Chamber of Commerce even sent a telegram to the British Foreign Secretary, Sir Edward Grey, urging neutrality. They weren't the only ones worrying. The Governor of the Bank of England had earlier warned Lloyd George about the potential of financial collapse in the event of war, leading to the closure of the London Stock Exchange on 31 July. As Lloyd George later wrote, 'Money shivered at the prospect. Big Business everywhere wanted to keep out.'

There were some anti-war demonstrations in provincial British towns and cities, organized by the Independent Labour Party, and a small demonstration for peace in Trafalgar Square on Sunday 2 August, in which the volatile nature of the public mood saw one speaker being pushed off the platform. In the words of one witness:

> As he fell somebody lifted an umbrella and whacked him over the head. A venturesome man climbed the lamp post on the island in the centre of the road and tied a Union Jack to the top. A great cheer went up but another youth swarmed up and pulled it down again.

King George recorded in his diary on 1 August that 'public opinion here' was 'still dead against our joining in the war', a mood reiterated by that week's edition of *Punch*:

> *Why should I follow your fighting line*
> *For a matter that's no concern of mine?*
> *I shall be asked to a general scrap*
> *All over the European map,*
> *Dragged into someone else's war,*
> *For that's what a double entente is for.*

Towards the other end of the social scale, on 3 August the South Wales Miners Federation expressed its determination to proceed as normal be refusing a government request to cut short the annual miners' holiday, and this was even reaffirmed by the union on 5 August.

The German invasion of Belgium began on 4 August. Belgium hardly had time to react to the situation at all, but its king, Albert, and his prime minister had had no hesitation in refusing the ultimatum, immediately appealing to the guarantors of Belgian neutrality under the 1839 Treaty of London, principally Britain. In many respects, the crucial decisions that led to involvement in the war were not taken by the Cabinet as a whole but largely by Asquith and Grey and, to a lesser

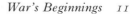

Marching as to war.
A stream of recruits
for Kitchener's 'New
Armies' march through
Regent's Park, London,
September 1914.

AT THE COURT AT BUCKINGHAM PALACE,

The 3rd day of August, 1914.

PRESENT,

THE KING'S MOST EXCELLENT MAJESTY IN COUNCIL.

WHEREAS there was this day read at the Board a Memorial from the Right Honourable the Lords Commissioners of the Admiralty, in the words following, viz. :—

> "WHEREAS we are of opinion that the present state of Public Affairs justifies Officers of the Reserved and Retired Lists being called into Active Service temporarily; we would humbly submit that Your Majesty will be pleased to authorize us to call on such Officers to hold themselves in readiness for Active Service, and to sanction our employing any of such Officers as we may think fit. We would also submit that compulsory retirement from the Active List on account of age be suspended in such cases as we think fit."

HIS MAJESTY, having taken the said Memorial into consideration, was pleased, by and with the advice of His Privy Council, to approve of what is therein proposed. And the Right Honourable the Lords Commissioners of the Admiralty are to give the necessary directions herein accordingly.

ALMERIC FITZROY.

All hands on deck. A memorandum records the King's assent for the calling up of naval reserves on the outbreak of war.

extent, Churchill. In the end it was only the threat of resignation by Grey and Asquith that forced the Cabinet to honour pre-war naval commitments to France on 2 August – to safeguard the Channel while the French Fleet deployed to the Mediterranean. It was the German ultimatum to Belgium, and not actual German invasion, that triggered in turn the British ultimatum to Germany, which expired at 11 p.m. on 4 August 1914. From that day, Britain – the third of the Entente powers – was at war with the so-called Central Powers of Germany, Austria-Hungary and their allies.

The Cabinet divisions encouraged, years later, an increasingly fashionable view that British entry to the war was unnecessary, even if the intervention of the British Expeditionary Force (BEF) on the Continent in its early stages probably did prevent a German victory. The Foreign Office had concluded that the 1839 treaty did not require Britain to go to Belgium's assistance in all circumstances, and some British military and naval planners had themselves contemplated violating Belgian neutrality, if necessary to do so, in order to take the war to German soil. There is also no doubt that the true extent of Britain's 'moral commitment' to supporting France, since the initiation of staff talks between the British and French general staffs in 1905, had been concealed from the public and many in government. Most ministers remained unaware of these talks until 1911, and the German invasion of Belgium was a political gift to Asquith in terms of preserving his Liberal government: only two Cabinet ministers and a junior minister resigned. It was not, though, in Britain's long-term strategic interests to allow Germany either to dominate the Low Countries and the Channel ports or to upset the balance of power in Europe. And even if Germany's immediate war aims had been limited by a need to keep Britain neutral, a victorious Germany would have soon threatened British interests. Unpleasant though the consequences were for Britain, the First World War was a necessary war.

Gathering the 'First 100,000'. Alfred Leete's famous recruiting poster of Kitchener was issued on 5 September 1914.

The violation of Belgian neutrality began to change the public mood, large crowds gathering in Trafalgar Square and outside Buckingham Palace on the last two days and nights of peace. The King had to appear no less than three times on the palace balcony on the evening of 4 August in response to the demands of the crowd, which would simply not disperse. The philosopher Bertrand Russell, later a notable pacifist, spent the evening of 3 August walking near Trafalgar Square, 'noticing cheering crowds' and discovering 'to my amazement that average men and women were delighted at the prospect of war'. By contrast, the journalist F.S. Oliver was delighted to find a resurgence of what he regarded as national spirit: 'I had not conceived it possible that a nation could be born again so quickly. This war even now has undone the evils of a generation.' Yet, in common with other crowds appearing in other European cities, the one in London was composed primarily of the middle class and the young. While the throng was somewhere between

6,000 and 10,000 in number, this was, after all, a city of 7 million people. For many other people beyond the heady scenes of Trafalgar Square, anxiety was the prevailing mood.

Amid some panic buying and food hoarding, mobilization of the British armed forces proceeded. The plans put in place before the war by the amply named 'Committee of Imperial Defence's Committee on the Co-ordination of Departmental Action on the Outbreak of War' went smoothly into effect, three successive editions of the so-called *War Book* having already appeared in 1912, 1913 and 1914. On 5 August the great imperial proconsul, Field Marshal Lord Kitchener, became Secretary of State for War and, on the following day, he appealed for 100,000 men to come forward to join the army, soon to be followed by an appeal for a further 100,000 men on 28 August.

A total war

Kitchener expected a long war – he thought at least three years. It was not a view shared by many, the public subscribing to the notion that it would be 'over by Christmas'. Lloyd George, as Chancellor of the Exchequer, had announced on 4 August that it would be 'business as usual'. Of course, it would not. Moreover, it would be a war that would have a profound domestic impact on Britain, at least in the short term. Government and people were, in due course, forced to confront the realities not only of massive casualties, but also of a conflict where it was just as vital to out-produce as to out-fight the enemy. Conscription, introduced in 1916, was one dramatic change from society before the war; but wartime mobilization also meant mobilization of the economy, with ever-increasing state control and intervention touching the lives of every man, woman and child. In this new kind of war, in which civilians on the home front were as important to sustaining the national war effort as servicemen at the fighting front itself, civilians themselves were now a legitimate target for attack.

In addition to such new and unexpected impositions as government interference in labour matters, the advent of rationing, licensing restrictions and British Summer Time, the British people also experienced aerial bombardment. Political leaders realized that the contribution of ordinary men and women to the war effort required political, social and economic reward; and women in particular were employed in industry in substantially larger numbers than ever before. Not all of these developments were to last, in the medium or longer term, and many people and interest groups sought to, and did, return to the pre-war status quo after 1918. Nonetheless, during the war years it seemed that the conflict had dramatically changed the way in which people lived, at all levels of society.

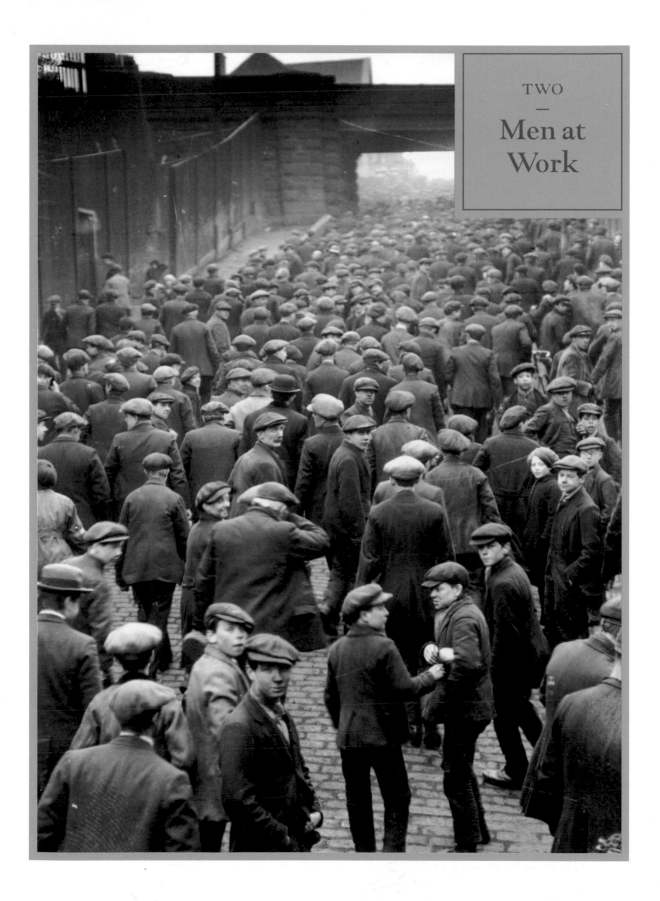

(*below*) Taking a rest. A shipyard worker from the Swan Hunter and Wigham Richardson yard.

(*right*) Hard physical work. Women at Glasgow Corporation's Gas Department empty a coal wagon, September 1916.

One measure of the transition to the kind of modern 'total' war that the First World War represented was that it became as important to mobilize industry and its workers as it was to mobilize men on the battlefield. The outbreak of war resulted, therefore, in increased government control marked by the appearance of new ministries, departments and agencies. More often than not, these appeared in key areas as a result of the incapacity of existing organizations, both public and private, to meet new demands. Control of the distribution of labour and of industrial production, especially that of munitions, was crucial. In the process, all aspects of the labour market and of people's working lives were to be increasingly regularized by the state.

In spite of this, production levels fell by about ten per cent between 1914 and 1917 through economic dislocation, resulting from trade disruption, shortages of raw materials and manpower problems. Inevitably, too, the concentration on war production involved a reduction in consumer production and generally altered the pattern of regional employment. Certain sectors of industry were obviously stimulated by the particular demands of modern war. In turn, pre-war trends could be further distorted by new demand. Coal, shipping and heavy industry, all previously in decline, were revitalized. Some industries contracted, either through the decline in exports such as cotton and wool, or through having little protection against recruitment, as with the building and

paper trades. In the case of the Scottish jute industry, based in Dundee, exports had been vital before the war. In wartime, military demand for sandbags and the need for sacks for food distribution resulted in large profits that more than compensated for the lost exports.

The war also stimulated the growth of industries that were little established previously, such as scientific-instrument making and the aircraft industry. War also naturally tended to strengthen larger manufacturers at the

expense of smaller ones. Through the need of the state to ensure war production, the position of working people generally improved in the short term. Wartime gains, however, were not always sustained.

Bigger government

The Defence of the Realm Act (DORA), which became law on 8 August 1914, was the first indication of the government's intention to give itself sweeping new powers. Its provisions were extended on 18 August and 27 November 1914 and again in both 1915 and 1916. The Defence of the Realm (Amendment No 2) Act in March 1915, for example, gave the government powers over engineering, as a first step

The new face of war.
These aircraft fuselages
were being housed in the
Hammersmith Palais
dance hall, London,
hence the unusual decor.

Dilution in action. A young women helps an older male worker operate a magazine drilling plate, at Swan Hunter and Wigham Richardson.

in placing the country on a total war footing: firms could now be forced to take government work if they had the necessary facilities to do so.

In most of the countries at war, railways were swiftly taken under state control in August 1914. In Britain this did not mean nationalization as such, since the individual rail companies were guaranteed the same level of profits they had enjoyed in 1913 and, through the Railway Executive Committee, the rail system was pointedly administered not *by* the government but *for* the government. Indeed, since control was initially intended to last for just one week, this necessitated renewal of the requisition measure every seven days for the duration of the war! Of course, the assumption in 1914 was that intervention would not be necessary for long.

The first significant new government agency was the Ministry of Munitions, created in May 1915. New committees also proliferated, such as those established to regularize Russian purchases of supplies. After Lloyd George became prime minister in December 1916, new ministries of Labour, Shipping, and Food were created, together with a Department of National Service. In all, the number of national government employees in Britain almost doubled in the ten years after 1911, and the number of local government employees increased by one-third. One should not assume, however, that state intervention had not occurred in these areas already, or that it automatically improved administration. The Ministry of Shipping was merely an extension of a web of shipping controls established in 1915 and 1916 through agencies such as the Ship Licensing Committee, Requisitioning (Carriage of Foodstuffs) Committee and Shipping Control Committee. Similarly, the Ministry of Munitions was actually a merger between the existing War Office Armament Output Committee and the Treasury Munitions of War Committee.

In terms of efficiency, the creation of both a Ministry of Labour and a Department of National Service, which became a full ministry in August 1917, actually confused labour and industrial-relations policy, since there was considerable overlap between them. The establishment of the Ministry of Reconstruction in August 1917 further complicated matters. Moreover, partial responsibility for labour relations was also vested in the Ministry of Munitions, the Admiralty, the War Office and the Board of Trade, whose old labour departments had been the nucleus of the Ministry of Labour.

The most marked change from the situation as it was before December 1916 was Lloyd George's determination to strengthen central control over departments. Interestingly, the Treasury lost much of its former centralizing influence. It increased its control over currency, the Stock Exchange, exchange rates and overseas finance, but it lost control over other government expenditure. One reason was simply the exigencies of war: Lloyd George, while still Chancellor, told the War Office in October 1914 that it did not need to seek Treasury approval for war purchases. A second reason was that many of the new ministries were never subjected to Treasury control, the legislation establishing them giving them control over their own staffs. The Ministry of Munitions, in particular, kept almost no staff records and did not even attempt to grade staff adequately.

Explosives come first

The most crucial industrial sector was munitions. As it happened, the armaments firms had been generally more innovative than other sectors of industry prior to the war. Thus, shortfalls in output were the product of the high additional orders placed with private firms by government in 1914 without regard for capacity, rather than of unrealistic expectations on the part of industry itself. Indeed, the shortfall in weapons-production targets by June 1915 ranged from 12 per cent in rifles to 55 per cent in machine guns and 92 per cent in high explosive shells. This 'shell shortage' then enabled Lloyd George to wrest control of munitions from the War Office, and the Ministry of Munitions appeared in May 1915 with its own sweeping powers under the Munitions of War Act to control all armaments factories.

Under Lloyd George, the Ministry of Munitions developed an innovative approach in such areas as managerial organization, cost accounting, welfare provision for labour, electrification and automation. The

The tools of the trade. Saw smiths of Sanderson Brothers and Newbould in action, photographed during 1914–18.

Tackling the 'shell shortage'. Men work on shell heads at a Ministry of Munitions' establishment, 1915/16.

'A PROTEST AGAINST LORD KITCHENER'

[*Following pages*] *The Chairman of the United Alkali Company of Liverpool, M. Muspratt, complains to the President of the Board of Trade, Walter Runcimann, on 19 May 1915 that the Secretary of State for War, Lord Kitchener, has unfairly blamed the private armaments industry for the 'shell shortage' facing the British army in France and Flanders.*

The publicity given by The Times *on 14 May to the failure of the British offensive at Aubers Ridge (9 May), supposedly attributed to a shortage of shells, had been orchestrated by the Commander-in-Chief of the British Expeditionary Force, Sir John French. It contributed to the collapse of Asquith's*

Liberal administration and its replacement by a coalition government on the very day Muspratt wrote to Runcimann.

Muspratt pointed out that the War Office had used too few private armaments firms in the past – it had relied largely on the Royal Ordnance Factory – and that too many skilled men had been allowed to enlist with Kitchener then refusing to release them from the army. Indeed, while 1500 men from Muspratt's firm had enlisted, Kitchener had refused to release even 12 of them.

Lord Moulton, to whom Muspratt refers, was a leading scientist and also a judge, who had been asked by Kitchener to take charge of the production of high explosives. (BT 13/62)

The President wd. like you to see: EBle 20/V/15 Sir HLLSmith

Read. Keep with the Armament papers
HLS
22.5.15

THE UNITED ALKALI COMPANY LIMITED.

TELEPHONE: 8213 CENTRAL.
TELEGRAMS: "UBIQUE."

30, JAMES STREET,
LIVERPOOL,

**Strictly private and
confidential.**

May 19th 1915.

Rt.Hon.Walter Runciman.M.P.

Board of Trade.

LONDON.

Dear Runciman,

This is not a time for recriminations, but,as Chairman
of the largest Chemical Company in this Country, I wish immediately
and emphatically to put on record a protest against Lord Kitchener's
implication that any delay in the production of High Explosives is
the fault of the Manufacturers.

Fault, if there is any, must be put entirely to the account of the War Office. The system which they have adopted in
the past has made them a tied-house to Nobel's and Kynochs' for
most Explosives, with a small coterie of little men for a few speci-
alities. If they really knew the likely requirements of this great
contest, they should have known that their system was totally incapable of meeting the new conditions; it was not, however, until
November that they even realized that something had to be done.

In appointing Lord Moulton, an excellent step was taken,
but even then the large manufacturers were not consulted and, although certain specific work was given to certain firms, there

(1)

SHEET NO. 2. FROM U. A. CO. LIM: TO Rt. Hon. Walter Runciman. M.P.

there/

was no co-ordination and Industrial competition was accentuated under the guise of patriotic effort.

In the meantime, all sorts of mushroom growths -- many of an experimental nature -- were encouraged and it was not until the end of April that the large manufacturers were called together and, even then, only to discuss one specific problem.

To show the effectiveness of this method, -- Lord Moulton asked for large quantities of Ammonium Nitrate and within half-an-hour was promised 500 tons per week within three months. Had this method been adopted at the commencement of the War, the same would have happened for any product required, as the large manufacturers would have been capable of dealing with the whole situation with about three months notice for erecting Plant, while the small men could, of course, have been called in to supplement.

One other point, is the refusal of Lord Kitchener to allow essential experts back from the Colours.

Over 1,500 men have joined from our Company and since January, I have been urging the return of 12 of these, who are urgently required for important and direct War Office work.

I do not wish you to take any action as matters are slowly clearing up, but I do wish to place these facts on record and, of course, you are at liberty to show this letter to anyone you wish, but, of course, in confidence.

Yours truly,

ministry commandeered raw materials, centralized foreign purchases
and dealt in the import market. Nonetheless, it was the munitions
orders placed by the War Office that sustained the war effort until the
spring of 1916; the results of the first orders placed by the new ministry
did not arrive until October 1915 and were often sub-standard. It was
also the case that the size of the bureaucracy – there were eventually
over 25,000 employees in 50 departments – created some organiza-
tional confusion. By 1918 the Ministry of Munitions directly managed
250 government factories and supervised another 20,000 'controlled'
establishments. Yet, from a situation in which only 500,000 shells were
produced in 1914, the British armaments industry produced 76.2 million shells in 1917. Indeed, by 1916, the Ministry of Munitions could
produce in just three weeks what had been a year's production of
eighteen-pounder shells in 1914; a year's pre-war production of
medium shells now took eleven days and a year's pre-war production
of heavy shells just four days. By 1918, too, 61 per cent of the entire

Warfare and welfare. The Gretna township, established by the Ministry of Munitions, housed over 16,000 workers.

male industrial labour force was employed on war work of some kind.

The impact on industry was considerable. In the case of Birmingham, for example, it was reported by visiting journalists in 1918 that:

Jewellers abandoned their craftsmanship and the fashioning of gold and silver ornaments for the production of anti-gas apparatus and other war material; old-established firms noted for their art productions, which had found a permanent home in most of the museums of the world, turned to the manufacture of an intricate type of hand grenade. Cyclemakers devoted their activities to fuses and shells; world-famous pen makers adapted their machines to the manufacture of cartridge clips; and railway carriage companies launched out with artillery wagons, limbers, tanks and aeroplanes, and the chemical works devoted their energies to the production of the deadly TNT.

The working conditions in munitions works could be highly dangerous. While attention has focused mostly on women workers who

(*left*) Transferable skills. These sailmakers are putting their expertise to different uses, roping a tent.
(*below*) Down, but not out. These Belgian soldiers were employed at the Birtley munitions factory.

GRILLO OLEUM PLANT.

ABSORPTION HOUSE.

MANUFACTURING EXPLOSIVES

Plans of the Grillo Oleum Plant Absorption House at the Ministry of Munitions armaments factory at Avonmouth, as drawn up by Messrs Holland and Cubitts Ltd, 30 September 1917.

Oleum – fuming sulphuric acid – was used to 'wash' sulphur trioxide as part of the production of sulphuric acid, an important industrial chemical used in the manufacture of explosives. This instal-lation was just one of many at the massive complex.

Over 30 firms were involved in construction at Avonmouth, the cost of the Holland and Cubitts plant with its attendant buildings alone running to over £132,000. The Avonmouth oleum plant was subsequently to generate more heat than that at Queen's Ferry near Edinburgh. (SUPP 10/1)

became industrial casualties, events such as the explosion at the munitions factory at Silvertown in East London, on 19 January 1917, not only killed 69 people and injured over 1000, but damaged an astonishing 70,000 houses through the hot metal fragments strewn over a large area. It was said that the blast was heard as far away as Cambridge.

Working for victory

The need to ensure war-related production inevitably gave government a greater role in determining policies regarding the workforce. The introduction of such policies was not always easy, given the prevailing assumptions in 1914 that the war would be short and the failure in consequence to control the movement of skilled manpower into the armed forces. In some areas, the loss of labour was critical. By December 1914 small-arms factories had lost 16 per cent of their employees to enlistment and chemical and explosive works had lost 23 per cent.

The net effect was to propel the search for alternative sources of labour, such as the unskilled and women. The introduction of new sources of labour then raised the difficulties of tackling the restrictive practices of the pre-war unions of skilled workers. The government, however, fought shy of compulsory labour direction and a voluntary national registration programme was introduced in June. In theory, the introduction of military conscription was an important step towards proper planning through the ability to manipulate exemptions from military service. A Manpower Distribution Board was established in August 1916, but both the War Office and the Ministry of Munitions resisted its attempts to coordinate policy. The board was replaced by the Department of National Service in December 1916, but the resulting National Service Scheme to release young and fit men

'TREATMENT OF CASUALTIES'
Part of a report on the Ministry of Munitions National Filling Factory No 23 at Chittening, near Bristol. It was prepared by H. Bing and C.T. Ritchie immediately after the end of the war and reveals the human costs of the charging and head filling of HS shells.

HS (Dichlorethyl sulphide) was produced when ethylene was brought into contact with sulphur monochloride: the result was popularly known as mustard gas. First developed by the Germans in July 1917, mustard gas was successfully produced in Britain only in July 1918 at the munitions plants at Chittening, Hereford and Banbury. Banbury housed

the main production line. The Nobel Explosives Company opened the Chittening plant in November 1917, but it began to produce HS shells only on 8 July 1918.

By 11 November 1918 Chittening had produced 85,424 mustard gas shells, but there had been 1213 cases of illness among the labour force between 21 June and 7 December, including conjunctivitis, inflammation, congestion, nausea and vomiting, erythema (a reddening of the skin) and blisters. Most suffered from persistent coughs. There were two deaths, but these were attributed to influenza. A small surgery and hospital were opened at the plant in November 1918.
(WO142/274)

(g) All workers to be instructed as to the properties of H.S. before working with it, particular stress being laid on the smell of H.S. and the importance of absolute personal cleanliness.

3.—Symptomatic Treatment of Casualties.

(a) *Conjunctivitis.*—Frequent lavage with warm 2 per cent. Sod. Bic. Solution followed by the use of Ung-Cocaine 1 per cent., and if there is Photophobia, the provision of eye shades and rest in a dark room.

The above was found to be the best method of treatment and gave the most satisfactory results in this condition ; after the acute symptoms have worn off, it becomes merely necessary to bathe the eyes twice daily with the Sod. Bic. Solution.

To relieve the acute congestion and distress, plugging the nostrils with cotton wool wrung out of 4 per cent. Sol. Cocaine gives almost instantaneous relief, which, however, is only of a temporary nature.

(b) *Inflammation of Nasal Mucous Membrane.*—Syringing nostrils with warm 2 per cent. Sod. Bic. Solution.

(c) *Congestion of the Fauces : Cough—Aphonia.*—The following methods and treatment were adopted from time to time :—

(i) Gargles	(a) 5 per cent. Sod. Bic. Solution.	
	(b) 2 per cent. Chloramine T. Solution.	
	(c) Garg. Pot. Chlor.	
(ii) Sprays and inhalations	(a) Tr. Benzoinae. Co.	
	(b) Pheno-Salyl	2 parts.
	Sod. Benzoate	5 parts.
	Sal Ammoniac	3 parts.
	Glycerine	50 parts.
	Distilled Water	450 parts.
(iii) Medicines	(a) Mist Expct.	
	(b) Iodine	2 parts.
	Acidi Tannici	4 parts.
	Distilled Water	360 parts.
	Sugar	640 parts.

Dose, one tablespoonful.

The above is a French prescription, and was suggested by Mr. Bing, Managing Director. It gave good results, and certainly relieves the harassing cough to which H.S. workers are liable.

Laryngitis and the more serious lung complications I did not have the opportunity of treating, for the reasons given in the concluding paragraph. It may, however, be stated that I am satisfied that the Aphonia is not due to laryngitis, but is simply a hoarseness from the acute congestion of the fauces. Lung complications directly due to H.S. were a scarcity in our workers, and I am unable to trace a single case of broncho-pneumonia or acute bronchitis directly due to this cause.

(d) *Nausea and Vomiting.*—This is a real and distressing symptom in H.S. workers. We found the best method of treatment was to give a full dose of Mist. Alba followed by Mist. Bismuth or Sod. Bic. Solution in conjunction with rest in the recumbent position for a few hours, followed by work not in the charging sheds.

(e) *Erythema.*—Eusol Solution applied on lint gave the most relief in conjunction with hot baths with a liberal supply of Sod. Bic. Solution. Lotio Calaminae relieves the irritation.

Erythema of the Scrotum was best met by equal parts of starch and boracic powder, and here it would not be put out of place to mention that casualties in the genital organs of the females were conspicuous by their complete absence, whereas in the male workers they were quite common. The conclusion is obvious that they were contamination casualties and not due to the condensation of the vapour.

(f) *Vesication.*—The ideal treatment of an H.S. blister is as follows :—Withdraw the serum by means of a large bore serum needle under strict aseptic precautions. Cut away the dead skin but not quite to the margin and apply Ambrine by means of a brush. If the case can be watched continuously splendid results will ensue, and we had a few good results ; but if, as in the majority of our cases, the patient is lost sight of for a few days, then sepsis results and healing is much prolonged.

---

* No protective clothing was available for the workers in the period under review, and strong reasons against its use are given by Lt. Vernon in the Tenth Report of this Series.—T. M. L.

from industry, by providing substitutes from non-essential work, was again voluntary when introduced in February 1917. Some 206,000 men registered, but, since most were engaged in essential work, only 388 actually moved to new employment.

Only the increasing manpower shortages enabled what was now a full Ministry of National Service to acquire powers over this area, in November 1917. A War Cabinet Committee on Manpower was then

Home-grown devastation. The North Woolwich Road in tatters, following the Silvertown munitions explosion, East London, 19 January 1917.

'SHELTER FROM RECRUITMENT'
A paper placed before the Cabinet by the Secretary of State for War, Field Marshal Lord Kitchener, on 8 October 1915.

It points out that while some 5 million men had been enlisted in the army and 1.4 million were classed as in reserved occupations, there were at least 1.7 million men still left potentially available for military service. Kitchener calculated that 1.2 million of these could be 'combed out' from non-essential occupations, particularly in banking, the retail and distributive sectors, and domestic services.

The pattern of voluntary enlistment since August 1914 had certainly been quite arbitrary, with wide regional and local variations, often reflecting local employment conditions and the age structure of certain occupations. Indeed, by February 1916 the Board of Trade was to suggest that, contrary to Kitchener's views in his Cabinet paper, a higher proportion of men in commercial and distributive trades had enlisted compared to those in industry, transport and agriculture. Since many men in key industries were exempted once conscription was introduced in 1916, there was little material change in the relative share of military service among different types of occupation. (CAB1/13)

[This document is the property of His Britannic Majesty's Government.]

SECRET.

Printed for the Cabinet, October, 1915.

Notes on Lord Lansdowne's Paper of 29th September.

Addendum to Memorandum on Recruiting for the Army circulated by Lord Kitchener, dated 8th October, 1915.

The figures in paragraph 9 lead up to the conclusion that the available recruitable population of England and Wales between the ages of 19 and 41 is 1,412,040

As shown in the notes on Mr. Long's paper of 5th October, 1915, an addition might be made for Scotland of about 180,000

And a further addition of those of the present age, 18, who will come during the next 12 months within the recruitable limits 135,000

Making a possible total for Great Britain of 1,727,040

According to the figures upon which the War Office have worked up to the present, the following is the position :—

Returns from Recruiting Areas up to date show, according to the Pink Forms, the total number of men between ages 18 and 41 in Great Britain as 5,039,181

The number of men whose Pink Forms have been " starred " and who may be set aside as not immediately available for recruitment is... 1,462,136

Leaving a balance of 3,577,045

Deduct 50 per cent. for unfits, &c. 1,788,500

Possible total for Great Britain 1,788,500

Additions for Ireland and extension of age to 45 would bring the totals up to 1,977,040 and 2,038,500 respectively.

One or two remarks should be made on the first set of figures.

It is to be noted that the total registered males between 15 and 65 in England and Wales is about $9\frac{1}{4}$* millions, and of these $7\frac{3}{4}$ millions are reckoned as being left in industries. Amongst the latter are the following :—

564,300 left in Banking, Finance, Insurance, and Commercial occupations.
535,700 left with Shopkeepers and other retail dealers.
109,230 left in Domestic and Personal Services.

Total 1,209,230, of whom about 302,500 are between the ages of 19 and 41. These seem to be occupations in which considerable further introductions of female labour than are reckoned upon in Lord Lansdowne's calculations could be effected. Similar comments might be made in regard to other occupations.

With reference to the deductions on account of men in starred occupations, there is some evidence from the North that men not normally employed in such occupations are seeking in them shelter from recruitment, and that in some cases protected firms are extending similar shelter to men of recruitable age who are employed on unskilled labour, while men of non-recruitable age are out of work. It will be a matter of some difficulty to prevent practices of this kind, as it will be to secure that individual employers in claiming exemptions do not seek to retain amongst their "indispensables" all or more than is really necessary of the physically fit in their employment, thus leaving for recruitment an unduly high proportion of unfits.

---

* The 8,404,274 given in Lord Lansdowne's paper is based on the Returns then received, namely, 90 per cent. only of the total. An addition of 10 per cent. is accordingly made throughout.

(B607) 40 10/15 H&S 2692wo

Dangerous work.
At the Gretna factory,
these workers appear
to be handling cordite,
July 1918.

established on 6 December and this finally effected a coherent policy, subordinating military demands to an overall assessment of priorities: merchant shipbuilding and the production of aircraft, tanks, iron ore, food and timber all took precedence over army manpower. Yet, even in June 1918, rather than impose labour conscription, the government still preferred to call skilled workers previously exempted from military service to register voluntarily as war munitions volunteers, albeit on pain of losing the exemption.

**'ALL INDUSTRIES —
GENERAL EXCEPTIONS'**
A circular issued by the Board of Agriculture and Fisheries on 26 April 1916 for the guidance of the farming community. It helpfully lists those occupations certified to be of national importance with effect from 1 May 1916, the first Military Service Act having introduced conscription for all single men and childless widowers between the ages of 18 and 41 in January 1916.

In each case, age limits were specified for those single men who could expect exemption as a result of being in a reserved occupation. Moreover, with the exception of those employed in mining or shipbuilding, the men had to be able to demonstrate that they had been in their occupations before 15 August 1915, when the National Registration Act had come into effect.

In June 1916 the second Military Service Act was to extend conscription to all men aged between 18 and 41, the age range being extended to those between 18 and 50 in April 1918. The list of certified reserved occupations was also adjusted fairly frequently. (WO106/372)

ALL INDUSTRIES—GENERAL EXEMPTIONS.

ENGINEMAN :—
Engineman or Engine Tenter 25*
Power Crane Driver 25
STOKER :—
Stoker or Boiler Fireman 25
ELECTRICAL FITTERS engaged in the maintenance and repair of motors and other electrical plant in factories 30
MECHANICS AND SIMILAR MEN engaged in the maintenance and repair of their employers' plant, machinery and tools 25
TOOL MAKER and DIE SINKER for machine tools 25
TOOL SETTER for machine tools 25
WORKS CHEMIST 30
COOPER :—
All classes (except those employed in making or repairing barrels or casks for beer, wine or spirits) 25
CARTER, LORRYMAN AND DRAYMAN (HORSE OR POWER)† :—
(1) Employed by carting contractors in connection with railways, docks, wharves and warehouses ... ...
(2) Employed by public carriers of goods by road 25
(3) Others, in all trades, not engaged in collecting from or delivering to private houses 25

MINING AND QUARRYING.

COAL MINING :—
Men below ground.—All classes. H.O.
Workmen above ground.—Colliery Fitter ; Colliery Mechanic ; Electrician ; Pumpman ; Weighman (including Checkweighman) ; Winding Engineman. H.O.
Central Rescue Stations.—Technical Staff and Permanent Rescue Corps. H.O.
COPPER MINING :—
All underground Workmen ... ...
Foreman (above ground) 30
FIRECLAY MINING AND QUARRYING :—
All underground Workmen in Mines ... ...
Foreman (above ground) at Mines and Quarries 30
Getter or Quarryman in Quarries ... ...
FULLER'S EARTH QUARRIES :—
Getter ; Kilnman ... ...
GANISTER MINING AND QUARRYING :—
All underground Workmen in Mines ... ...
Foreman (above ground) at Mines and Quarries 30
Getter or Quarryman in Quarries ... ...
GYPSUM INDUSTRY :—
Foreman 30
Miner or Quarryman ; Miller ; Furnaceman ... ...
IRON MINING OR QUARRYING :—
All underground Workmen in Mines ; Getter or Quarryman in Quarries ;
Surface Workmen (all classes) ... ...
LEAD MINING :—
All underground Workmen ... ...
Foreman (above ground) 30
LIMESTONE QUARRIES SOLELY ENGAGED IN SUPPLYING IRON AND STEEL WORKS :—
Foreman 30
Getter or Quarryman ... ...
OIL SHALE MINING :—
Workmen below ground.—All classes
Workmen above ground.—Colliery Fitter ; Colliery Mechanic ; Electrician ; Pumpman ; Weighman (including Checkweighman) ; Winding Engineman ... ...
SHALE OIL WORKS :—
Shale Oil Workman ... ...
SALT-MINES AND WORKS :—
Rock Salt Miner ; Shaftman ; Salt Fireman ; Waller ; Lofter ...
TIN AND WOLFRAM MINING :—
All underground Workmen ... ...
Foreman (above ground) 30
PATENT FUEL WORKS :—
Foreman 30
Beltman or Loader ; Trolleyman 25

METAL, ENGINEERING AND SHIPBUILDING.

AGRICULTURAL IMPLEMENT AND MACHINE MAKING, ERECTING AND REPAIRING :—
Foreman 30
All other classes of workmen except Woodworkers and Painters 25
ANCHOR MAKING :—
All classes of workmen ... ... —
BLACKSMITH (INCLUDING FARRIER) 25
CAST AND WROUGHT IRON DOMESTIC AND SANITARY WARE MANUFACTURE :—
Foreman or Charge Hand 30
Cupola man ; Moulder ; Grinder ; Drop Hammersmith ; Lathe Hand (Spinner or Trimmer) ; Annealer ; Tinner ; Enameller ; Pickler ; Burner or Fuzer ; Galvanizer 41
CHAIN MAKING :—
Block Chains—all classes of workmen ... ... —
Other Chains—all classes of workmen (except men engaged on chains of less than 7/16 inch diameter) ... ... —
DAIRY APPLIANCE MANUFACTURE :—
Foreman 30
Sheet Metal Worker ; Blacksmith ; Tinner ; Fitter and Erector ... 25
ELECTRICAL ACCUMULATOR MANUFACTURE :—
Departmental Manager ; Foreman 30
Caster ; Mixer ; Paster ; Lead Burner ; Forming Man ; Battery Erector 25
ELECTRICITY METER MANUFACTURE :—
Calibrator ... ... —

Metal, Engineering and Shipbuilding—*continued.*

FLOUR MILLING ENGINEERING :—
Mechanics engaged in the repair and maintenance of flour milling machinery ... ... —
GOLD REFINERIES :—
All classes of Workmen ... ... —
HEAVY EDGE TOOL, PICK, SPADE, SHOVEL AND HOE MANUFACTURE :—
All classes of Workmen except Wood Turners 30
IRON AND STEEL ROLLING MILLS, PUDDLING FURNACES :—
All classes of Workmen ... ... —
LEAD SMELTING :—
All classes of Workmen ... ... —
MARINE ENGINEERING :—
All classes of Workmen ... ... —
MICA MANUFACTURE (FOR ELECTRICAL OR SCIENTIFIC APPLIANCES) :—
Departmental Manager ; Foreman 30
Mica Machine Worker 25
NEEDLE AND FISH-HOOK MANUFACTURE :—
Departmental Manager ; Foreman 30
Grinder ; Hardener (not Improver) ; Scourer (not Improver) ; Boot-hook Maker ; Bearding Machine man 30
PIG IRON MANUFACTURE, BLAST FURNACES :—
All classes of workmen ... ... —
RAILWAY WORKSHOPS AND SHEDS :—*See Transport Trades.*
SCYTHE, SICKLE, REAPING HOOK, HAY KNIFE, AND AGRICULTURAL MACHINE-KNIFE MANUFACTURE :—
Foreman 30
All other classes of workmen except Wood Turners 25
SHIP AND BARGE BUILDING AND REPAIRING :—
All classes of Workmen ... ... —
SHOE AND ACCOUTREMENT MACHINE-KNIFE (DIE) MANUFACTURE :—
All classes of Workmen 30
SLAG WOOL MAKER ... ... —
STEEL MANUFACTURE :—
All classes of Workmen ... ... —
SURGICAL INSTRUMENTS AND APPLIANCES, AND FURNITURE AND EQUIPMENT FOR OPERATING THEATRES, MAKER OF ... ... —
TIN BOX MANUFACTURE :—
Foreman 30
TIN SMELTING :—
All classes of workmen ... ... —
TUBE AND TUBE FITTINGS MANUFACTURE, IRON, STEEL, COPPER AND ALLOYS (for Engineering and Shipbuilding) :—
All classes of workmen ... ... —
WEIGHING MACHINES, SCALES AND BALANCES :—
Adjuster and repairer 30
WHEELWRIGHT 25
ZINC SMELTING :—
All classes of workmen ... ... —

TEXTILE MACHINERY ACCESSORIES.

BOBBIN MANUFACTURE :—
Foreman ; Overseer 30
Rougher and Turner ; Bobbin Maker-Ready ; Machine Man ; Bobbin Finisher 41
CARD, COMB, HACKLE, AND GILL PIN MAKER 41
COMB AND GILL LEATHER MAKER 30
HEALD AND REED MAKER 30
JACQUARD CARD MANUFACTURE :—
Foreman 30
Machine Man 30
LOOM TEMPLE AND ROLLER MANUFACTURE :—
All classes of Workmen 30
PAPER TUBE MANUFACTURE :—
Foreman ; Overlooker 30
Paper Cutter ; Paper Grinder ; Stoveman or Drier 30
PICKER MAKER 30
SHUTTLE MANUFACTURE :—
Bodymaker ; Forger ; Finisher 30
TEXTILE COMB, HACKLE, GILL AND FALLER MAKER ... 30
WOOD CARD-CLOTHING MAKER 30

TEXTILE AND ALLIED TRADES.

COTTON TRADE, INCLUDING SEWING COTTON MANUFACTURE :—
Foreman ; Tackler (including "Harness Tyer" in Scotland) ; Overlooker ; Spinning Master ; Carder 30
Blowing-room Man (Scutcher and Opener) ; Stripper and Grinder ; Taper ; Sizer ; Slasher ; Warp Dresser ; Twister (hand and machine) ; Drawer-in (hand and machine) ; Hand Presser (hydraulic) 25
Mule minder ; Mule Piecer ; Twiner Doubler 26
WOOLLEN AND WORSTED INDUSTRY :—
Foreman ; Overlooker ; Loom Tuner ; Scribbling Engineer ... 30
Cloth Scourer, Miller, and Fuller ; Hand Presser (hydraulic) ... 30
Card Fettler ; Comb Grinder ; Comb Jobber ; Comb Minder ... 41
Woollen Mule Spinner (married men to be recruited up to 30 years of age ; single men up to 41)* 41
Worsted Warp Dresser ; Blanket Raiser 25
Assistant Scribbling Engineer ; Card Nailer ; Pin Setter ... —
Wool Carbonising :—
Foreman 30
Carboniser 25
Rag Carbonising and Extracting :—
Foreman 30
LINEN MANUFACTURE :—
Foreman ; Loom Tenter 30
Beamer or Warper (canvas only) ; Dresser or Starcher ; Cloth Lapper 25
JUTE TRADE :—
Foreman 30
Batcher ; Dresser or Beamer ; Tenter ; Calender Man 25

---

* Where the man in charge of the principal power engines at important works is under 25 and is the only engineman left in charge of a set of engines he should be exempted.
† These exemptions are in addition to the exemption of carters, lorrymen and draymen under specified trades, viz.:—in the coal trade, in railway service, at flour mills and on farms.

(B 6393) Wt. —g746 62M 4/16 H & S

* In those districts where women and girls have not hitherto been usually employed in woollen (mule) spinning as piecers and minders, the calling up of all married spinners and piecers and of single spinners and piecers over 25 years of age should be postponed until 4th June, 1916.

Circular.

Local Tribunals.

Appeal Tribunals.

LOCAL GOVERNMENT BOARD,
WHITEHALL, S.W.
23rd May, 1916.

SIR,

1. The President of the Local Government Board has been asked to bring the following further information to the notice of Tribunals on the subject of skilled workers useful for munitions work but not badged, to which reference was made in section 6 of the Circular of the 4th ultimo (R. 71).

As already intimated, the certificate given by the Ministry of Munitions in regard to certain occupations (formerly marked M.M. in the list of certified occupations) expired on the 1st May ; and it is probable that many employers of skilled workpeople engaged in those occupations have applied or will apply to the Local Tribunals for the issue of certificates of exemption to such workpeople, on the ground that it is expedient in the national interest that they should continue in their present occupation instead of being employed in military service. This is one of the grounds of application recognised in the Regulations and Instructions, and may therefore be admitted by the Tribunals even when the workpeople concerned are engaged on private work ; in fact the Ministry of Munitions themselves have in many cases declined to transfer men from private work to munitions work on the ground that they were indispensable in their existing employment.

In other cases, however, especially in the case of unmarried men under (say) 25 or 30 years of age, the Tribunals may not think it necessary to issue a certificate of exemption in respect of the private work upon which such workpeople are engaged ; and the question will then arise whether they possess qualifications specially required for munitions work. As indicated in the Circular Letter of the 4th ultimo, where this is the case, the national interest will probably best be served by making the issue of the certificate of exemption conditional upon the applicant's obtaining work entitling him to wear a War Service Badge within a month, or such longer time as may be necessary to enable his badge to be issued.

The occupations for which there is at present a most urgent demand for munitions work for men of all ages are the following :—

Engineering :

    Millwright.
    Fitter and Erector (engineering).
    Turner (engineering), excluding capstan and automatic lathe turners.
    Planer (engineering) who sets up his own machine.
    Slotter (engineering) who sets up his own machine.
    Miller (on universal and slab machines) who sets up his own machine.
    Grinder (on precision grinding machines).
    Sheet Metal Worker (engineering).
    Marker off (fitter, turner and draughtsman only).
    Draughtsman (engineering, not tracer).
    Coppersmith.
    Examiner (fitter or turner only).
    Viewer and Gauger (fitter or turner only).
    Tool Setter for machine tools.
    Tool Fitter.

Era of the airship. This was the last 'blimp' produced during the war at the Wormwood Scrubs factory, West London. It was probably for naval use.

Flexing the labour muscle

Deciding on manpower policies in turn led the government to direct involvement in labour relations. War, of course, distorted the normal working of the labour market. The position of labour generally improved through the premium that was now put on skilled workers, and trade union membership rose. At the same time, and as a consequence of labour's increased bargaining position, industrial militancy grew after initial periods of industrial truce.

In Britain, the first agreement on 'dilution' – the introduction of women and unskilled labour instead of skilled labour – was negotiated in November 1914 between the Engineering Employers Federation and the unions. In March 1915, however, the government itself negotiated the Shells and Fuses Agreement with the same parties to speed

'A MOST URGENT DEMAND'
A circular issued on 23 May 1916 under the signature of H.C. Monro, the Secretary to the Local Government Board, as guidance to the local tribunals established to handle claims for exemption from conscription.

The previous exemption for many skilled men not 'badged' for exemption – that is to say, those issued with an 'On War Service' badge for employment in key occupations – had just expired and their cases would be coming before the tribunals. Those employed in key

engineering tasks in munitions factories were still to be exempted and consideration was to be given to those engaged in shipbuilding. Otherwise, tribunals were asked to take account of those skill shortages notified by their local labour exchanges. In fact, tribunals were far more lenient than often supposed, 2.5 million men still being classed as in reserve occupations in October 1918.

Walter Long, a prominent Unionist, who is mentioned, was the President of the Local Government Board in the Asquith coalition government. (WO106/372)

dilution. Then, following the recommendations of the Board of Trade's Committee on Production, the so-called Treasury Agreements were reached with 35 unions to prevent workers taking advantage of their strengthened position. The agreements outlawed strikes, introduced more flexible working practices, permitted dilution on war work, and referred industrial disputes to official arbitration.

These voluntary agreements were incorporated in the statutory provisions of the Munitions of War Act in June 1915, Clause VII of which effectively tied workers to their place of employment, by preventing them from taking up alternative work for six weeks unless they obtained a leaving certificate from the existing employer first. The Act also effectively nominated trade union leaderships as the means through which the government would negotiate for dilution and changes in working practices. Indeed, the Trade Card scheme introduced in late 1916 to exempt workers in war industries from conscription made the unions themselves responsible for deciding exemption. Extended from engineering to other skilled unions, it was not actually put into effect, since it was recognized as unworkable when unskilled workers were just as necessary for war production. However, rising food prices, high rents, restricted mobility of workers and wartime profiteering all contributed to a growing discontent on the factory floor that could not be controlled by the union hierarchies.

The increasing power of shop stewards was illustrated by the role of the Clyde Workers Committee (CWC) in orchestrating unrest in the Clyde shipyards and engineering works through the winter of 1915–16.

Mending the roads. Tar spraying was one of the less glamorous occupations to open up to women during the war.

'A DEAD-LOCK HAD ENSUED'
[*Following pages*] *W. St D. Jenkins, Assistant Director of Admiralty Contracts in the Cardiff Docks, writes to the Director of Contracts, Sir Frederick Black, on the situation in the docks at Barry, Cardiff and Newport on 20 January 1915.*

Together with the Superintending Transport Officer, Captain R. Parker, Jenkins had met representatives of the Dock, Wharf, Riverside and General Workers Union at Barry. A dispute had arisen as a result of the differential pay rates between the general dock labourers and the platers, who were represented by the separate Boiler Makers and Iron and Steel Ship Builders Society. Platers were permanently employed while the general labourers were only casually employed, receiving part of their pay from the

employers and part from the platers. Matters had also been exacerbated by the perception that the owners of dry dock facilities were earning large profits. The labourers wanted 7s.6d a day more – they earned £1.13s.0d a day – and to work fewer hours.

While admitting that profits were being made, Parker and Jenkins stressed the importance of the pressing naval and military needs and the high costs of freight, successfully staving off strike action. Jenkins felt that the Admiralty would have to bring pressure to bear on the Boiler Makers though, subsequently, he also expressed the view that there was not much economic hardship among the labourers and they were taking advantage of the situation, the dispute ultimately going to arbitration.
(MT23/385)

C A R D I F F.

January 20th 1915.

The Director of Transports.,

ADMIRALTY....S.W.

We beg to report that a number of the members
of the Dock, Wharf, Riverside & General Workers Union engaged at
Barry Docks have been on strike for the last two weeks with
consequent delay to the repairing of Military and Collier transports
in Drydock.   The majority of the men resumed work this morning
but as 80 or 90 platers' helpers refused to resume despite the
advice of their organising Secretary, Mr Ben Tillett, and local
Secretary, Mr Rogers, we visited Barry Docks this afternoon and
after a preliminary talk with Mr Rogers at the Dockers Hall,
addressed the men.

We did not enter into the merits of the dispute
and we understand that Mr Cummings of the Board of Trade visited
Barry last week and went into the matter.

The ringleader who, Mr Rogers informed us, was
responsible for the "down tools" policy, said that their grievance
was not against their employers but against the platers who were
earning at the present time enormous wages whilst they, who were
only casual helpers, were sent from one job to another made to
work harder without getting any extra remuneration.

It appears that only 6/- per week is paid to
these helpers by their employers, the remainder of their pay being

received from the platers themselves.

The platers belong to a different organisation viz., The Boiler Makers & Iron & Steel Ship Builders *Society* of which Mr John Hill J.P., is the Secretary. It appears that the men had early in January made certain demands upon the platers, and when after 9 days delay they received no reply, downed tools. Mr Tillett applied to Mr Hill on their behalf for a joint conference on the subject, but made it clear to the men that so long as they refused to resume work and adopted unconstitutional means nothing could be done to enquire into their case. The men had pressed for a conference and as they would not resume work without a conference being guaranteed, a dead-lock had ensued.

We addressed the man and pointed out to them the serious effect their action was having upon the Military and Naval transports and promised that if they resumed work tomorrow morning, we would do our best to bring both parties together. As far as we could gather there were only six extremists amongst the men by whom the remainder were practically intimidated.

After we had retired the men conferred together and informed us that on condition that a conference would be arranged within 14 days they would resume work next morning. If by then the conference had not met they would immediately stop work again. We had to be content with that and desire strongly to submit that pressure be brought to bear by the Admiralty upon the Boiler Makers Society to arrange with Mr Ben Tillett for an enquiry into the mens' grievances with a view to a settlement.

It is suggested therefore that the Admiralty or Board of Trade should get into touch with both Mr Hill and Mr Tillett

(*below*) Sweat and toil. Employees of Glasgow Corporation's Gas Department clean fire bricks, September 1916.

(*right*) 'We want justice'. Demonstrators, including servicemen's children, support the Glasgow rent strike, October 1915.

The image of 'Red Clydeside' was forged from the migration of workers into the area, exacerbating an existing housing shortage, forcing up rents and contributing to a rent strike in Glasgow. When 18 of the 20,000 participants in the rent strike were served summonses, the shipyards went on strike. Ultimately, the concession of rent controls eroded the wider sense of grievance and isolated the CWC, enabling the government to break the committee in March 1916 by the arrest and deportation of ten of its leaders from the Clyde. The fact that the engineers as a whole were isolated within the labour movement by being widely perceived as an elite also enabled the government to act. Visiting the Clyde during the dispute, and receiving a rowdy reception, Lloyd George was introduced to the men by one leading agitator, David Kirkwood, who proclaimed that 'we regard him with suspicion, because every Act with which he is associated has the taint of slavery about it'. The minister was also described ironically in the Independent

'TO SPREAD DISLOYALTY'

[*Following pages*] *Dr J.T. Macnamara, Financial Secretary to the Admiralty, writes on 21 October 1915 to the First Lord of the Admiralty, Arthur Balfour, about the growing labour problems on the Clyde.*

Macnamara reveals that action against agitators had been under consideration for some time. He felt a small number of agitators were responsible and that the Admiralty authorities on the Clyde should take steps to identify instances of

incitement so that individuals could be prosecuted. In a handwritten note Balfour adds his endorsement to the suggested course of action and indicates that the note should be sent on to the Scottish Office and the Home Office as well as to Admiralty officials on the Clyde.

Subsequently, Macnamara, who had meanwhile spoken to Lloyd George, considered that the Admiralty itself could not observe the workforce more closely but that specific reports could be followed up. (ADM1/8436/311A)

FIRST LORD

Some months ago I had a paper before me
containing a report to the effect that an agitator
in the Clyde District had advised the workmen to
extend their holiday in defiance of the Government's
wishes.   So far as my recollection goes, it was
suggested that the question should be referred to the
Director of Public Prosecutions with a view to taking
legal action against the man in question.   I have
never been able to learn what became of that paper,
though I have frequently asked for it.

I have for some time past been quite convinced
that there is a small section of men, particularly on
the Clyde, who lay hold of every petty grievance in
order to foment disaffection amongst the men.
Elsewhere I have suggested that all means should be
taken to see that the genuine grievances of the men
are fairly met, and of course if this were done systemat-
ically, much of the advocacy of the persons about whom I am
now writing would become abortive.   Nevertheless, I
think it is the duty of the Government to proceed much

more

more seriously under the Defence of the Realm Act than
is at present the case where men seek deliberately to
spread disaffection amongst their fellows.   And I
suggest to you that the Home Office and the Director of
Public Prosecutions should be invited to watch much
more carefully than at present for such evidence as
would enable prosecution to be pursued.   Further, I
am not sure that we ought not to send a confidential
communication to our Competent Naval Authorities asking
them to bring to our notice well authenticated cases
of deliberate incitement to strike, deliberate endeavour
to interfere with men in the discharge of their duties,
and deliberate intention to spread disloyalty amongst
the men.

21st October, 1915.

Labour Party journal, *Forward*, as Britain's 'best paid munitions worker'. Publication of the journal was then suppressed for a time. By contrast, Lloyd George had readily conceded national pay bargaining to the leaders of the South Wales miners, who had gone on strike in July 1915. Generally, the government learned to tread more warily in the case of large-scale disputes that enjoyed popular local support. Lloyd George also continued to cling to the idea that union leaders could deliver on industrial peace, if incorporated into government through service on various committees. In practice, however, as did employers, unions increasingly viewed the intervention of the state in industrials relations as something to be avoided.

Although food prices and restrictions on labour mobility were also involved, the government's intention to withdraw the dormant Trade Card scheme and to impose 'dilution' on non-war production provoked widespread unofficial strikes in April and May 1917, involving as many as 200,000 engineering workers in the North and resulting in an estimated loss of 1.5 million working days. Once more, the union leadership – in this case that of the Amalgamated Society of Engineers (ASE) – was unable to control the Joint Engineering Shop Stewards' Committee, even after substantial concessions were made on the conscription of skilled men. A government investigation concluded that high food prices, the restrictions on labour mobility, the lack of worker accommodation, fatigue through Sunday and overtime hours, inadequate compensation for injuries, and the conscription of those who had believed themselves exempt had all contributed to the unrest. Engineering workers were again on strike in April 1918 in Leeds and Birmingham, at the height of the German Spring Offensive. It was,

'POWER OF ARREST'

[*Facing page*] *A memorandum to the Home Office on 19 February 1916, written by the Commissioner of the Metropolitan Police, Sir Edward Henry, relating the ongoing case of Tom Rees, secretary of the London District of the Amalgamated Society of Engineers (ASE).*

Rees had refused to accept arbitration in a dispute involving the Royal Arsenal at Woolwich, in which the night shift was paid time-and-a-quarter but the day shift got time and half if they worked after 8 p.m. Woolwich employed 1500 men and produced 5 million rifle cartridges every week. The memorandum indicates the intention of the Ministry of

Munitions to bring in police to protect non-strikers if events escalated; but it also points out the possibility of legal challenges to any outlawing of picketing under pre-war legislation that might or might not be deemed to have been superseded by wartime emergency legislation. A civil servant has noted on the document that he telephoned Henry to inform him that the problem had already been referred for legal opinion.

Rees duly appeared before the magistrates at Bow Street where the case was adjourned for a fortnight. Ominously, the men cheered Rees as he left court. In the event, the ASE accepted arbitration and the case was dropped on 18 March 1916. (HO45/10804/308532)

A man named Rees, who is Secretary of the District Committee of the Amalgamated Society of Engineers, appears at Bow Street this afternoon on a summons under Regulation 42 of the Defence of the Realm Regulations, the charge against him being that he put pressure upon Munition Workers at Abbey Wood to cease working.

The Ministry of Munitions are of opinion that Rees may receive sympathy and support from a considerable number of Munition Workers employed at Woolwich Arsenal, where a strike, which may be on a large scale, is expected, should he be convicted.

The Ministry of Munitions have informed me of the intention of the Government to afford adequate protection to all workmen willing to remain at work, and this may necessitate action on the part of the police to prevent what is known as peaceful picketing.

I propose, therefore, in the event of a strike taking place, giving directions that picketing is to be deemed an offence under Regulation 42 of the Defence of the Realm Regulations, for which the police have power of arrest, (under Regulation 55).

This action on the part of the Police would doubtless be challenged, as violating a right conferred by Section 2 (1) of the Trades Disputes Act, 1906; and it seems desirable, therefore, to take the opinion of the Law Officers upon the point raised, viz., whether Regulation 42 of the Defence of the Realm Regulations does or does not abrogate, whilst these Regulations are in force, as regards Munition Factories, the right conferred by Section 2 (1) of the Trades Disputes Act.

E. R. H
19.2.16

Before the necessary this I spoke
to Sir E. H. on the telephone & told
him that the point had been put to the
L. O. in my note of yesterday to Mr. Mellor
C.J 19.2

however, the blunting of the offensive at a time when leaving certificates were reintroduced (they had been abolished in August 1917) that brought renewed engineering strikes in Coventry and Birmingham in July 1918. The strikes ended with the threat of conscription. Some of the other unions, however, resented the attitudes of the engineers, whom they saw as a pre-war labour elite. The journal of the Workers' Union commented: 'They have no conscientious objection to manufacturing munitions of war for someone else to use. They are determined to push anyone into the Army; all may go, but not them.'

Overall, Britain had by far the highest rate of industrial militancy of any of the warring states, with strikes that were both longer, and from an earlier date, than elsewhere. On the other hand, there was far less militancy than during the peacetime industrial unrest of the period between 1910 and 1914. Figures vary slightly but one estimate is that there were 3227 strikes in Britain between 1915 and 1918, involving 2.6 million strikers and costing the loss of 17.8 million working days.

Trade union membership increased from about 4.1 million in 1913 to 6.5 million by 1918. Where trade unions were already strong, they

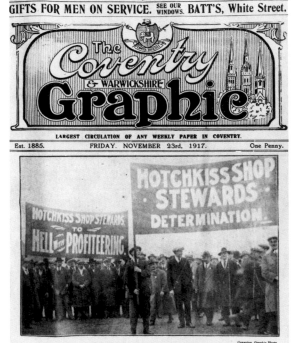

'Determination'.
Men and women from
the Hotchkiss plant,
Coventry, protest at
the high food prices,
November 1917.

COMMITTEE ON LABOUR TROUBLES.

The present position is that the A.S.E. have voted by a majority of 9 to 2 against the proposals of the Ministry of National Service for calling up men for the Army, and that this may be followed, [when these proposals are put in operation,] by a strike. The indications, however, are that no general strike is likely to take place. The danger is that there may be a local strike, e.g., if one or two shop stewards were called upon the Clyde or at Sheffield, and that a strike once begun in one area may spread to others and become general. If the A.S.E. were to strike, the E.T.U. would be likely to follow.

We have considered what action should be taken in that event. This will necessarily depend on circumstances, and no exact scheme of action can be laid down beforehand.

The suggestion that leaders should be deported under D.R.R. 14 was mentioned, but we were unanimously against it.

If drastic action is necessary, we think that, if evidence is available, the instigators of the strike should be prosecuted under D.R.R. 42 and proceedings taken to prevent the payment of strike pay. In order to facilitate action under these heads the Ministry of Munitions have suggested two amendments in the D.R.R:-

increased their strength, but considerable gains were also made in areas where unions had been previously weak, such as agriculture and white-collar occupations, and among the unskilled. Moreover, the number of trade unionists formally affiliated to the Trades Union Congress (TUC) increased from 2.2 million in 1913 to 4.5 million by 1918.

The war stimulated amalgamation among unions, with the Iron and Steel Trades Confederation coming into existence in 1917 and six other new federated unions in early 1918. The trend continued after

feel able to sign it, though he did not apparently regard it
as inequitable.   Later on Sunday morning there was a
meeting called of all the men in the Hotchkiss Works by the
illicit Shop Committee, at which Mr. Cassidy (Army Ordnance)
presided, supported on the platform by Mr. Dingley, Mr. Chalin
and Mrs. Sullivan the ring-leaders of the self-constituted
Shop Committee.   At this meeting, attended by about 300 men
there was a lot of wild talk condemnatory of the Union leaders,
and in support of the "Rank and File" movement, and the men
were being worked up into considerable excitement, when the
Joint Committee of Unions appeared on the scenes, and demanded
to be heard from the platform.   After some trouble Mr. Davis
and others got a hearing and Mr. Davis made a very courageous
speech, explaining the Agreement, and asking the men to be
reasonable and accept it.

This seems to have made a favourable impression -
but I have not yet heard the result - But Mr. Davis was of
opinion that the Agreement would be accepted.

It must be remembered that the Hotchkiss Works
having come recently on the scenes, and recruited with great
rapidity and little discrimination, contains a considerable
number of the Workers' Union. undesirable men , and a large number of

Mr. Squires, the manager, is an American and, it
would seem, not very familiar with English ways.   It cannot
therefore be said that these works are typical of the whole
of Coventry.

Of the Union Leaders Mr. Davis (Iron Moulders Union)

the war with the establishment of the Amalgamated Engineering Union in 1920 and the Transport and General Workers Union in 1921. Increased unionization and federation, the latter often prompted by rank and file members, may suggest a greater sense of solidarity within the working class. At the same time, though, the older voluntary working-class organizations declined as the state took over their role; and the subsequent decline in union membership in the 1920s might also suggest that members saw them only as a means to an end in acquiring greater bargaining power, rather than as an expression of class cohesion.

Winners and losers

The need for government to ensure continued production generally had the effect of reducing working hours and raising wages. It is estimated that, between 1914 and 1918, average working hours fell from 50 hours per week to between 44 and 48 hours per week, and the average annual wage rose from £51 in 1911 to £103 by 1924. This did not necessarily mean higher wages in real terms, since what mattered to the individual was the actual purchasing power of money in relation to wartime inflation, and the amount of disposable income available.

All statistics need to be treated with care because averages tend to hide considerable differences between one industry and another, and there could be wide variations even within the same industry. They also hide the initial downturn in people's paypackets through economic uncertainties in 1914. Thus, in the cotton industry the average wages of workers slipped down to 30 per cent of the pre-war level in August 1914 and were still 10 per cent below pre-war levels in December 1914.

'A LOT OF WILD TALK'
Part of a report by W.C. Bridgeman on unrest in the Hotchkiss munitions plant at Coventry, visited on 21–22 April 1917. He indicates that Coventry had been regarded as a problem area well before the more serious unrest in 1918. A Shop Stewards Committee had emerged, of which the official union leadership knew nothing and, with the local representative of the Ministry of Munitions, W.H. Phillips, feeling unable to rule on matters of recognition, the various parties had thrashed out a solution in London.

The Shop Committee was given official recognition. Interestingly, no employee under the age of 18 was permitted to vote in the ballot for shop stewards. One local union representative did not agree with

the London agreement and there was considerable opposition on the part of the workforce, but one of the official union leaders, called Davis, from the Iron Moulders Union, had apparently gained a measure of acceptance for it at a public meeting.

Bridgeman attributed the unrest not only to a reduction in wage rates but also to the rapid expansion of the workforce, involving the employment of many 'undesirables', and to the American manager, W.H. Squire, who knew little of British working practices, Hotchkiss being an American firm best known for the production of machine guns. Bridgeman believed that if the official union leadership was sufficiently supported it should be able to stop unrest. (LAB2/254/6)

Solidarity and camerad-
erie. Coal miners gather
for a drink and to discuss
the impending strikes,
February 1917.

Generally, wage differentials narrowed between skilled and unskilled labour, between men and women, and between older and younger workers, although, again, there were wide variations. As might be expected, those workers employed in war industries generally did better than those employed in occupations more marginal to the war effort. By 1917, for example, while average wages in Britain had risen by 55 per cent, those in the cotton industry had still risen only by between 14 per cent and 20 per cent. At that date, the largest increases had been secured by miners, unskilled engineering workers, iron-ore miners, blast-furnacemen and iron and steel millmen.

Information about wages is difficult to calculate because of the additional complication of 'piece rates' (payment by results), time rates, bonuses, overtime payments and other variations. Unskilled engineering workers were paid on piece rates, and the skilled by the hour, whereas the reverse was true in steel and shipbuilding. There were, however, considerable opportunities for high cash earnings through additional payments, especially as the reduction in standard working hours allowed for more overtime. At the same time, reduced working hours increased demands for better hourly rates, which rose far higher than pay worked out on a weekly basis. Such bonuses may have kept actual earnings approximately in line with inflation, at least in war industries. There were fewer opportunities for additional payments in agriculture.

Many of the earlier descriptions of the effect of labour 'dilution' and the narrowing of differentials in industry were based on the British engineering industry. The experience of labour in other sectors, such as shipbuilding, was very different. Differentials between the skilled and unskilled were certainly eroded, since labour rather than skill was what was predominantly required. Indeed, the introduction of women and the unskilled into the labour force did tend to prove that skilled men were less necessary than had been imagined, especially with the advances of wartime automation. Similarly, arbitration on the part of

'LEAVE THE NIPPERS IN AT 5D'
E. Pearson, the Construction Manager of Messrs. S. Pearson & Co, writes to Lieutenant Adrian Corbett of the Explosives Department of the Ministry of Munitions on 6 November 1915 for clarification on the distinction between general labourers and others involved in construction work at the Gretna munitions site, near Carlisle.

Labourers were paid less than platelayers and other more skilled men and wanted more guaranteed work. That morning, frost had prevented work starting on time and the labourers had walked out, union representatives wanting guaranteed minimum hours when it had already been ruled out by arbitration. Feeling he could hardly control the weather, Pearson was inclined to let the men strike until they were forced back to work by want, but he knew that the government would not allow this. Corbett confirmed, however, that there could be no pay for hours not worked.
(MUN 7/255)

MINISTRY OF MUNITIONS OF WAR.

H. M. FACTORY, GRETNA.

TELEGRAMS, "SONRAEP-GRETNA".

TELEPHONE, 541 CARLISLE.

S. PEARSON & SON, LIMITED.

CONSTRUCTION MANAGERS.

Gretna.

November 6th. 1915,

Lieut. A. Corbett (2).

drivers etc.

In view of the shortage of platelayers, and the urgent necessity of getting our roads in quickly, I some time ago authorised men who were thoroughly accustomed to plate-laying to have an extra ½d. over the ordinary labourers' rate, and I am still keeping to this arrangement, which means that platelayers will get 8½d.

I think also it will be necessary for us to put in a new rate for youths, which I am proposing to put in at 6½d. We shall still leave the Nippers in at 5d.

We seem to be getting plenty of tradesmen, but we are not getting sufficient labourers, or rather the men that we are getting are practically useless, and to push this work, it is absolutely essential that we should get the right type of navvy.

We have had a little trouble with the men this week. Wednesday morning, we had rather a sharp frost, with the result that the men could not start brickwork the first thing. When I arrived down here, just before 9, I found the labourers leaving their work, as they said they were not going on until they heard the decision of the Arbitrators. By the time they had been smothed over, the brickies came out, wanting to know whether they were to be paid for the time they had lost owing to the frost. Eventually, however, they went back. I may say that this only affected part of the men on No. 2 site, but it is an indication of the restlessness amongst them.

Men of steel. These workers are engaged in a seemingly streamlined process at the Sanderson Brothers and Newbould steel warehouse during the war.

wartime tribunals tended to advantage the unskilled, since flat wage rises were often the result. In engineering, the general improvement of the unskilled in relation to the skilled was in the order of 14 per cent, but it averaged less than 7 per cent in other heavy industries such as mining and shipbuilding.

Wartime 'winners' included engine drivers, railway platelayers and railway porters, while wartime 'losers' included textile workers and male shop assistants. While it can be argued that the greatest gains were made by those who, before the war, had been the most poorly paid, it does not mean that the skilled were actually losers, however. Even in engineering, 'dilution' most often meant that the skilled would be

'UNDER THIS SEVERE HANDICAP'
James Ramsay, Secretary of the Maybole and District Shoe Manufacturers Association, puts the case for resisting additional war bonus demands by the National Union of Boot and Shoe Operatives to Sir George Askwith, on 5 December 1916.

The firms concerned – A.L. Scott & Co, the Scottish Co-operative Wholesale Society, F. & J. Dick, and S. Gallery & Sons – believed that paying higher war bonuses of the kind enjoyed by workers in Glasgow would be fatal to a

local industry that had been in decline before the war, and for which there were far higher carriage costs.

The union, represented by Thomas Baird, wanted 5s.od for all men and 2s.6d for women and girls, the existing bonuses paid since March 1915 being 2s.od a week for men and 1s.od for women and girls. The manufacturers had offered 3s.od for men and 1s.6d for women and girls when the dispute arose in June 1916. Askwith found in favour of the manufacturers on the grounds that the union had not established its claim. (LAB2/26)

MAYBOLE AND DISTRICT SHOE MANUFACTURERS'
·ASSOCIATION·

St. Cuthberts Works,   Decr.
Maybole.   5th.
1916.

Submission to Sir George Askwith on behalf of the above
Association in dispute with the National Union of Shoe Operatives
regarding payment of the Glasgow Award in Maybole District.

Herewith copies of all correspondence from October 20th. till
November 14th.

In framing the demand the Union have completely ignored the fact
that the terms , if conceded, would make the War Bonus in this
district one shilling per week more to adult male operatives and
sixpence per week per week more to females and youths 18 years of
age and over, than is at present being paid in Glasgow.
Since June 1916 the extra payment in War Bonus in this District
has been three shillings per week to all male operatives 21years
of age and over, and one shilling and sixpence per week to all
youths and females 18 years of age and over. The boys and girls
under age have also been in receipt of a War Bonus of one shilling
and sixpence per week from the same date.
From October 1914 the minimum wage in Maybole District has been
advanced four shillings per week , from 28/- to 32/-, under protest,
and a corresponding advance averaging at least 4/- per week has
been paid to females and youths of age, whilst the wages of the
young help has been increased over fifty per cent.
The geographical position of Maybole is a severe handicap on the
progress of the shoe industry. The difficulty of effecting repairs
to machinery necessitates the institution of mechanical staffs in
the various factories whilst the distance from the main distributing
centre entails a heavy oncost for carriage and transport. The cost
of this item alaone represents three shillings per week on the
minimum wage.
Under this severe handicap it is obvvious that the trade in this
district must continue to decline. Twenty years age there were nine
engaged in the manufacture of shoes in Maybole with a collective
output of over twenty thousand pairs per week. In July 1914 prior
to the outbreak of war the total output did not exceed eleven
thousand pairs per week from the three firms still remaining.
This is reflected in the decrease of the population of the town,
from six thousand to well under five thousand during the last ten
years, and attributed mainly to the decline in the shoe industry.
The principle of adjusting wage rates as between city and country
has already been recognised and provided for in framing the
National Agreement, and the present effort of the Union to equalise
the Glasgow and Maybole conditions can only hasten the final
collapse of the industry in this district.

moved to supervisory roles. Moreover, the skilled remained in a sufficiently strong position to recover any temporary loss in relative earnings both during the war and after it.

Earning a living wage

In calculating how much Britain's working people gained, much depends on the relationship of wages to prices. On average about 75 per cent of British household expenditure had been devoted to food, fuel and housing before the First World War. During the war, people felt that living standards had declined. Ministry of Food calculations suggest that working-class families spent about 60 per cent more on food between 1914 and 1918. Increased earnings, transfer payments such as separation allowances, and changes in consumption generally offset some of the effects of inflation.

In any case, inflation did not affect all items uniformly, food and clothing prices rising far faster than those for fuel. Housing was often in short supply, but rents were controlled and the increasing amounts spent on tobacco more or less cancelled out decreasing spending on controlled beer, wine and spirits. Clothing prices probably represented the most significant additional financial burden, but economies could be made on clothing so that a greater proportion of working-class income was available for food than was the case before the war. Yet, an average increase in retail prices of perhaps 25 to 30 per cent per year still represented a considerable break from the pre-war experience of increases of only 1 or 2 per cent per year. Generally, it can be said that wages in real terms *did* keep ahead of inflation, although they would not actually catch the cost of living until the very end of the war.

The craft of war.
A worker carefully checks
an aeroplane propeller, at
the factory of Frederick
Tibbenham Ltd, Ipswich.

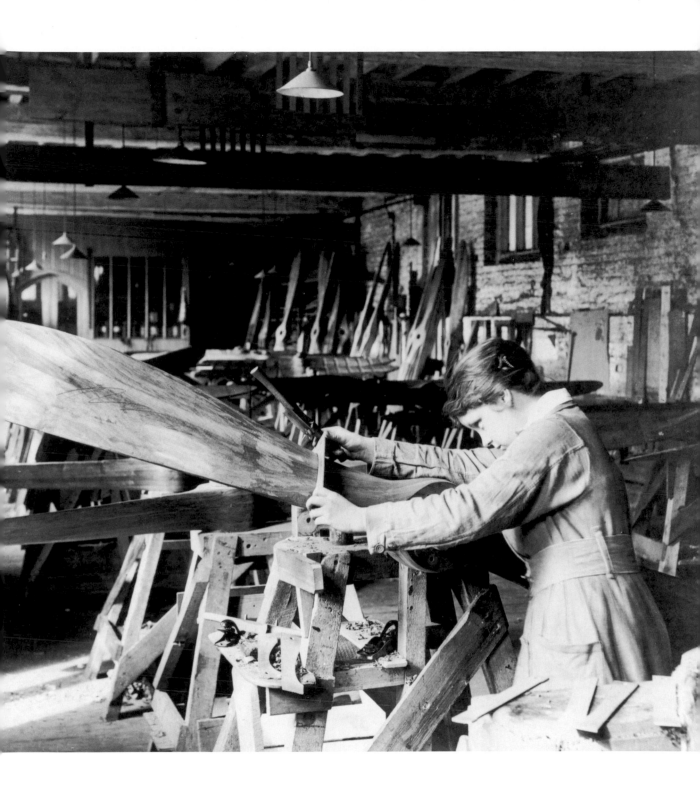

(1)

Alfred Bradburn, a 46-year-old munitions worker at a munitions factory in Bristol, living in nearby Cotham, writes to his older brother Sam in Liverpool on 13 November 1915 describing his work.

———

I AM STILL *on 18 pdr H.E. shells and have got with the skilled class of work; forming the nosing and cutting nose end. We all work to gauges, mine are 3.285 inches for base of nose & 2.195 inches for nose end, & a fraction say 1/500 of an inch small spoils that shell. It's harder work than the first & second rough turning, in as much as you cannot leave hold of the guide to tool cutter for one second; & one cutting of the tool at rough cutting would go for 7 or 8 mts without any attention. But it's better pay, and is skilled work. I have an insurance and out of work card & etc. in the proper working man line.*

The conditions of labour have advanced beyond all conseption [sic] since I was last a working man. They work less, are more independent, and get more money. There might not be such a thing as the Master.

Then the general run of the men are not nearly as skilled as formerly and I can quite see how easy it has been for Germany to get ahead of us; and unless our men alter very considerably we will still be far behind after the war. Our methods of working will always be easily beaten by the German method. Our men say "Oh, let them beat us" we will have tariff charges to keep their goods out; we will do less work and get more money for it after the war.

And all this makes me feel that the war is useless, so far as we are concerned. Germany today is what England was in Drakes &

Raleigh's days in Queen Elizabeth's day; with a national spirit which cannot be broken; I cannot see how we as a Nation are to do it; unless as I say, we alter considerably.

[IWM, 95/16/1, Bradburn Mss.]

(2)

A second letter from Alfred Bradburn to his brother on 16 January 1916. Clearly, a patriotic man with little time for industrial militants, he left the factory in September 1916 to enlist as a specialist in the Royal Engineers. He comments on financial difficulties in wartime and the presence of Belgian refugees among the munitions workers at Bristol.

———

E M RETURNED *on Friday feeling very much better, but the Dr. says that she must go slowly for some time, as any extra strain might cause a return of the old trouble, & another spell of illness. Elsie will not return to school this term, the funds won't run to it. She should keep up studies, & we have thought, seeing her health is now so much better, that she might have some little tuition at home, & sit for say the Cambridge Exam, which would give her something to do, & also the pass would be very useful to her if she needed to turn to any work in the school line later on. But things are going to be very tight in the money line with me for the next 12 months or so. As my income will be mostly what I get from munitions my average £2-15-0 a week. The bottom part of House is empty; there was some letter over the door bells and lighting & the 'lady' got the power one day & started slinging her weight about in a general sort of way, thinking I was out; shouting things to no-one in particular. I rather fancy she had been drinking; so I gave her notice there and then and she cleared out in due course. There are some other folk after the rooms, but unless we are sure of them the little money gained is not worth the discomfort of having any one undesirable in the house.*

We are at full swing at Munitions. All along we are aiming at 4,000 a week & there is a bonus attached to the 4,000 of £15. We have been up to 3,500 & then 3,800 & last week we did 4,050. That is we had that number passed by the War Office inspector; & perhaps about 300 rejected as well.

So we all feel very bucked. I am on outside turning & did 582 in 7 days 8 hours shift from Friday to Friday; we finished up at 4.30 on Sat. morning. Start again at 6 on Monday morning.

I've had quite a pathetic incident last week. We have 4 Belgians working there, from Monday night another came & the Boss fixed him to me for teaching, as each beginner has to be passed by a 'skilled' man before he gets to work on his own.

This man – call him A. – is Flemish & I did not make very much headway with his lingo, but he did his work well, & I started him on Tues. night on his own in my section of the shop. Then another Belgian came in on Tues., with a note from the Boss to me, & as he had been working at it before I put him with A., until we got another lathe going which had broken down. And so the man B. got started on his own about 3.0 a.m. on Weds. Morning (or Tuesday night).

A. told me he was a Manager of a large cloth factory in Brussels, just outside; the whole place smashed up, & he got away with some of this things & all his family & had been in England about 16 months; he is a very good stamp of a man.

B. told me 'I am a Baker in Brugh' [Bruges]. I suggested that he ment [sic] was but not 'I am a Baker in Brugh'. But I said 'Brugh is in ruins'. 'Oh yes' he replied 'the Germans did that, but its [sic] only for a time'. He described his shop & bakehouse & family, Father & Mother & sisters two brothers in army. He has been in England 14 months & lost all he had in the smash up, & had not heard a word of any sort of any member of his family. He came to Bridgwater from London & then on to Bristol about 4 weeks ago to 'do' shells.

On Weds. night, or rather Thurs. morning about 2.0 he asked me if he could go & have a chat with the other Belgian A. I should have said no, get on with your work; but I felt so sorry for the poor beggar that I had to allow him: they both were working in my section in same room but at extreme corners.

A few mts after there was a fearful shout & row, & A. & B. were in each other's arms shouting & crying & dancing like mad men, & I had to go along to see the fun; B. was shouting 'Glory to God' at the tope of his voice – in French. Then I got the story. B. told A. his story & where he came from, Oh, said A., I am living in the same house with people from Brugh, & it turned out that they were B's family, Father & Mother & his sisters & his sweetheart, all safe & sound. Of course I had to tell the rest of the chaps of our shift about 80 of us, & there was more shouting & handshaking; & after all that we got settled to work again.

I asked B. if he would like to knock off. 'Oh no' he said 'I have waited and sorrowed & cried for 14 months – like 14 long black dread years – and I wait for morning, & daylight, my day of rejoicing, tonight I make shells'. I tell you

*Sam old man, a fearful mad fury to turn out
shells settled on the whole of us, & we did the
record. I fancy that B. is something of a Poet his
language is very fine, he can give it rip.*

*Two things stand out with all the Belgians I
have met, a very deep feeling of hope, expressed
in the words 'I AM a Baker in Brugh' away
only for a time; and a fearful mad hatred of
the Germans.*

*I told the Boss the above the next day &
he cried.*

*I sometimes hope that some of our workmen
had a taste of what Belgium have had; they
would make up some; & get on with work.
I would shoot some of the S. Wales Blighters.*

[IWM, 95/16/1, Bradburn Mss.]

It is well known that the First World War brought substantial increases in women's employment. Traditionally, it has been said that this enhanced the status of women so much as to bring about the extension of the vote to (some of) them in 1918. Although debatable, at the very least it can be said that with the expansion of the war economy, the whole emphasis of a woman's role in society changed.

Knitting and nursing

Initially in the war, women were expected only to encourage their menfolk to enlist and to provide material comforts for those who did so. Mrs Montague Barstow (aka Baroness Orczy, author of *The Scarlet Pimpernel*), for example, created the Active Service League, asking women to pledge to persuade men to enlist and 'never to be seen in public with any man who, being in every way fit and free for service, has refused to respond to his country's call'. Other women handed out the notorious white feathers to able-bodied men not in uniform, deemed to be evading service. A variety of support groups and comforts funds for refugees, servicemen, and British prisoners of war were also created, such as the Victoria League, Queen Mary's Needlework Guild, and the Queen's Work for Women Fund. Unlike the others, the last of these was not a voluntary enterprise, but an attempt to provide some employment for women thrown out of work by the initial wartime economic uncertainty. Some 9000 women were being paid 3d per hour, with none permitted to earn more than 10s.0d a week, by early 1915, at which time other, more lucrative, opportunities were becoming available.

The knitting of 'comforts' for troops became an almost universal initial response to the war, with the result that vast quantities of unwanted garments flooded the army. Captain John Liddell of the Argyll and Sutherland Highlanders, later killed in action, wrote to his family in November 1914 criticizing the oddities being sent:

> The people who send them mean very well, but apart from the fact that these huge bales stop everything else coming through the post, the Government ones are far more appreciated by the men, and with reason, as they really are tophole garments, and some of the efforts that arrive are very thin and shoddy. Especially do I condemn the atrocity known as the heelless sock.

The Central Committee on Women's Employment, established to find gainful employment for the many women who became unemployed on the outbreak of war because of the economic uncertainties, also pushed (among others) a scheme for knitting 'useful' garments for Poor Law hospitals and maternity wards.

Upper- and middle-class women also undertook the morality patrols

A deluge of socks. Members of the Women's Emergency Corps busily knit, in one of the more traditional support roles.

mounted by the Women's Police Service and the Women's Patrols Committee of the National Union of Women Workers in the vicinity of army camps in response to the 'grave rumours of uncontrolled excitement' reported in September 1914. It was an activity then extended to factories by agreement with the Ministry of Munitions in July 1915. Some quasi-military organizations, such as the Women's Emergency Corps and the Women's Volunteer Reserve, were also created under the patronage of titled women, although even they aroused suspicion through donning uniform, which appeared to take them beyond acceptable feminine roles.

Traditionally, women had taken on the role of nursing, although this was considered more acceptable when middle-class and upper-class women undertook it. The pattern was continued by Queen Alexandra's Imperial Military Nursing Service; the Territorial Force Nursing Service; the Voluntary Aid Detachments (VADs), containing both men and women; and the aristocratic First Aid Nursing Yeomanry (FANY). Excluding some 74,000 VADs, the number of military nurses rose from 2600 in 1914 to over 18,000 by 1918.

'HOPELESSLY SILLY AND VULGAR'

A report card on the cinema at 53 The Strand, London, by Miss Hicks of the National Union of Women Workers.

The National Council of Public Morals believed indecency was taking place in cinemas and, while the Commissioner of the Metropolitan Police was sceptical, he instituted a survey of 248 cinemas to report on (1) how many children were in attendance, (2) whether there was separate supervised seating for children, (3) whether the auditorium was too dark, (4) whether indecency was facilitated by dark corners or other structures, (5) whether any particular age, sex or class of patron was present, and (6) any general comments. Interestingly, Miss Hicks also commented on the quality of the American film being shown, many of her colleagues finding Chaplin's films especially vulgar.

The Commissioner, Sir Edward Henry, concluded as a result of the survey that cinema auditorium were generally too dark, that the regulations introduced in May 1916 for supervised children's seats were often ignored, that spitting should be banned, and that there should be censorship of films depicting violence and immorality. (MEPO2/1691)

In search of delinquents. Two members of the Women's Patrols Committee of the National Union of Women Workers quiz some boys.

53 Strand   Time 8.35 - 3.10 June 15

Cheapest 6ᵈ and stax 1ᵈ. Children half price
Better 1/. I think nothing higher.

1. I could not see one. A young woman, and a lad showed people to seats.

2. Apparently quite in front

3. It would be difficult. But the narrow seats would also make such behaviour difficult.

4. No.
   I think everyone could see their neighbour, but the dim light, and slope, made it difficult to see far. I moved towards the children in front, but was told the front seats were 1/. Seats

5. Struck by number of young men, civilians as well as soldiers. Two girls at least there to pick up acquaintances.

6. A hopelessly silly and vulgar American performance

Marching into controversy. Nurses from Elsie Inglis's Scottish Women's Hospital Organisation leave Buckingham Palace after meeting the King, February 1918. In 1914 her offer of services had been given short shrift by the authorities.

Beyond the kinds of roles described above, there was considerable reluctance to encourage women in any other capacities. Famously, when Dr Elsie Inglis offered to raise an ambulance unit in 1914, a War Office official replied: 'My good lady, go home and sit still!' Subsequently, Inglis took her Scottish Women's Hospital to Serbia. However, women's work in the munitions industry forced the army to reconsider. In April 1915, therefore, the Army Council authorized the employment of women as cooks and waitresses in Britain in Lady Londonderry's

'CHARGES OF INDECENCY'
[*Opposite and overleaf*] *Acting Superintendent Short and Inspector Phillip of the Metropolitan Police report on 21 August 1916 that two constables of the Women's Police Service – Miss Salisbury and Miss Peebles – had been reluctant to go on patrol as they did not wish to appear in court as witnesses to acts of indecency.*

In the event, they went on patrol and the constable accompanying them had arrested Corporal Richard Lee of the

3/11th London Regiment and a Harrods' clerk, Edith Arnlat, for indecency. The soldier was fined 10s.6d and the woman bound over, without the women constables having to attend court.

The problem was a delicate one, another superintendent at Harrow believing that women constables should not be required to 'mix themselves up in these filthy cases'. Generally, it was expected that women constables should attend court except in cases of homosexuality, from which they would be spared. (MEPO2/1708)

Metropolitan Police.

Reference to Papers.

E.T. memo.
15.8.16.
Ex a
106103.
20 Reg 158

GR134573

Hyde Park STATION.   *a* DIVISION.

21st August, 1916

Women Patrols.

I beg to report that at 7p.m. 19th inst. when Women Patrols miss Salisbury and miss Peebles attended this station for Patrol work they both asked me if it was now considered necessary that all women Patrols who were witnesses in charges of indecency should attend Police court. I told them that it was. They then said that if they had known that, they would not have come, and would not come here again as they could not attend court. They asked if they might go out that evening since they had attended, and they were posted with P.C. 454 *a* Thompson on the understanding that if a charge of indecency arose they would keep entirely out of it. This they agreed to do.

At 10.20p.m. the Constable arrested Richard John Lee, corporal 2892, of 3/11 Battn. 11th London Regiment, and Edith Amlot, a clerk of Harrod's Stores, for having sexual intercourse. The women attended the Station with the Constable and volunteered the information that they had seen all that took place, but when

Station P.S. Lane, who was on duty, was about to take down their evidence, they again said that they could not attend court, and their names were not entered on the charge sheet.

The prisoners appeared at Marlboro' Street Court before T. Mead Esq. on 21st inst. and the soldier was fined 10/6, the girl being bound over. They both pleaded guilty.

Having regard to Commissioner's memorandum of 15th inst. I beg to ask directions as to allowing a constable to patrol with women who are not prepared, when they are witnesses, to follow up an arrest by attending court.

E. Phillips, Insp

Submitted for directions as at "A". Unless the women patrols are prepared to attend Police Court to corroborate cases in which they are witnesses their usefulness is greatly impaired.

Stuart.
Act'g Supt
21. 8. 16.

The acceptable face of women's work. Clerical staff of the Women's Royal Naval Service go about their jobs. The WRNS was founded on 1 January 1918.

Women's Legion, which received official recognition in February 1916. The Legion eventually numbered some 6000 women. If women could replace men at home, then there was no logical reason why they should not do so overseas. Thus, in March 1917, the first cooks of the new Women's Army Auxiliary Corps (WAAC) arrived in France. The 41,000 women who served in the WAAC – renamed Queen Mary's Army Auxiliary Corps in April 1918 – were mostly working class or lower middle class. Consequently, there was a tendency to view them as lacking the more altruistic patriotic motivations attributed to their social superiors. A Women's Royal Naval Service (WRNS) also came into existence in January 1918, followed by the Women's Royal Auxiliary Air Force (WRAAF) in April.

Before the First World War the most common employment for women had been domestic service, which employed 1.6 million women in 1911, or approximately a quarter of the female workforce. Relatively large numbers had also been employed in millinery, dressmaking, pottery, weaving and light industrial work in the North and Midlands. Some, however, did manual labour at coal tips and neither 'light' work in the cotton mills of Lancashire nor domestic service meant anything other than long hours of hard and repetitive toil. Many women were employed casually in 'sweated trades', child minding, taking in washing and in agricultural work, but such invisible employment was not recorded in the census returns. About 90 per cent of the women employed before the war were single and overwhelmingly working class. Even among the working class, the expectation was that most women

would cease employment on marriage, although married women were more common in the cotton industry of the North of England, since this was regarded as a mark of respectability.

Whether supplementing family income or otherwise, the usual expectation for married working-class women was many years of childbearing, ten pregnancies being the average, though many children did not survive into adulthood. While many diseases had been arrested by scientific discoveries, others, such as whooping cough, diphtheria and scarlet fever, still claimed many lives. On average, 20 per cent of infants still failed to survive the first year of life in the larger regional conurbations such as Birmingham, Salford, Sheffield and Wolverhampton.

Hard work, high wages. These apparently happy 'coke heavers' faced hard, heavy work and long hours, but it was far better paid than the more traditional women's jobs.

Back to the farm

Women had largely ceased to be a significant element in the agricultural labour force by the time war broke out. The exact number of women engaged in full-time or part-time agricultural work before 1914 is unknown, but it was probably around 130,000. There were, however, actually 20,000 fewer women employed on the land in July 1915 than at the outbreak of war, largely because of expanding employment opportunities elsewhere. Accordingly, there was an attempt to recruit more women for the land.

Women's War Agricultural Committees were established to draw up a voluntary register of women willing to work on the land, but the results were limited. The same was true of the Board of Agriculture's Women's National Land Service Corps of February 1916, although efforts were supplemented by private organizations such as the Women's Defence Relief Corps, the Women's Legion Agricultural Branch and the Women's Farm and Garden Union. Significantly, such organizations tended to call for women of 'high social standing socially living in dairying districts' to learn how to milk, so that 'their social inferiors will not be slow to follow their example, and employers of labour will take them seriously'. In fact, believing that women were incapable of performing heavy agricultural work, farmers – as it was reported in Hampshire as late as January 1918 – would 'take on anything that comes along, boys, old men, cripples, mentally deficients, criminals, or anything else' rather than women.

In March 1917 a new Women's Land Army (WLA), open to women of all classes, emerged. It had the intention of providing a permanent skilled and mobile female labour force for work on farms and in forestry, although a separate Women's Forestry Corps continued to be administered by the Board of Trade. Significantly, the WLA members, numbering only about 16,000 by September 1918, were paid less than

Working the land. Wartime necessities reversed a decline in women working in agriculture.

DEVON WOMEN'S WAR SERVICE COUNTY COMMITTEE.

REGISTRATIONS   Women Registered.   2.574

Incomplete - most part time workers
and immoveable.

KIND OF WORK   Not stated.

W A G E S.   "   "

ATTITUDE OF FARMERS.

Farmers are managing in general to carry
on without the help of women.
Individual farmers who have tried woman
labour are more than satisfied - the
labour of old men and young boys is
preferred as being cheaper - school
children are being exempted. Local Tribunals vary considerably in their deal-
ings with agricultural labour, and in
many districts women will not show any
readiness to work on the land until more
of the farmers sons are gone. Farmers are
not willing to take untrained workers.
Also many farmers have small holdings
which they work with their own families.

TRAINING.   Three sets of students have been trained
at Seale Hoyne Agricultural College -
most of these have found places.

DEMONSTRATION.   A very successful demonstration of Women's
work on the land was organised by Miss
Calmasty Hamlyn - about 2,000 people
attended including many farmers who were
obviously impressed especially by the
business like way in which several women
sheared sheep.

SUGGESTIONS.

OBSERVATIONS.   "Experience has shown that local part
time workers are not always made use of
if left to themselves and unorganised,
but in the hands of a good keen Registrar
they become a valuable asset.   There
are districts where one scheme fails of
success for some definite reason such as
the presence of some woman's industry
connected with the war - or the sloakness
of the Local Tribunal, but in general
it may be said that the women are ready
enough to work and that the success or
failure of the scheme depends upon the
individuality of the Registrar.

Much work is being done in cultivating
gardens and waste plots,Tavistock having
been particularly successful(report
attached). Little girls are learning to
milk.

NATIONAL SERVICE
WOMEN'S
LAND ARMY

GOD SPEED THE PLOUGH
AND THE WOMAN WHO DRIVES IT

Serve God and the war. Despite posters like these, the Women's Land Army, established in March 1917, attracted only 16,000 women, who were paid much less than unskilled male labourers.

the unskilled male agricultural labourers, although an elaborate welfare network was created for them. There were also attempts to demonstrate women's potential through various competitions and demonstrations of ploughing, milking, hoeing and harrowing. Reporting one such competition in Hertfordshire in July 1917, *The Times* waxed lyrically about 'the land women, bronzed and freck-led' and 'splendidly healthy', clearing ditches, piling carts with manure and harnessing horses. The WLA's own handbook reminded its members that they were 'doing a man's work and so you're dressed rather like a man, but remember just because you wear a smock and breeches you should take care to behave like a British girl who expects chivalry and respect from everyone she meets'. Neverthe-less, the Board of Trade estimated that there were still only about 148,000 women employed in agriculture in 1918, but it is possible that the true figure was closer to around 260,000. The emphasis on finding a role for women in greater food production was to have a more lasting significance in the establishment of the first Women's Institute in Anglesey, in September 1915, the movement having begun in Canada in the 1890s. By 1919 there were to be over 1200 women's institutes in Britain, establishing part of the social fabric that has survived into the 21st century.

'MORE THAN SATISFIED'

A report from Devon in September 1916 on the reaction of farmers to the campaign to employ more women on the land, the Board of Agriculture and Fisheries having initiated the national effort in February of that year.

Farmers in Devon had proven resist-ant, although those who had employed women were generally satisfied with their work. Women, on the other hand, had resisted volunteering while it was per-ceived that many farmer's sons had yet to enlist in the armed forces. Nonetheless, *there had been a good demonstration of women's agricultural work and some women were already undertaking cultiva-tion while girls were also milking cows. Across the country, farmers' opposition to women workers was greatest where male labour was still available. By that time, some 57,497 women had registered for agricultural work and 28,767 of them were employed, although only 30 counties had thus far reported. On average, women were earning 3d to 4d per hour for an eight-hour day, with board and lodging provided.* (MAF 59/1)

'WOMEN'S LAND ARMY'

An armlet of the Women's Land Army. The baize armlet with the scarlet crown was approved in March 1916 for issuing by Women's Farm Labour Committees to women who had registered to work on the land and had completed at least 30 days' work. There had been some thought of issuing distinctive knickerbockers instead but the President of the Board of Agriculture, Lord Selborne, thought this improper as did his female advisors! Initially, 50,000 armlets were produced by the Co-operative Wholesale Society at a cost of 3d–4d each, to which expense the Treasury agreed.

The Co-operative Wholesale Society was also enlisted to supply suitable clothing to Women's County Committees, but, when women were earning only 3d–4d a day, recommended prices such as 6s.11d for overalls were too high. The Society withdrew from the clothing scheme at the end of 1916, ostensibly on the grounds of its own labour shortages. (MAF42/8)

'SERVING HER COUNTRY'

A certificate of service in the Women's Land Army signed by Selborne and President of the Board of Agriculture and Walter Runcimann as President of the Board of Trade. The certificate was approved on 20 January 1916. (MAF42/8)

'PUPILS MUST BE PUNCTUAL'

[Facing page] Rules of the Monmouthshire Women's War Agricultural Committee for its training centres, as forwarded to Miss Meriel Talbot, the Director of the Women's Branch of the Board of Agriculture, by Lady Ada Mather-Jackson in July 1918.

Concern had arisen about the lack of discipline in the Women's Land Army, Lady Mather-Jackson reporting that some girls – mostly recruited from mining districts – had run away, most stayed out late, and many kept asking for weekends off and did the least work they could. Monmouthshire, therefore, had issued these rules in the hope of enforcing them,

Every woman who helps in agriculture during the war is as truly serving her country as the man who is fighting in the trenches or on the sea.

President of the Board of Trade.

President of the Board of Agriculture.

but Lady Mather-Jackson believed it would be necessary to put some girls in front of the magistrates and that gang hostels might also be desirable.

Miss Talbot replied on 27 July that military-style discipline could not be expected and that a recent case in Gloucester, where Grace Smith had been given 14 days' hard labour for being absent without leave, was unhelpful. Women of influence would now be appointed as welfare supervisors to instil esprit de corps. (MAF42/8)

MONMOUTHSHIRE WOMEN'S WAR AGRICULTURAL COMMITTEE.

Principal.—

Hostel Matron.—

Forewoman or Instructress.—

District Representative.—

RULES FOR TRAINING CENTRE.

RULES to be observed by Pupils in Training under the Women's War Agricultural Committee—acting for the Board of Agriculture.

1.—The Pupils must immediately on arrival report themselves to the Principal.

2.—The Pupils must obey the Rules of the Hostel and keep strictly to the hours.

3.—Pupils are expected to make their own beds and keep their own rooms neat and they must not use their bedrooms during the day.

4.—Pupils must be punctual at meals. No meals will be provided out of hours.

5.—When work is finished all farm boots must be changed in the Common room before taking tea.

6.—The use of improper language, rowdy behaviour, or inattention to Rules, will be considered sufficient reason for expulsion.

7.—The Pupils must be punctual in starting for work on the Farm and must keep to the hours in accordance with the Time Table.

8.—Pupils must wear the Uniform provided when at work, and no jewelry must be worn. Out of working hours pupils may wear civilian clothes, but if so they must not include any portion of their Uniform.

9.—All Pupils must attend some place of Worship on Sunday mornings unless prevented by their Farm Duties.

10.—No leave of absence is granted without the direct permission of the Principal, at the written request of Parents or Guardians.

11.—Pupils must carry out any form of practical or manual work that may be demanded at such time and places as may be required.

12.—Pupils must take Notes at Lectures and keep a record of the work done. These Notes must be in legible form and properly arranged and must be handed in for inspection when required.

13.—All Pupils will be reported upon at the end of their Course, as to their attendance, conduct, diligence and capacity.

14.—Pupils having any complaint to make should do so through the Forewoman or direct to the Principal.

TIME TABLE.

HOURS.

RISE ....6 a.m.

BREAKFAST ....6.45 a.m.

DINNER .... 12.15 p.m.

TEA .... 6 p.m.

BEDTIME—SUMMER .... 9.30 p.m.

WINTER .... 9 p.m.

During the Summer Session Pupils are not allowed out after 9 p.m. and during the Winter 8 p.m.

HOURS FOR WORK AT THE INSTITUTE :

7.30 a.m. to 12 Noon.

1 p.m. to 5.30 p.m.

Pupils are expected to work 9½ hours a day exclusive of Meal Times.

N.B.—Overtime will be paid at the District rate.

Nature and nurture. These members of the Women's Land Army care for newly born piglets, in this touching image.

Expanding their horizons

With the outbreak of war, there was a steady expansion in the female work force in industry as men enlisted. It is worth remembering, though, that, in the first twelve months of the war, while some 400,000 women came into employment, so did a million men: the first recourse of employers was to unemployed men. Positive recruitment of women came only after the establishment of the Ministry of Munitions in May 1915 and, especially, after the introduction of conscription in January 1916. Thus, little use was made of the women who came forward under the government's voluntary registration scheme in March 1915: two months later only around 1800 out of almost 79,000 who had registered had gained employment. Many of these were also filling such tangential jobs in London as lift attendants in stores, theatre assistants, and waitresses in men's clubs. Indeed, Mrs Emmeline Pankhurst organized a major 'Women's Right to Serve' demonstration in London on 17 July 1915 with 30,000 women walking behind banners proclaiming: 'Women's Battle Cry is Work, Work, Work.' Typical of many responses was that of the London Postal Service to the suggestion that women be employed in sorting mail. It initially refused, on the grounds that women would need separate rest rooms and separate offices in which to sort post, and special seats because of the height of the sorting boxes; that women could not cope with the night work; and that, in any case, they would find the work too arduous. Moreover, women had actually been worse hit than men by the initial increase in unemployment, stemming from initial wartime business uncertainties. An additional difficulty was women's relative inability to move to find new employment in the way that men could. Finally, by including re-employment with wholly new employment, official statistics tend to imply a larger increase in women working than was actually the case.

(*left*) The formidable Mrs Emmeline Pankhurst, pictured in 1908. The suffragette movement divided in 1914, with Sylvia Pankhurst splitting from her mother and her sister, Christabel, to oppose the war.

(*above*) Vital work, dubious reputations. The munitionettes' working-class origins and new spending power led to accusations of selfishness and extravagance, despite the essential jobs they did.

Figures vary, however. One contemporary commentator, A.W. Kirkaldy, estimated that 1.6 million more women were employed in Britain in 1918 than in 1914, the total rising from 3.2 million to 4.8 million. Kirkaldy, however, omitted those in domestic service and other groups such as the self-employed, women employed by their husbands, and those involved in small-scale dressmaking. Taking all these other categories into account it is likely that the number of women in paid employment rose from 5.9 million to 7.3 million, representing a slightly smaller wartime increase of 1.4 million.

Particularly large increases were recorded in transport, commerce and administration, where women were judged far more acceptable. In clerical work, for example, the number of women rose from 124,000 in 1911 to 591,000 by 1921, while those involved in national and local government increased from 262,000 to 460,000. The largest proportional increase was in transport, where the number of women increased from 18,200 to 117,200.

A respectable way to
help. This driver and her
ambulance belong to the
Voluntary Aid Detachment
(VAD), formed in 1909 and
a socially acceptable means
of assisting the war effort in
a traditional nursing role.

In fact, approximately half of the women brought into employment to substitute for men in uniform were employed in commerce rather than industrial occupations. Indeed, the number of women employed in industry rose from 2.1 million to just 2.9 million, representing an increase from from about 26 per cent of the total labour force to about 36 per cent. The increases in some fields resulted from decreases elsewhere, as the better pay available in war industries lured women from traditional and 'invisible' employment. Accordingly, the numbers employed in domestic service declined by 400,000 and the numbers in the clothing industry by 76,000. At the Gretna National Cordite Factory, some 80 per cent of the female labour force had been previously employed, 36 per cent of them in domestic service. Similarly, 71 per cent of the female labour force at Armstrong Whitworth, on the Tyne, had been previously employed, with 20 per cent coming from domestic service. This movement in itself changed the lives of many upper- and middle-class women as servants became scarce. One officer's wife recalled: 'Neither my Mother, sister or myself had ever done any serious housework or cooking of any kind, so it was an entirely new experience to be confronted with meals to cook, rooms to clean, and required an entirely new mental adjustment.'

Wartime propaganda exaggerated the extent of 'dilution', the introduction of more women and unskilled labour into the workforce. Unions and employers alike resisted it, and women were employed for very specific functions. In many cases, women did not actually supplant skilled male labour. In practical terms, dilution was not substitution as such, but a reorganization of working practices, so that the unskilled could perform more tasks. It is calculated that only about 23 per cent of the women who came into the munitions industry were actually doing men's work.

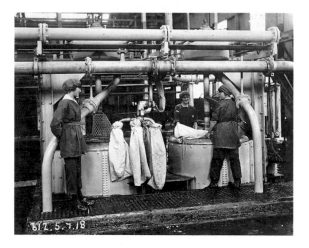

Stealing their clothes. These women, working at the Gretna factory in 1918, wear trousers rather than skirts, an increasingly common sight among wartime women workers.

4th December, 1916. I'A

Lieut. Colonel L. E. O. Charlton,
    A. O. 1,
    <u>Adastral House.</u>

        The attached reports will enable some opinion to be formed as to the percentage of women labour being employed on machine tools in certain London factories at the present time in relation to the total number of employees.   They will also indicate what machines are being worked by women and to what extent.

        It seems to be the general opinion of the Works Managers that training women as skilled hands on machine tools takes much the same time as training a youth, but for ordinary simple operations women labour is giving satisfactory results, provided the work is properly supervised and the machines are set up by skilled men.

        For repitition of manufacture women can be utilized much more than they are at present but in connection with jobbing work where difficult and varied operations have to be carried out, they are of little use not having had sufficient experience.

        Women appear to work with the men quite satisfactorily.   In some factories women supervisors are employed, in others, such as Napiers, they take their place side by side with the men and are under the control of the usual male foreman.

        The disadvantages are those pertaining to accommodation, but all the factories intend to employ more female labour in the immediate future and are making provisions for the necessary accommodation.

                      Captain.
          Inspector of Transport.

'WOMEN CAN BE UTILIZED'

A report by Captain C. Jarrott, Inspector of Transport, to Lieut. Colonel L.E.O. Charlton, the principal Royal Flying Corps staff officer at the War Office, on 4 December 1916. It concerns the employment of women in London factories.

In response to a decision to examine ways of drawing upon female labour in the RFC's own supporting services, Jarrott visited The Associated Equipment Co Ltd, The Napier Motor Co Ltd, and The Fiat Motor Co, all of whom were engaged in manufacturing aero engines as well as vehicles. All had employed women as well as boys and had found the former more satisfactory workers on lathes, and drilling and milling machines, as well as in fitting small parts.

Opinion varied on the time women required to become proficient, but it ranged between six and eight months. In every case, women were started at £1 per week, but they could eventually earn between £2 and £2.10s.0d. per week.

As a result of Jarrott's report, RFC depots were asked to comment upon the opportunities for women. Most believed that women could undertake only repetitive work and would require special accommodation and other facilities. Consequently, most depots suggested opportunities for increasing female employment existed only in clerical positions or in the stores.
(AIR2/10/87/9035)

More women, please.
A Ministry of Munitions poster of 1918 appeals for more female workers for the aircraft industry, stressing maintenance allowances and training.

This working life

The majority of the 'new' women who entered employment during the war were either working-class women entering the workforce earlier than might have been the case previously, or married women returning to employment. Many of the latter only did so after the cushioning effect of separation allowances had been eroded by rising prices. In a sense, therefore, wartime work was not a novel experience for many women and, whatever the financial rewards they received, the work would not have had a particularly liberating effect. Nonetheless, the disquieting flight of women from domestic service, the increased purchasing power available to munitions workers, combined with their working-class origins, resulted in accusations of selfishness and extravagance. There was a marked increase in sales of soap during the war and it was also claimed that money was being 'wasted' on clothes, underclothes and jewellery. 'Munitionettes' also earned the same kind of reputation for promiscuity as the WAAC.

For many women long hours, albeit on shift work, and manual labour was a new experience, especially as facilities such as cloakrooms and canteens were sometimes slow to emerge. Conditions could be extremely unpleasant. At the Royal Arsenal, Woolwich, for example, the works were badly ventilated, poorly lit and overrun with rats. Work shifts attempted to make things more bearable by organizing concerts and competitions, such as hat-making, while also creating some kind of collective identity through a work song or different coloured hair ribbons, since most personal items such as purses or jewellery had to be removed before going on shift for safety reasons. One woman working in a munitions factory at Morecambe, Lancashire, walked three miles to the factory for her twelve-hour shifts from a room she shared with five others in lodgings; when a fire burned down the factory in October 1917 she was paid off and subsequently entered the WAAC.

There was also often hostility from male workers. One woman, who worked on machining parts for aero engines, recalled that the men would not allow her to use their tools and rarely spoke to her: not long after she first arrived, her tool drawer was nailed up and, on another occasion, oil was poured into it. In another case, a woman who became a tram conductress in Lancashire reported that the drivers would suddenly put on the brakes and send her flying, male conductors would refuse to hand over their ticket books, and some male passengers would refuse to show her their tickets.

In addition to such problems, women were running much greater physical risks than before the war. Hazards included TNT (trinitrotoluene) poisoning, the chemical attacking red corpuscles in the blood and the tissues of organs such as the liver. Those who worked with the

All change, please. Women tram drivers, like this one in Lowestoft, represented one of the first new forms of women's work to emerge in the war, in the face of some hostility from male colleagues and the travelling public.

599.2.7.18

Out-producing the
enemy. Women munitions
workers, such as these at
the Gretna plant, were
integral to the new form
of mass-production,
mechanized warfare.

chemical generally became known as canaries from the toxic jaundice that turned faces bright yellow, which many of them contracted. It could also mean loss of memory, sight disorders, convulsions, and delirium. In extreme cases, it meant death: 109 women died from the condition during the war. The 'dope' varnish applied to aircraft canvas was also extremely hazardous, causing many women to collapse unconscious. Then there were industrial accidents. An explosion at the National Filling Factory at Barnbow, near Leeds, killed 35 women in December 1916, while 35 women died in another incident at Chilwell, near Nottingham, in July 1918. Many women were among the 69 fatalities of the massive explosion at Silvertown, in East London, in January 1917.

War work was probably more liberating for the minority of middle-class women who came forward and who enjoyed a degree of subsequent economic independence as a result. Whether middle- or working-class, however, many women might not have regarded wartime employment as permanent. Accordingly, they might have returned relatively willingly to domesticity, where they already held much influence within the family, despite often appreciating the opportunities employment had given them. In many cases, wartime employment had been a necessity rather than a desire.

Equality at work?

It certainly did not mean equal pay with men, which government and unions alike resisted. Indeed, while a Ministry of Munitions circular, called 'L2', of October 1915, appeared to suggest that women should get the same pay as men, this was only a requirement where women could work unsupervised. It was largely intended as a sop to unions, who feared 'dilution' might be used as a means of lowering the rate for particular jobs. Moreover, it was common to pay women on time rates rather than the piece rates (by results) to which equality had been applied by the regulation. In the case of municipal tramways, for example, each corporation was free to set its own pay rates. In Leeds, women received 14s.0d a week less than men for the same work, while the decision in Bradford to increase women's bonuses in 1918 out of line with other towns drew such strong protests that the scheme was abandoned. Only in munitions work did women's pay keep pace with inflation, but it was still less than that of men. On average, women's wages rose from 13s.6d a week in 1914 to 35s.0d by 1918, but this represented an increase from about half of average men's earnings to only about two-thirds. Female employment during the war was seen as a cheap source of easily exploitable labour, which could be dispensed with in peacetime.

A role for the more genteel. Dr R. Murray Leslie lectures some well-to-do trainee nurses at the Institute of Hygiene, September 1914.

In entering wartime employment, women also joined trade unions of course, contributing significantly to the general rise in membership. Overall, women trade unionists almost tripled from 437,000 in 1914 to 1.2 million by 1918. Although 383 British unions accepted women, some, such as the Amalgamated Society of Engineers and the Amalgamated Society of Carpenters and Joiners, declined to admit women. In becoming unionized, many women were also increasingly prominent in strike action. Most women's industrial unrest initially surrounded welfare issues, but equal pay became more of an issue in 1918.

Reversing the trend

At the end of the war, the number of women employed in industry began to decline rapidly. Some 750,000 women were made redundant by the end of 1918 alone, the press changing its coverage abruptly from praise for women workers to hostility towards them. Two-thirds of women who had entered employment during the First World War had left it by 1920. But the picture was still a varied one. The decline was even greater in the more traditional working roles, such as the textile industry and domestic service: in the latter case, former munitions workers in particular refused to contemplate a return to what they regarded as servile labour. Expectations had altered. And the number of women actually increased in newer industries such as chemicals and light engineering. To some extent, women also maintained their wartime position in white-collar work.

Most people assumed that women would return to the home. Wartime regulations were changed so that women visiting labour exchanges would find it difficult to insist on industrial or even office employment on pain of losing unemployment benefit; and married women were excluded entirely from the benefit by 1922. The Amalgamated Society of Engineers pressed in the courts for full implementation of the Restoration of Pre-War Practices Act (1919). Even a traditional women's occupation, such as the laundry trade, was opened to disabled

(*left*) The machinery of war. Women from the Britannia Works of Marshall, Sons & Co in Gainsborough, Lincolnshire, work amid contraptions reminiscent of a Heath Robinson drawing.

(*right*) A new kind of plumber's mate. The variety of 'male' roles that women could now fulfil was considerable, as this plumber/general jobber demonstrates.

soldiers and there was considerable government propaganda to reinforce the desirability of domesticity and the concept of a marriage bar. Indeed, the Sex Disqualification (Removal) Act (1919), intended to prevent gender or marriage from being a bar to civil and judicial employment, was interpreted selectively by the courts.

The achievement of the franchise for a proportion of women in 1918 tended to fragment the women's movement and ironically it left women without an effective political voice; and unionization proved of little assistance in defending women's employment. Women did gain a degree of equality in terms of divorce and custody of children through the Matrimonial Causes Act (1923) and the Guardianship of Infants Act. But, just as few women were sufficiently well placed to take advantage of the supposed easier access to the professions, so the latter pieces of legislation were of more relevance to middle- and upper-class women than to the majority of working-class women.

Winning a voice

The question of how women's contribution to the war effort related to their achievement of the franchise is a difficult one. Few politicians supported women's suffrage on the grounds of the work they had performed during the war; but most were in favour of electoral reform, and the Representation of the People Act of February 1918 was a war measure and not a women's measure. The argument for electoral reform was fuelled by the potential disenfranchisement of men, who had lost their residence qualification of 12 months' continuous occupation through service overseas; the need to reward those without the vote who had fought for their country; and the need to allow all those who had contributed to the victory to determine the country's future. The intention was to enfranchise only stable, mature women as a means of balancing the extension of the vote to the 40 per cent of males who had also not voted before 1914. Such women were more likely to identify politically with their husbands than the predominantly young, single, working-class 'munitionettes'. The eventual legislation enfranchised some 7 million women over the age of 30 in 1918, who were either ratepayers or married to ratepayers. With some 5 million or so women over the age of 21 excluded, the terms ensured that women would not be a majority of the electorate, although, as it happened, women often acted as proxies for absent male voters in 1918's General Election.

In effect, therefore, the war limited the potential scope of the franchise so far as women were concerned. Having lost the political initiative through the virtual suspension of the issue in 1914, when they might have been close to success, the women's movement accepted what was on offer in 1918 – which in itself was no more than had been

Roll out the barrel. Women also entered the wartime brewing industry, even as government legislation was reducing the available time to consume the industry's products.

proposed in legislation (lost on a parliamentary technicality) in 1912. In fact, the majority of those engaged in the pre-war suffrage movement, as epitomized by Millicent Garrett Fawcett's National Union of Women's Suffrage Societies (NUWSS), had been essentially constitutional, conservative and middle-class and concerned with the narrow objective of the franchise rather than wider issues of equality. The Pankhursts' Women's Social and Political Union (WSPU) had been more militant, but it had fragmented before the war: by September 1914 both Emmeline Pankhurst and her daughter, Christabel, had thrown themselves into the war effort. And suffragettes were often prominent in handing out white feathers to men not in uniform.

Family values, sex and morality

Some have argued that women's real contribution to the war was actually in the traditional role of keeping home fires burning and raising children in the absence of fathers. In so doing, they dealt not only with deprivation and separation, but also the possibility and all-too-often reality of untimely widowhood. Certainly, the difficulty faced by many women in feeding their families in conditions of rising prices and shortages of foodstuffs, while conducting their own full-time employment, should not be underestimated. The National Food Economy League, for example, published a series of wartime guides such as *Housekeeping on Twenty-five Shillings a Week, or under, for a Family of Five*, which was priced at one penny.

It is has also been suggested that British family ties may have been strengthened by the war. This view tends to be based on the popularity of that tribute to the benefits of marriage, Marie Stopes's *Married Love*, published in March 1918 and reprinted four times before the armistice. It was followed by *Wise Parenthood* in November 1918, in which Stopes raised issues of birth control absent from her earlier book, and, subsequently, by the somewhat risible film *Maisie's Marriage*. In fact, family and household patterns do not appear to have changed substantially even in the absence of servicemen, although individual family situations would depend, obviously, on different circumstances.

Mention of Marie Stopes, however, raises the matter of social values generally. As the establishment of female morality police in Britain suggests, sexual mores were often those that most concerned

(*above*) Suffragette kitsch. This novelty moneybox was produced for the Christmas market in 1913. The precise impact of the war on the long-standing issue of female suffrage remains contested.

(*right*) 'Maisie's Marriage'. Marie Stopes's controversial film had an original wartime title of 'Married Love', which was banned.

(*far right*) Some compensation. A notification of increased separation allowances, which played an important financial role for the families of married servicemen.

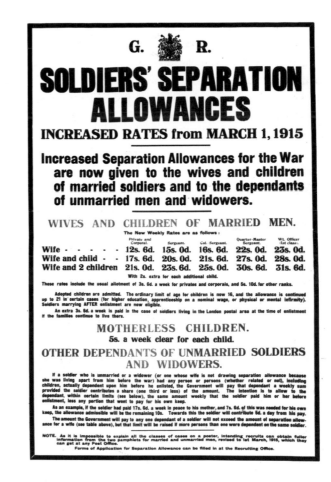

contemporaries. Prostitution and venereal disease were understandably of perennial concern to the military authorities, and the supposed 'khaki fever' for men in uniform displayed by young women in 1914 aroused particular alarm. It was also the case that, albeit briefly until public outrage led to its curtailment, police took an interest in the wives of men on active service lest they be tempted to stray from the straight and narrow through drunkenness, promiscuity, neglect of children or criminal activity. Separation allowances, which were also not initially paid to 'wives' not legally wedded or for children born out of wedlock, could be withdrawn in such cases. The local authorities in Chesterfield went so far as to post up a notice in its schools warning of 'Cessation of Separation Allowances to the Unworthy'. Moreover, the WAAC and 'munitionettes' were equally alleged to be promiscuous, and, in some places, women were initially prohibited from entering public houses after 7 p.m. 'War babies' became a press sensation in 1915, though, as it happened, that year saw an unusually low number of illegitimate births and an unusually high number of marriages, many of the latter no doubt encouraged by imminent wartime separation as men went overseas. As Sylvia Pankhurst expressed it after the war:

> Alarmist morality mongers conceived most monstrous visions of girls and women, freed from the control of fathers and husbands who had hitherto compelled them to industry, chastity and sobriety, now neglecting their homes, plunging into excesses, and burdening the country with swarms of illegitimate children.

Nonetheless, as one diplomat reported on returning to Britain after having spent the entire war overseas, 'When I left England in 1911 contraceptives were hard to buy outside London or other large cities. By 1919 every village chemist was selling them.' As Mary Agnes Hamilton put it, in recalling the war:

> How and why refuse appeals, backed up by the hot beating of your own heart, or what at the moment you thought to be your own heart, which were put with passion and even pathos by a hero here today and gone tomorrow.

Another manifestation of public concern was the extraordinary 1918 libel case brought against a British Independent MP, Noel Pemberton Billing, who had won a by-election campaigning for better air defences in March 1916. Pemberton Billing, who alleged that the Germans had a list of 47,000 British men and women open to blackmail for sexual

'THE CUSTOM OF DRINKING INTOXICANTS'

A report by the Restrictions Committee of the Central Control Board (Liquor Traffic), on 1 July 1915. It concerns a petition demanding a new prohibition on women under the age of 21 being sold liquor or allowed on licensed premises in Birmingham until three months after the end of the war.

The issue had been raised by the Birmingham branch of the White Ribbon Band, a Christian teetotal organization that had collected 37,155 signatures on a petition to this effect. There were 2205 public houses or other licensed premises in the city, or one for every 404 inhabitants, together with over 1700 unlicensed feeding houses, 65 cinemas, 8 music halls and 5 theatres. The White Ribbon Band's female monitors claimed to have counted 7753 women leaving 150 licensed premises within a period of just over 129 hours, of whom 79 were drunk. Similar reports came from Woolwich and Blackburn.

The Birmingham police did not believe that women were drinking to excess, but they supported the restriction as a sensible precaution. The Committee resolved to undertake its own report and suggested a prominent member of the Board, Sir George Newman, should head it. The report refers to Neville Chamberlain, then Lord Mayor of Birmingham. Chamberlain subsequently became Director General of National Service. (HO185/238)

July 1 1916

8593/16.

REPORT OF RESTRICTIONS COMMITTEE.
PETITION OF BIRMINGHAM WHITE RIBBON BANDS.

The Committee have considered representations from
Birmingham that the custom of drinking intoxicants and of frequent-
ing public houses is on the increase among girls, and a Petition
that the Board should make an Order prohibiting any girls under
the age of 21 in Birmingham and District from being served with
intoxicating liquor, or being allowed on licensed premises, together
with a statement of facts in support of the Petition.   The statements bear closely upon the condition of girl workers in munition
factories, and it has been ascertained from the Director of the
Welfare Department of the Ministry of Munitions that he would welcome
investigation of this matter.   The Committee recommend that the
Board should undertake such investigation with a view to seeing whether
and how far, their powers could be used to remedy any evil which
may be found.   They suggest that Sir George Newman, who they have
reason to believe is willing to do so, should undertake the task
on behalf of the Board, and that he should have the assistance of
Miss. Macadam whose services are offered by the Welfare Department
for the purpose, and of a woman factory Inspector, if the Home
Office can lend one, and possibly also of a lady from Birmingham.
On this latter point it would be well to consult Mr. Neville
Chamberlain, both as to whether a Birmingham lady should be asked
to assist in the investigation, and if so, as to the lady who would
be suitable for the purpose.

_____

L.T.F.

1.7.15.

depravity, stood accused of libelling Maud Allan, a dancer and actress well known for her performance as the biblical temptress Salome, as a lesbian and sexual pervert. In the event, he was acquitted.

The perceptions at the time do not necessarily correspond with reality. In theory at least, more women were aware of contraception, as were the soldiers issued, sometimes reluctantly by the authorities, with wartime prophylactics. Indeed, while the wartime illegitimacy rate in Britain did rise by 30 per cent, with a big rise in 1916, it needs to be borne in mind that since the overall birth rate declined, fewer women were actually having illegitimate children. Similarly, an official enquiry established in February 1918 to investigate the widespread accusations of immorality aimed at the WAAC could find no evidence to support such a contention. Nonetheless, there was a perceived change in attitudes among women, as evidenced by the appearance in female fashion of shorter hairstyles, more makeup, lighter fabrics, bras rather than camisoles, and shorter mid-calf skirts, of which the newspapers owned by Lord Northcliffe particularly disapproved. To the *Daily Mail*, an 'absurdly short' skirt was six inches off the ground, one revealing 'the feet, and ankles and even more of the stockings'. In factories, women were even to be seen wearing trousers, though one wartime pamphlet issued by a woman welfare superintendent at St Helens recommended a 'woollen combination' over a one-piece dress, which 'should not reach below the boot tops, i.e., eight or ten inches from the ground'. More women also took up smoking and alcohol. It also became commonplace to see women unescorted in restaurants and pubs. As the *Daily Mail* commented in April 1916:

> The wartime business girl is to be seen any night dining out alone or with a friend in the moderate-priced restaurants in London. Formerly she would never have had her evening meal in town unless in the company of a man friend. But now with money and without men she is more and more beginning to dine out.

The traditional chaperones, indeed, had entirely disappeared, Mrs C.S. Peel later writing that the elderly 'didn't feel like having to walk home after late nights'. In many factories, even women's football teams were formed.

A challenge to family life

It was impossible that family relationships would not be affected by the war. Many mothers' lives were transformed, and ultimately husbands and fathers might return strangers, or disabled, or not at all. In the meantime, wartime absence was generally thought to have substantially contributed to increases in juvenile delinquency, particularly

War's young victims. These war orphans are pictured outside Buckingham Palace, after returning from playing in Hyde Park.

among those children aged 11 to 13. Cases of birching of boys ordered by the courts increased from 2415 in 1914 to 5210 in 1917. In cities such as Manchester, Birmingham and Glasgow, there were reports of youth gangs: one, in the Ancoats area of Manchester, wore distinctive pink neckerchiefs and carried prominently displayed razorblades for cutting the plaits off young women. Many observers also blamed the cinema. The National Council of Public Morals pointed more to the social and economic pressures of war as the cause while the State Children's Society suggested that the military requisition of many schools was also a factor.

As far as education was concerned, the government had been intending to bring forward new legislation had war not broken out in 1914. There was a general consensus on the need to improve education, in view of the greater efficiency of German schools and the fact that 75

per cent of British children left school at the age of 14. Greater numbers of working-class children attended fee-paying secondary schools during the war, but by 1917 an estimated 600,000 children had also left school early to take up wartime employment. Many children were employed on the land on a seasonal basis before the war, during school holidays or before and after school hours. It was not altogether surprising, therefore, that farmers took the lead in requesting that by-laws on child labour be relaxed, a pressure to which government and local authorities soon surrendered, though doubts continued to surface as to the wisdom of allowing younger children to work. For those children who did remain in the classroom, the syllabus took on an increasingly militaristic hue, with an emphasis on celebrations such as Empire Day (24 May) and Trafalgar Day (21 October). Moreover, they, too, could be pressed into useful war-related activity, such as war savings campaigns, the knitting of garments for servicemen, vegetable growing, and the organized collection of acorns, blackberries and horse chestnuts.

The President of the Board of Education, H.A.L. Fisher, sought to encourage greater secondary provision, ending the practice of 'half-timing', raising the leaving age from 12 to 14, and improving teaching as a career. His legislation ran out of time in 1917 when opposition arose to perceived over-centralization. Employers were also concerned at the potential loss of cheap labour through the ending of half-timing. Indeed, wartime relaxation of child employment regulations now permitted children of 14 to undertake up to 13½ hours of work per day and up to 60 hours per week. Amended legislation was reintroduced in March 1918, but, with the onset of postwar economic difficulties, the continuation classes Fisher had envisaged for children aged 14 to 18 never materialized. The number of free places at secondary schools remained limited and there was no acceptance of the principle of universal secondary education.

'THE COMFORT AND MORALS OF ITS PATRONS'

[Facing page and overleaf] A letter from the Chairman of the Cinematograph Exhibitors' Association, F.R. Goodwin, to the Home Secretary, Sir George Cave, on 5 January 1917.

Goodwin objects to the assumption that cinemas are to blame for increased prostitution, following a case in which a local authority had demanded the greater illumination of auditoria. The Association acknowledged the (implausibly exaggerated) claim that there were 60,000 prostitutes operating in London, of whom no less than 40,000 were French or Belgian refugees, and that they had been driven off the streets into teashops, cafés and cinemas; but it believed that stronger levels of light would actually assist rather than diminish sexual activity.

The Association proposed deportation of foreign prostitutes and compulsory identity cards for women. In fact, the Metropolitan Police had no evidence of prostitution taking place in cinemas and seriously doubted the figures given for the number of prostitutes. (MEPO2/1691)

THE

<u>CINEMATOGRAPH EXHIBITORS' ASSOCIATION OF GREAT BRITAIN & IRELAND.</u>
                                                                Limited.
                        President T.P.O'Connor, Esq, M.P.

                        Broadmead House, Panton Street,

                                Haymarket, London, S.W.

                        London District Branch,
                          Broadmead House,
                          Panton St., Haymarket, S.W.

                                        5th January, 1917.

        Rt.Hon.Sir George Cave K.C. M.P.
        Home Secretary.
        Home Office,
        Whitehall,
        S.W.

        Dear Sir,

                On behalf of the above Association we venture to
        approach you to direct your attention to, and to make some
        observations upon an extremely urgent matter which affects
        the well-being of the public in general, and the Cinematograph
        Trade in particular.

                Certain abnormal conditions unfortunately exist in
        the West end of London at the present time which tend <u>gravely
        to endanger the good name of the Cinematograph Trade, and the
        comfort and morals of its patrons,</u> and which without the aid
        of the State cannot be altered.

                It has recently been stated that there are at the
        present time 60,000 prostitutes in the County of London, 40,000
        of such being of alien birth. Many are refugees from France
        and Belgium, and very many are ordinarily resident and have been
        so for many years in this country. Recent arrangements and
        adjustments have closed certain quarters in which the women in
        question have been used to ply their occupation, and the result
        has been that in addition to using the streets in vastly increased
        numbers, such women are found to be endeavouring to establish a
        new market place by invading the tea shops, cafes and cinemas in
        the West end and vicinity. Having abandoned the glaring garb
        of the music hall for a more sober raiment the abnormally
        darkened conditions of the vestibules of cinemas in the early
        evenings make it exceedingly difficult to detect the character
        of women seeking admission.

                A campaign for more illuminant within the auditoriums
        has considerably aided the women in their calling. It has been
                                                        suggested

suggested that indecent and immoral conduct takes place within cinemas.   This is entirely without foundation, and the cry for more lighting came from this unfounded charge; the real evil being that the women seek to solicit and are aided rather than otherwise by any attempt to raise the standard of indoor lighting.   The difficulty of dealing with this matter is well known.   Actions for libel are so easy to manufacture, while the calling for these women is so lucrative that any fine inflicted is paid with ease.

The Association prays for help in this matter, and ventures to place before the Department a series of proposals having for their object the better control of the health and morals of the town.

Under the National Registration Act of 1915, steps might be taken to re-register the woman of power of the country, and by this means exact details of the age, occupation, and means of support of every female over the age of 14 would be obtained. A personal card would be issued to every female giving certain particulars, and this card would be producible on demand by any authorised person.

No opposition should be offered to this course, which only equalises the conditions between the sexes.

Suitable penalties could be inflicted for failure to produce identity cards, and it might be found possible that in future a convicted prostitute would have the identity card marked to that effect.

The result of this registration would be to tabulate clearly the numbers and nationalities of the pests now poisoning our city.

Deportation should follow of the foreign element, and some method of isolation and reclamation for the British nationals adopted forthwith.   Woman labour is wanted we understand in vast quantities, and it appears to this Association that no better work could be undertaken than the provision of a working settlement in which these women could be placed for stated periods of time, during which organised effort could be made for their better education and reformation.

The Association begs the consideration of His Majesty's Secretary of State for Home Affairs of the information contained in this letter, and hope that some means may be devised to deal with evils alluded to.

We have the honour to remain,

Your obedent Servants,

(sgd) F.R.Goodwin.
Chairman.
(sgd) E.W.P.Peall.
Secretary.

The Earl of Lytton and
the Rt Hon. Sir Albert
Spicer, respectively
Chairman and Vice
Chairman of the State
Children's Society,
address the President of
the Board of Education,
H.A.L. Fisher on 30
March 1917 regarding
juvenile delinquency.
The view of the Society
was that the military
occupation of so many
schools, particularly
elementary ones, was a
major contributory factor
in the rise of delinquency.

Though not believing
wartime delinquency was
likely to lead to perma-
nent increases in crime,
the Society felt that one
solution appeared to be
establishing open-air
schools and play centres
for the summer months in
areas where schools had
been closed. Suitable temporary buildings would
be a cost to the state, but
could be offset in terms of
fewer children being com-
mitted to reformatory
or industrial schools by
magistrates, the value
of which appeared slight.

Fisher also received
a suggestion from the
teachers' association in
Newcastle-upon-Tyne
that, since many school-
masters called up for
military service were unfit
for the front line and had
been relegated to clerical
duties, they should be
recalled to the classroom.
(ED11/114)

The State Children's Association
(With which is incorporated The Boarding-out Association).

The late Rt. Hon. VISCOUNT PEEL, Chairman, 1896-7.
The late Rt. Hon. LORD HERSCHELL, Chairman, 1897-9.
The Rt. Hon. EARL GREY, Chairman, 1899-1900.
The Most Hon. The MARQUESS of CREWE, Chairman, 1901-5.
The Rt. Hon. LORD BURGHCLERE, Chairman, 1906-7.
The Rt. Hon. The EARL of LYTTON, Chairman, 1908-15.

Office hours, 2 p.m. to 6 p.m. Interviews at other hours by appointment. The Office is closed on Saturdays.

Hon. Sec.:
Mrs. S. A. BARNETT.
Secretary
F. PENROSE PHILP.

53, VICTORIA STREET, S.W.

March 30th, 1917.

To the Rt. Hon. Dr. H. A. L. Fisher, M.P.
Minister of Education.

Sir,

The State Children's Association, having been privileged
to take a large share in the establishment of Children's Courts
and the Probation system in this country, is naturally deeply
interested in juvenile delinquency which has, owing to the war
and the changed conditions it imposes on homes and schools, so
unfortunately increased of late. While deploring this increase,
we do not regard it as permanent and believe that, if handled
with spiritual courage and insight, it need not cause anxiety
with regard to the future, though, if wrongly dealt with, it has
in it the seed of real criminality in the children and moral
retrogression in those who would stay it by methods of punishment
and repression.

It cannot, we fear, be denied that one of the main
causes of the present juvenile wrong-doing is the taking over of
so many elementary schools - more especially in poor neighbour-
hoods - by the military authority for military purposes, thus
leaving many of the children so displaced and those whose school-
buildings they share, at a loose end for half the day. We notice
that various local authorities are being pressed to provide
increased hospital accommodation to meet the expected needs of

(1)

Mrs Dorothy Poole, a well-educated and highly capable individual, was trained for munitions work on a course run by the London Society for Women's Suffrage in January 1916. Ultimately, she became a Demonstrator Operative for the Ministry of Munitions, then a Woman's Dilution Officer in, first, an aircraft fitting works and, second, at a makers of capstan lathes. Her employment was terminated soon after the Armistice in November 1918. Here she recalls (in 1919) her initial employment in a small workshop at an aircraft engine works near London, between February 1916 and April 1917.

————

CONDITIONS *at G's were not ideal in those days. It was an old established firm that was increasing at a great rate, and they took on a considerable number of women, although there was quite inadequate accommodation for them. The only cloakroom for women was that in our shop, and the consequent crowding was a great discomfort. It meant that all classes came to our shop, too, and there were continual complaints of thefts.*

Hours were 7.00 a.m. till 12.00, 1.00 till 5.30 p.m. and overtime 6.00 to 8.00 p.m. Overtime was called optional, and in our shop was so for many months, but later it became customary though not really compulsory. A quarter of an hour for tea at 4.00 p.m. was very soon given to the women, and later another quarter for lunch in the middle of the morning. But such was our zeal for work that some of us worked right through the lunch quarter instead of going to the canteen. (The state of our resources, too, did not admit of extra meals.) There was a crowded canteen, served by voluntary workers. Food was of course rough and roughly served, and men and women shared the same canteen. I, and most of the others in my shop, lived close by and always went home to dinner.

We found the cold in the shop intense that winter, as warming apparatus was very inadequate, and coke buckets which were added only warm a small circle, and fill the whole shop with fumes which add insult to injury.

But while speaking of conditions I must add that before I left in April 1917, things had changed considerably. The canteen was enlarged and run on more business-like lines while meals served in relays prevented overcrowding; a large cloak room had been built for the women, and hot water laid on; steam fed radiators had been put on in the shops, stools were supplied to the girls, a 'welfare supervisor' had been appointed; and a rest room built. Red Cross work which had originally been done by one of the clerks in the pay office, was put in charge of two trained nurses on day and night shifts. These changes and improvements are, of course, only such as were going on all over the country in 1916 and 1917.

In the matter of pay we fared badly at G's. New hands began with 15/- for four weeks unless they had attended a course of training of some sort in which case they received £1 – i.e. 4 d an hour for a 53 hour week. This was the standard rate of pay for women, and was supposed to be only augmented by piece work prices. But in our shop there was no piece work for months because there was no output, and one girl at any rate received this pay for six months. For myself, I had understood there would be rises, and when I found this was not so I gave notice, as I could not possibly live on £1 a week. I was then offered another penny an hour which I accepted, although it was impossible to make ends meet even with this. By the time I left I had worried 8d an hour out of Mr M. and he admitted I had been worth more than I had been getting all the way along.

We were all of us content to put up with the bad pay for the sake of the conditions. We felt that we might go further and fare very much worse. We all got on well together, the shop was large and light and airy, and no manager could have been more considerate to work under.

There was considerable discontent about money all through the works, because of the inequality of piece work prices. If a job had been a man's job, the price set on it was based on a man's rate of pay, and a woman put on to it would earn £3 or £4; whereas the price set on what was originally a woman's job was based on her rate of pay and she made a total averaging 28/- or 30/-, and though these inequalities became more level as time went on, I heard that in 1918 the Milling Section were still the best paid, as they had been in 1916, although the work was neither so skilled or so responsible as some of the other sections and this because it was some time before women were put on to the work.

As for the work itself – I have said that we were making a small accessory for an aero-engine. This part had progressed not much further than the blue prints when I first joined the shop, having never been constructed, tested, or passed by the Admiralty.

For the first few months the work was mostly tool making – tool holders for two small turret lathes, mandrels, cutters, arbors, gauges of many sorts, templates, jigs, etc. besides the turning of some of the more straightforward parts, washers, distance washers, spindles, gudgeon pins etc. But soon castings began to arrive and we were able to start on casings, cylinders, pistons and so on. At first there were only a few lathes, two small

turret lathes, a sensitive drill, and a universal grinder in the shop; but soon a milling machine was added, and other lathes and capstans, and new hands were taken on as fast as the machinery was set up. I was the only one with a preference for bench work, and though I did some turning at first I very soon had enough to occupy me at other things. At first, too, I was the only operator of the milling machine, as there was no repetition work ready for it; and I had also always to set up and test any new set of cutters on the turrets and capstans. For the rest my work consisted of cutter shaping and fitting, jig making, and various simple tool-fitting jobs. If work was slack I shaped and hardened a stock of tools for the turners.

Later when we began to turn out work, there was of course much less tool-fitting to do, and I was given all the viewing and assembling. The latter included a good deal of drilling and tapping and some nice filing. The only repetition work I had was the hobbing of certain gear wheels that we used – not a nice job, as the gear was not adjustable, and it was difficult to steer between jamming and too much back-lash. I also had certain pinions to harden. We used to send them to the hardening shop, but they always came back warped so we did them ourselves. Before I left I had three girls working under me at viewing, fitting and assembling.
[IWM, Wom. Coll, Mun. 17]

(2)

Mrs Elizabeth Fernside of Fulham writes to her son, Sergeant Fred Fernside, serving with the Royal Artillery at Inchkeith on the Firth of Forth, on 20 January 1917. Apart from revealing the effects of food shortages, she gives a highly coloured and exaggerated account of the explosion at the Silvertown munitions factory. In reality, there were 69 fatalities, a number of whom were women workers.

———

Now for *'All the latest'. Some news this time.*

First let me tell you we are frightened of burglars. We have got 6 lb of sugar in the house. We held a War Council to arrange who should be on guard all night & like all *other War Councils, we went to sleep before we arrived at any conclusion. Not much sleep last night though. We have a* most terrible *explosion at Silvertown. Though it was so far away, the noise was so terrific that I thought the Huns had dropped a surprise packet about 3 doors away, so opened the door to look but as there was nothing to be seen, decided to remain in the kitchen and 'wait & see'. The doors & windows shook & so did the ground. This morning the sky is very strange, showing it must have disturbed the elements. Makes me think of something I read years ago 'Force Force everywhere, & we ourselves a mysterious force in the centre of that'. Never in my life have I experienced that force as I did last night. There are thousands killed, great cracks & gaps in the roads, people 3 miles off were blown out of their homes & were running about, seeking a place to shelter. All the London hospitals are full, the ambulances have been busy all night. A lady was at R.A.Music [Royal Academy of Music] & says it set all the organs playing. The extent of the disaster will never be known if any one does know, they will not dare to tell. There was a small explosion at White City last week, but this is impossible to exaggerate. Some years ago I went to a Training Home for Social Workers & looked out the window to see the 'Dreadnought' floated which had been built just then. We stayed to tea in the pretty house which some of our members had helped by subscribing. This house overlooked some vacant land leading to the Thames. On this the factory was built, the people who used to be there were W Brumon Mors (German firm) but it has lately been taken over by the Government. I expect that house & all its inhabitants are missing.*

England has never experienced anything so terrible. People on the whole kept calm though there was panic in some of the picture palaces. Plenty of rumours as to how it happened but that will never be solved. They think a German has done it. The report will be modified so as to keep it from Germany. City shops are boarded up, all widows broken, & houses within a mile radius all down. Don't think we have got the pip, am only writing the news *of the week.*

Finished in a hurry as our young lady has just come.

[IWM, 92/49/1, Fernside Mss.]

The growth of government as a result of the incapacity of existing public and private organizations to meet new wartime demand, as well as the sweeping powers the state gained through the Defence of the Realm Act (DORA), ensured that everyone's lives would be affected by the war.

But, if the state was making greater demands on its citizens in wartime, the degree of sacrifice being made demanded an appropriate reward in the subsequent peace rather than simply a restoration of the status quo. That implied public acceptance that government should provide not only the resources for, but also control over, services previously left to charitable organizations. Before the First World War, British workers had been particularly suspicious of state welfare provision, cherishing the self-help mechanisms of the Friendly and Co-operative societies. Indeed, the tradition of voluntary organizations and self-help continued to be evident in the readiness to support war charities of all kinds, with no less than 18,000 new such funds springing up during the war to join established charities such as the Red Cross,

Charity at home. The Liverpool Conservatives' tombola scheme, to aid the city's prisoners of war, and the Belgravia War Hospital Supply Depot's sweepstake (May 1918), awarding war bonds, were just two of many money-raising wartime efforts.

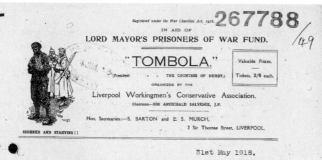

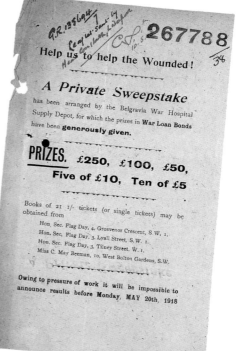

Helping the hospitals. Queen Alexandra, the Queen Mother, was associated with both Queen Alexandra's Imperial Military Nursing Service and Queen Alexandra's Royal Naval Nursing Service.

which collected over £22 million in Britain during the war. In August 1915 the 'Million Egg Week' exceeded its target of sending fresh eggs to British soldiers in France and Flanders. In October 1918 a specially constructed 'ruined' French village erected in Trafalgar Square for the Feed the Guns Campaign raised a staggering £29 million, which was invested in new war bonds in just eight days. However, what has been characterized as a kind of 'moral economy' dictated some correction of perceived inequalities and the emergence of what has been called a 'war welfare state'. Living standards were at the very heart of the process.

Deepening debts, spiralling prices

Inevitably, war meant inflationary pressures, the rise in the circulation of paper currency between 1913 and 1918 amounting to an extraordinary 1154 per cent. The £1 note or 'Bradbury' (named after the Bank of England official who signed them) and the 10s note made their first appearance during the war. The national debt was increasing every four months by more than the total debt incurred during the entire period of British participation in the French Revolutionary and Napoleonic Wars between 1792 and 1815. Accordingly, prices rose, though there were a variety of factors pushing inflation, including the worsening shortages of transport and shipping.

Some care needs to be exercised when considering prices and the cost of living, particularly when based on a notional 'basket' of everyday goods. All kinds of factors – variations in quality and quantity, wartime substitution of other products, varying ideas of what constituted basic requirements, and so forth – could skew the picture. At best, therefore, the figures demonstrated general trends, as in a table of retail prices produced by the Ministry of Labour in November 1918. The Board of Trade's overall cost of living figures for the British working class rose 45 per cent from July 1914 to July 1916, with food prices rising 61 per cent in the same period.

In reality, of course, ordinary people were very aware of how the war was affecting the prices they paid and the shortages they encountered. The General Federation of Trade Unions noted in February 1915 that 'pallid and unappetising' brisket had already risen from 4½d to 8½d or 9d per lb. By 1916, the basic 4lb loaf was selling for 10d, up from around 6d two years earlier. Such was the high price of fish that the Archbishop of Westminster felt compelled to allow Roman Catholics to eat cheaper cuts of meat instead on fasting days. For families dependent on separation allowances from former breadwinners now serving in the army, everyday existence could be a real struggle. The pre-war suffragette, Sylvia Pankhurst, working among the poor of London's East End, found one wife of a Territorial serviceman with two small children receiving just 1s.5d a day in separation allowances but paying 6s.0d a week rent – leaving only 3s.11d a week for food, fuel and all other essentials.

The war also had the capacity to make more subtle changes in people's lives: by March 1917, for example, shoppers in Leeds were expected to supply their own paper bags as paper shortages now precluded shops freely handing them out with goods. One urban council

Food.

According to returns of retail prices of the principal articles of food, which have been collected from retailers in large towns and in a representative selection of small towns and villages, the average percentages by which prices at 1st November, 1918, exceeded the normal prices of July, 1914, are as shown in the following Table. The amount of increase is also stated in terms of money.

Article.	Large Towns (populations over 50,000).	Small Towns and Villages.	United Kingdom.	
	Percentage Increase from July, 1914, to 1st November, 1918.			Amount of Increase (in Money).
	%	%	%	
Beef, British—				
Ribs	100	106	103	10¼*d.* per lb.
Thin Flank	133	120	126	8½*d.* „
Beef, Chilled or Frozen—				
Ribs	178	173	175	1*s.* 0¾*d.* „
Thin Flank	215	198	206	10*d.* „
Mutton, British—				
Legs	103	102	102	10½*d.* „
Breast	117	96	106	6¾*d.* „
Mutton, Frozen—				
Legs	216	195	206	1*s.* 2¼*d.* „
Breast	224	211	217	9*d.* „
Bacon (streaky)	147	137	142	1*s.* 3¾*d.* „
Fish	190	145	167	—
Flour	50	54	52	5½*d.* per 7 lbs.
Bread	58	52	55	3¼*d.* per 4 lbs.
Tea	78	69	73	1*s.* 1½*d.* per lb.*
Sugar (granulated)	251	231	241	5*d.* „ †
Milk	140	142	141	4¾*d.* per quart.
Butter—				
Fresh	104	109	107	1*s.* 3½*d.* per lb.
Salt	112	112	112	1*s.* 4*d.* „
Cheese	133	128	130	11¼*d.* „
Margarine	105	89	97	6¾*d.* „
Eggs (fresh)	436	389	412	4*s.* 11½*d.* per 12.
Potatoes	72	47	59	2¾*d.* „ 7 lbs.

* Of which 7*d.* duty. † Of which 2½*d.* duty.

'BEEF, CHILLED OR FROZEN'

A Table of Retail Prices between 1914 and 1 November 1918 produced by the Labour Statistics Department of the Ministry of Labour.

Noting that food, rent, clothing, fuel and light were the most important items for ordinary working-class families, it shows prices generally running further ahead in large towns than in small towns and villages. Nearly all food commodities had increased by at least 50 per cent – the one exception being potatoes in small towns and villages – with most by over 100 per cent, a handful (like mutton and sugar) over 200 per cent, and eggs over 400 per cent. An important qualification, however, was that consumption patterns had changed as well, so that average spending had increased at a lower rate than average prices.

Taking into account rent, clothing and fuel, average prices had increased between 120 per cent and 125 per cent since 1914. As it happened, food prices in October 1918 had increased by 5–6 per cent over those of the previous month, representing the largest monthly rise since August 1914. (LAB2/274/1)

in Kent even tried to economize on paper by printing all its official papers without punctuation!

Not surprisingly, there was a change in patterns of consumption during the war, fuelled by inflation, and with food prices representing arguably the most significant factor affecting everyday life.

Eating less, queueing more

Britain imported about 60 per cent of its food before the First World War. In trying to make up the wartime shortfall, British agriculture was faced with many difficulties. Farms were expected to produce more food with fewer workers and fewer horses, though women, school children, soldiers and prisoners-of-war made up some of the deficiencies. Fortunately, British agriculture was comparatively over-stocked with horses and was more mechanized than continental agriculture. Agricultural machinery suppliers still maintained a sufficient level of normal production, while also switching to war production such as munitions. Increasingly, too, tractors were imported from the United States, the war marking their large-scale adoption in Britain.

Initially, there was little state intervention in agriculture. Controls were, however, soon introduced to secure the continued importation of commodities such as sugar, grains and meat. However, a suggestion to encourage more domestic cereal production through guaranteeing the minimum prices for wheat and a compulsory plough policy were felt too radical a break with existing practice.

The poor North American wheat harvest in 1916 necessitated a re-evaluation of this hands-off position, and a Food Production Department of the Board of Agriculture was instituted in January 1917. Subsequently, the Corn Production Act of August 1917 guaranteed

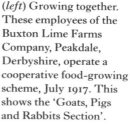

(*left*) Growing together. These employees of the Buxton Lime Farms Company, Peakdale, Derbyshire, operate a cooperative food-growing scheme, July 1917. This shows the 'Goats, Pigs and Rabbits Section'.

Using every scrap.
Men and women unload
salvage from a barge onto
railway wagons, 18 May
1918. The war's end
would generate so much
surplus material that
a National Salvage
Department was estab-
lished in the War Office.

minimum prices for wheat, oats and potatoes for six years to encourage investment by farmers, as well as guaranteeing minimum wages. Under what now became a compulsory plough policy, an additional 2.1 million acres were cultivated, the amount of tilled land in 1918 being the highest achieved between 1886 and 1942. Common land was taken up and unused private land requisitioned for allotments. The King even had the flowerbeds at Buckingham Palace replaced with vegetables.

As a result of such measures reliance upon imports was reduced, but the achievement was modest, and it has been calculated that the

BUXTON LIME FIRMS. PEAK DALE SECTIO[N]

percentage of homegrown food increased by barely one per cent. Britain could feed itself for only an additional 30 days a year by 1918. Nonetheless, the essential stability in production meant that the calorie level of the average British diet declined by only three per cent, although the protein intake declined by six per cent.

An effort to control consumption accompanied the attempt to increase food production. In December 1916, for example, lunches in public eating-places were restricted to two courses and dinners to three courses. Fines were introduced for feeding pigeons or stray animals. Another example of effort to reduce consumption is the Food Control campaign mounted by the National War Savings Committee in 1917. One Ministry of Food leaflet introduced the public to 'Mr Slice

The army of the land. These organized agriculture workers, also at the Buxton Lime Farms Company (1917), look as if they are on military parade.

'EAT LESS BREAD'

In March 1917 the National War Savings Committee was asked by the Ministry of Food to mount a Food Control Campaign, which later included a Householder's Pledge in response to that by the Royal Family to reduce its own consumption.

A proposed badge to be worn in support of the campaign was rejected in May 1917 as the Ministry of Munitions could *not guarantee to release sufficient metal to manufacture them, so a purple ribbon was substituted, bearing the legend 'I Eat Less Bread'. There was even a campaign song, 'Wear the Purple Ribbon', issued to schools, while a proclamation by the King on 29 May 1917 emphasized the effort to voluntarily reduce bread consumption by a quarter and to avoid flour in pastry.* (NSC 7/37)

By the King
A PROCLAMATION
GEORGE R.I.

WE, BEING PERSUADED that the abstention from all unnecessary consumption of grain will furnish the surest and most effectual means of defeating the devices of Our enemies, and thereby of bringing the War to a speedy and successful termination, and out of Our resolve to leave nothing undone which can contribute to these ends or to the welfare of Our people in these times of grave stress and anxiety, have thought fit, by and with the advice of Our Privy Council, to issue this Our Royal Proclamation, most earnestly exhorting and charging all those of Our loving subjects the men and women of Our realm who have the means of procuring articles of food other than wheaten corn as they tender their own immediate interests, and feel for the wants of others, especially to practise the greatest economy and frugality in the use of every species of grain, and We do for this purpose more particularly exhort and charge all heads of households

TO REDUCE THE CONSUMPTION OF BREAD IN THEIR RESPECTIVE FAMILIES BY AT LEAST ONE-FOURTH OF THE QUANTITY CONSUMED IN ORDINARY TIMES

TO ABSTAIN FROM THE USE OF FLOUR IN PASTRY AND MOREOVER CAREFULLY TO RESTRICT OR WHEREVER POSSIBLE TO ABANDON THE USE THEREOF IN ALL OTHER ARTICLES THAN BREAD

Given at Our Court at Buckingham Palace this Second day of May in the Year of Our Lord 1917 in the Seventh Year of Our Reign

GOD SAVE THE KING

NOW WE THE UNDERSIGNED MEMBERS OF THIS HOUSEHOLD HEREBY PLEDGE OURSELVES ON OUR HONOUR TO RESPOND TO HIS MAJESTY'S APPEAL

Arthur

May 29th 1917

THE NATIONAL WAR SAVINGS COMMITTEE, SALISBURY SQUARE, E.C.4.
FOOD ECONOMY CAMPAIGN
(Undertaken at the invitation and under the authority of the Ministry of Food.)
TWO FOOD CAMPAIGN SONGS FOR SCHOOL CHILDREN.

WEAR THE PURPLE RIBBON.

o'Bread', proclaiming that 48 million slices were wasted every day:

> I am the 'bit left over'; the slice eaten absentmindedly when really I wasn't needed: I am the waste crust. If you collected me and my companions for a whole week you would find that we amounted to 9,380 tons of good bread – Wasted.

It was similarly claimed that a teaspoon of breadcrumbs saved by every person every day would amount to 40,000 tons in a year.

The difficulty was that for many working-class families meat had always been a luxury, and to them less consumption meant less bread. What became known as 'Government Bread' itself was also increasingly doctored after March 1917 by reducing the amount of white flour and substituting other grain or potato flour. Attending one public meeting in 1917, a speaker for the Ministry of Food realized that the official line was unpalatable and she therefore merely asked for the audience's goodwill. Subsequently, a man present told her he had refrained from hurling rotten tomatoes when she had not demanded reductions: 'Ye see, we don't want ladies comin' to tell *us* to eat less, but we was glad to listen to what *you* did say.'

There were also ever-lengthening queues. In April 1917, for example, *The Observer* reported that queues for bread and potatoes at Edmonton had been so long that the police had to regulate them, while at Wrexham a wagon selling potatoes was 'surrounded by hundreds of clamouring people, chiefly women, who scrambled on to the vehicle in the eagerness to buy. Several women fainted in the struggle, and the police were sent for to restore order.' In December 1917, *The Times* reported that 1000 people had been queuing for margarine, which had largely replaced butter, in New Broad Street in the heart of the City of London and as many as 3000 were doing so in the Walworth Road. Men were even taking time off war work to keep places in queues while their wives took a break. Often shops were entirely emptied. One young

The practical low-carb diet. The point of this particular poster in 1917 was to reduce the amount of imported wheat on ships, at the height of renewed unrestricted German submarine warfare.

middle-class wife, who was 18th in a queue, hoped to secure some silverside of beef:

> But after twenty joints had been carved from one small piece of 'animal', there seemed but little chance of my obtaining my silverside. I approached the butcher furtively. 'Have you any silverside?' I whispered. 'No, no silverside – breast, scrag or bit o'brisket', he yapped at me impatiently. In those days I was not as experienced a housewife as I am now, and one feels somewhat weak after half an hour spent standing in a butcher's shop glaring at ugly insides. I gasped 'brisket', and then found myself on the pavement clasping lovingly a very minute parcel of stringy meat.

Another woman, this time in Fulham, London, reported to her son in December 1917 that she had queued for a quarter pound of butter, 'then changed my hat & fur ran back in time to get another. Can't help laughing at the tricks now.'

The authorities assumed that ensuring a constant supply of food would stabilize prices, but this did not prove the case. A price spiral began almost at once, from a combination of financial dislocation and panic buying: wheat prices were up by 80 per cent and meat prices by 40 per cent during the first 12 months of war. Shipping shortages drove up prices further, and as prices rose they fuelled the demands for higher wages. Yet, self-regulation of business was much preferred to price fixing, and a modest public education programme and the encouragement of allotments was preferred to either wage increases or rationing. Covert purchases by the Grain Supplies Committee were intended partly to arrest higher prices by releasing grain onto the market at less than cost price. But this became known to the private sector in March 1915, and the policy had to be abandoned in the face of strike action by wheat merchants. Public dissatisfaction resulted in the establishment of the Royal Commission on Wheat in October 1916 to control all grain purchasing abroad, as the Royal Commission on Sugar Supplies had been doing for the sugar trade since August 1914. Inevitably, there was careful monitoring of the production of wheat, barley and oats.

The diets of ordinary families changed over the course of the war in relation to prices and supplies. In Glasgow, for example, oatmeal was the cheapest source of energy and protein in 1914, but in 1915 beans represented the cheapest source of protein and rice the cheapest source of energy. In 1916 lentils and oatmeal represented respectively the cheapest sources of protein and energy. Potatoes were the cheapest food of all in 1915, but early frosts that autumn drove prices up accordingly in the following year. One cookery book published in 1915, which aimed to help housewives 'to whom existence under the new conditions is a problem', suggested lentil, pea and haricot soups as an alter-

native to meat 'with the additional advantage of giving warmth to the blood, and having a tonic effect on the stomach'. A rival publication that same year recommended tinned fish and powdered egg as still affordable commodities, whereas veal, lamb, bacon and ham were all already out of the reach of most. Bones were recommended, for stock and gravy, as well as cheaper meat cuts and 'methods of utilizing cold meats where a joint might once-in-a-way be bought'. Showing considerable enterprise, the manufacturers of the yeast-extract drink Bovril claimed that a teaspoonful before each meal as digestive aid would enable consumers to reduce their daily food consumption by one-fifth. By 1918 the *Illustrated London News* was extolling the virtues of sorrel, dandelion leaves and nettles as vegetables. Ironically, some families were earning far more than they had in peacetime, and some of their expectations rose as a result. Robert Roberts recalled one woman, the wife of former foundry labourer now making good money in munitions (as was her husband), coming in to his father's corner shop in Salford during the war. She demanded to know when the shop would be stocking 'summat worth chewin' for Christmas, such as tins of lobster or jars of pickled gherkins. Roberts's father 'damned her' from the shop. '"Before the war", he fumed, "that one was grateful for a bit o' bread and scrape!"'

Government intervention was inevitably extended as the war dragged on. Three months after the establishment of the Wheat Commission, Lord Devonport was appointed as first Food Controller of the new Ministry of Food in January 1917. Devonport extended the food economy campaign and prepared for the introduction of rationing, the two themes being linked by encouragement of a voluntary rationing scheme in February 1917. His successor, Lord Rhondda, introduced a bread subsidy in September 1917, together with a relaxation on brewing

Rethinking Mrs Beeton. A certain Mrs Weighall and her cook demonstrate the uses of potatoes and rice as substitutes for flour, 7 February 1918.

restrictions and a range of price controls, in which the cost of a 4lb loaf was reduced from 1s.0d to 9d.

Practise what you preach. Minister of Food, Lord Rhondda, commandeers margarine shortly before meat and fats were rationed in London and the Home Counties, 1 January 1918.

Rationing arrives

The plan was to bring in sugar rationing in the autumn of 1917, but difficulties were encountered in establishing a workable system. Price controls also proved unpopular when they were set higher than the public wished, while some overseas traders took commodities to other markets. The only solution was compulsory rationing, a policy long advocated by the ministry's second secretary, William Beveridge. Prompted by some local authorities taking matters into their own hands, the government introduced nationwide sugar rationing on 31 December 1917, followed by the rationing of meat and fats in London and the Home Counties in February 1918. Rationing was then extended nationwide in April. Weekly rations were fixed at 15 oz of beef, mutton or lamb, 5 oz of bacon, 4 oz of fats and 8 oz of sugar. Queues became largely a thing of the past, though some shopkeepers attempted to sell

'RATION THE BUTCHERS'

A Cabinet paper reporting the meeting between the Minister of Food, Lord Rhondda, and the Prime Minister, Lloyd George, on 22 February 1918, with regard to the meat situation.

Rhondda pointed to the disparity between the pre-war average consumption of 2 lbs of meat per week and the ration of 1 lb per head per week, the ration being fixed on the basis of what was available after the Army had been supplied.

As a result, Lloyd George requested specific figures on the quantities of meat required to supply an additional 100 per cent to workers undertaking hard manual labour and of 50 per cent for those 'half way between sedentary occupation and hard manual work'.

Also at the meeting were the Unionist leader and member of the War Cabinet, Andrew Bonar Law, and the Secretary to the War Cabinet, Sir Maurice Hankey. (CABI/26)

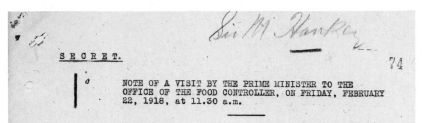

SECRET.

74

NOTE OF A VISIT BY THE PRIME MINISTER TO THE OFFICE OF THE FOOD CONTROLLER, ON FRIDAY, FEBRUARY 22, 1918, at 11.30 a.m.

THE PRIME MINISTER was accompanied by MR BONAR LAW and SIR MAURICE HANKEY.

The greater part of the visit on this date was confined to a discussion of the meat situation.

LORD RHONDDA said that before the War the normal consumption of the population had been 2¼ lbs. of meat per head per week. The ration to be given by the Food Controller from Monday next onwards amounted to 1 lb. per head per week. This was all that the people were getting at present. There had been no great dissatisfaction, and the people had taken the restrictions very well. The ration had been fixed at 1 lb. because that is all that the supplies enabled him to give.

In reply to THE PRIME MINISTER he said that the 1 lb. per head ration was to be universal for the present. Later on it was contemplated to differentiate and to give more to the manual worker. The reasons for the shortage of meat were that, in normal times about 40 per cent. of the meat supply of the population was imported. Owing to the great demands of the Army for meat, very nearly the whole of the imported supply, especially as regards beef, had been allocated for military purposes. In the autumn the slaughterings of home-grown cattle had been very large, and he himself and his advisers had wished to ration the butchers. Owing to the lack of feeding-stuffs the value of the cattle was only about 15 per cent. of what it was in normal times. The shortage this winter had been fully anticipated, although it had proved more acute than had been expected. People, however, had put up with it very well, and he did not anticipate any serious trouble.

In reply to the PRIME MINISTER, LORD RHONDDA further said that colliers now were going down to the pits in the morning in many cases with nothing but dry bread, although this was not universal.

1.

above the fixed price or to favour particular customers. In practice, rationing achieved not so much a general reduction of consumption but 'a levelling of consumption of essential foodstuffs'.

The result of the government's food policies overall was reasonably successful: no serious food shortage and an adequate supply of energy in the national diet throughout the war.

In London, coal rationing was also introduced in October 1917, consumers registering with specified coal merchants and receiving two hundredweight a week for up to four rooms and three hundredweight a

Getting cold to keep warm. Children queue for a coal ration at a depot in London's King's Cross. Coal rationing was introduced in London in October 1917.

week for five to six rooms, and so on. As with food, coal queues had become commonplace. Back in April 1917 it had been reported that people were queuing up for coal in London with prams, wheelbarrows, sacks and baskets. As it happened, many working-class families had been unable to afford coal before the war and it was their greater buying power through wartime earnings that had created greater demand.

Welfare in war

It was not only food shortages and prices that adversely affected British civilians. Economic dislocation arising from the disruption of normal trade, shortages of raw materials and manpower problems equally had an impact. Together with high rents, the difficulty of moving around for work and the problems of wartime profiteering, they contributed to growing discontent on the factory floor. In response, the government acted to maintain and, indeed, improve the material conditions of its people. In 1914, however, about 16 per cent of the total population of 40.8 million were classed as living below the 'poverty line', a concept originated by Seebohm Rowntree in a classic study of the working class in York in 1901.

War, the great leveller. Meat rationing was introduced in 1918, at first in London and the Home Counties and then nationwide. Even the King was not exempt, as his own ration card shows.

'A GOOD DEAL OF MODERATION'
Sir George Newman's request, as Chairman of the Canteen Committee of the Central Control Board and the Health of Munitions Workers Committee, to V. L. Raven, Chief Superintendent of the Royal Arsenal, Woolwich, for guidance on the demands of a workmen's deputation asking for a drinks break, 14 December 1915.

Newman, who had met the deputation and sympathized to some extent, had become aware of conflicting evidence on the working conditions at Woolwich. In a subsequent reply, Raven assured Newman that shortening the drinks break would not be detrimental, since it would only prolong the working day to allow a half-hour break in the morning.

Newman ultimately resolved that there should be no change unless it was felt more convenient to bring the working hours in line with other factories in London, which tended to close at 9.30 p.m.

(SUPP5/1049)

The health and safety provisions of the pre-war Factory Acts were waived for the duration, but the Health of Munitions Workers Committee of the Ministry of Munitions was empowered to inspect working premises. Over 900 factory canteens were established from the proceeds of the Excess Profits tax. Typical canteen fare included sausage and mash, mince and mash, stewed fruit, and milk pudding. National Kitchens were also established to offer cheap basic meals to the needy. The first of these establishments was opened by Queen Mary in Westminster Bridge Road on 21 May 1917. The queen herself served meals. One old man received his meal without realizing who had served it: 'The fact that it was the Queen must have been pointed out to him by the crowd outside, for shortly afterwards he returned, edged his way back to the serving-counter and solemnly waved his hat three times at her.' The ministry also set up cloakrooms, washing facilities and day nurseries. At the Gretna National Cordite Factory – with workers at Gretna, East Riggs and Carlisle – and where over 11,000 women were eventually employed, a two-storey institute had the ground floor for men and the first floor for women, the latter including

No-frills food. National Kitchens, like this one pictured here, were an important innovation of the Ministry of Food in May 1917, serving cheap, basic meals to the needy.

Private

14th December 1915.

Dear Mr. Raven,

On Friday morning at the Liquor Traffic Board we received a deputation of six men from Woolwich, led by Mr. Barefoot, J.P.   After stating various general objections to the Board's Restriction Orders, and animadverting upon the sobriety of the men at the Arsenal - which was all quite proper and suitable - they asked for exceptional treatment in the following two respects, viz:-

    1st.- that there should be an opening hour between
          7.30 a.m. and 9 a.m., and

    2nd.- that the closing hour should be 9.30 (as in the
          rest of London) and not 9 p.m.   They
          proposed to take off half an hour in the
          middle of the day, and thus leave the total
          opening hours at 6½ instead of 5½.

The reason why they made this claim was that it was desirable that men coming off night work and men going on day work should have morning facilities for drinking. They were not able to prescribe an hour which could be worked without difficulty, but with a good deal of moderation and plausibility they pressed their claim.

I am writing privately to ask you what you think of this proposal. In all matters of this kind the/Board are *Liquor Traffic* desirous of consulting the responsible Officers at the head of Munition Works affected.   Of course, we are anxious not to change our Order if we can avoid it.   The reason why the closing hour at night is 9 (and not as in the rest of London, 9.30) is that the hour of closure was 9 before our Order was

                              applied,

Vincent L. Raven, Esq,,
    Chief Superintendent,
        Royal Ordnance Factories,
           Woolwich.

a reading and writing room, a lounge with sewing machines, and a games room with a piano and a gramophone. The ministry led the way in providing facilities for its own employees and spent some £4.3 million on housing for its workers, building 10,000 permanent homes on 38 sites such as the Well Hall estate in Woolwich and at Gretna. One example of the bargaining over working conditions occurred when a workers' delegation from the Royal Arsenal, Woolwich, was received by a joint committee of the Central Control Board and the Ministry of Munitions in December 1915.

Local authorities were encouraged to maintain milk supplies for mothers and babies and, in 1916, women working in the production of TNT were provided with a free daily pint of milk in the (mistaken) belief that it nullified TNT's toxicity. Building on the pre-war interest in infant and maternal welfare, the relatively lax Notification of Births Act (1907) was amended in July 1915 to require compulsory registration of births within 36 hours, thus providing local authorities with information on which to act to ensure child health. Midwifery training also came under greater scrutiny in 1916.

The Maternity and Child Welfare Act in August 1918, again building on the pre-war system, required local authorities to establish formal committees to provide services for mothers and infants under five. The new concerns were characterized by the nationally organized 'Baby Week' in July 1917. Older children benefited equally from the extension of the provision of school meals for the needy for the whole calendar year. In the words of one historian, child welfare in wartime was an area where 'collective virtue and national interest clearly coincided'.

Similarly, the Rents and Mortgage Interest (Rent Restriction) Act of December 1915, which represented the principal victory of industrial unrest on the Clyde, eased the pressures of housing shortages in an area suffering from worker migration. (Some 20,000 people had been involved in a rent strike against private landlords there.) The Act was a major contribution to improving working-class life, although there was no actual penalty for contravening its provisions and it was frequently evaded. In some cases, landlords even rented out lodgings to one group of workers by night and another by day. Problems with evictions experienced with a change of landlord brought about the Increase of Rents and Mortgages (Amendment) Act in April 1918. The efforts of the Ministry of Munitions constituted the only really significant wartime housing development, since there was no wartime private construction. Much substandard and condemned property was, instead, brought back into habitation by landlords. They often declined to maintain such property on the grounds that the restriction of rents left

Maternal militants. Mothers with their children protest against increasing wartime milk prices, on 21 October 1916.

them with no means of affording improvements. A Billeting of Civilians Act in 1917, enabling local authorities to commandeer spare rooms for workers, was unpopular and did not materially assist the housing shortages. In fact, there had already been a perceived shortage of between 100,000 and 120,000 homes in 1914. The Commission of Enquiry into Working Class Unrest in June 1917 reported adversely on

Welfare before the welfare state. Children and their carers during the war, at the Singer Company creche, Clyde Bank, Glasgow.

working-class housing. In Barrow, for example, it was a 'crying scandal', while in Wales the towns and villages were 'ugly and overcrowded; houses are scarce and rents are increasing, and the surroundings are insanitary and depressing'. By 1918 the proportion of families sharing a dwelling with others had increased from 15 per cent to 20 per cent.

Escaping it all

Public leisure, pastimes, the very patterns of social life – all were inevitably affected by the war. The Defence of the Realm Act's many restrictions included prohibitions on public clocks chiming between sunset and sunrise, on whistling for taxicabs between 10 p.m. and 7 a.m., and on loitering under railway arches! Restaurants and hotel dining rooms had to switch off their lights at 10 p.m., and all places of entertainment had to close at 10.30 p.m. Shop-closing orders were also brought in. British Summer Time was introduced in May 1916, one measure that would become permanent.

Another marked change was the greater control exercised over

'EARLY CLOSING OF SHOPS'
Malcolm Deleuvigne, Under Secretary of State at the Home Office, had written to the Commissioner of the Metropolitan Police, Sir Edward Henry, on 8 December 1916 to enquire as to the impact of shop closing orders in the capital.

The Commissioner replies here on 29 December that the order was not affecting all classes equally. Larger stores like Harrods and Selfridges did not open anyway in the evening, but backstreet shops used to late opening, and catering for the working classes, were suffering. There was some qualified support by those shopkeepers glad of the rest, and no noticeable increase in Sunday trading, while even some small businesses near factories were increasing trade. The order was generally working well.
(MEPO2/1706)

128,001/129.

29th December, 1916.

Sir,

    With reference to your letter of the 8th instant, 322254/33, I have to acquaint you, for the information of the Secretary of State, that the Police have now had opportunities of observing the affect of the Order, of the 27th October last, for the Early Closing of Shops.

    The public have not experienced any serious difficulty in doing the necessary shopping or getting it done before the closing hour. Any difficulties that have arisen in the case of that section of the public which is engaged in business or labour during the day have been overcome by purchasing goods early, on the way home, or by asking friends to make small purchases during the hours of absence at work.

    It cannot be said that the Order has affected all classes of shops equally. The large shops in town, such as Harrods, Selfridges, Maples &c., never remain open in the evening and are therefore totally unaffected by the Order. With this exception, however, the different classes of shops have, for the most part, been equally affected. The extent to which small shops have lost their custom to large shops is not, in all probability. very great, although the greater means of serving customers which are at the disposal of the large establishments , must certainly put the smaller shops at

some/

The Under Secretary of State,
    Home Office,
      S.W.

licensing laws in 1914, the average closing hour of public houses being brought forward from 12.30 a.m. to 10.00 p.m. One early move was made by magistrates in St Helens to persuade the government to act nationally on liquor control in August 1914, a move supported by the Church Army. As with the introduction of British Summer Time, liquor control was ostensibly to improve industrial production, Lloyd George memorably justifying restrictions in March 1915 on the grounds of national necessity: 'We are fighting Germans, Austrians and Drink, and so far as I can see the greatest of these deadly foes is Drink.' Such was the concern over soldiers potentially falling victim to the patriotic zeal of civilians offering them free drinks that 'treating' was outlawed. One husband was even prosecuted for buying a drink for his wife. Buying drinks 'on the slate' was also prohibited. In fact, the

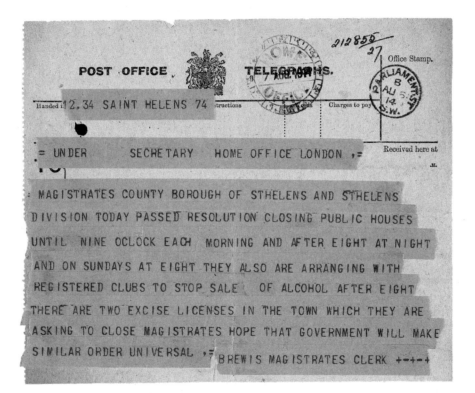

'STOP SALE OF ALCOHOL'
Prebendary Wilson Carlile of the Church Army had urged Field Marshal Lord Roberts on 22 August 1914 to support the closing of public houses at 9.00 p.m. As indicated by this telegram to the Home Office, magistrates in St Helens had already acted on 7 August to close public houses and private clubs between 8 p.m. and 9 a.m., though the legality of their action was doubtful. Roberts agreed with Carlile, noting that the City Remembrancer in London had proposed a similar course. The Intoxicating Liquor (Temporary Restriction) Bill was shortly to be introduced to legalise such action by local benches. One of the great Victorian military heroes, Roberts was to die while visiting the Indian Corps on the Western Front in November 1914. (HO45/25827)

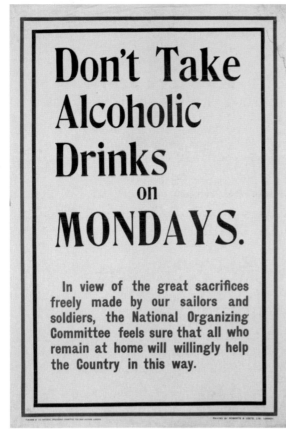

Don't Take
Alcoholic
Drinks
on
MONDAYS.

In view of the great sacrifices freely made by our sailors and soldiers, the National Organizing Committee feels sure that all who remain at home will willingly help the Country in this way.

Monday, dry day.
The National Organising
Committee for War
Savings urges temperance
as a contribution to the
war effort in 1916. Liquor
control was introduced
in 1914.

advocacy of liquor control by Lloyd George, including the weakening of spirits and the watering-down of beer, was primarily a device to move Liberals generally towards state control. In the event, state purchase of the liquor trade was not implemented, but licensed premises were actually taken over by the state in Enfield Lock, Carlisle and Gretna through the agency of the Central Control Board (Liquor Traffic). These state-owned pubs – many of which were taken over so that they could be closed during the war itself – were sold off only in the 1970s; and the English and Welsh licensing laws began to be relaxed again only in 1985. The impact of the measures in the First World War was that the consumption of alcohol fell by about a half and convictions for drunkenness by about three-quarters over the course of the war. As it happened, however, alcohol consumption had already declined before the war and continued to do so at much the same rate, irrespective of the new licensing laws and other restrictions such as increased prices. Smoking, however, increased, despite more duty being imposed on tobacco in successive wartime budgets – to the dismay of one cigarette manufacturer, who ingeniously urged its patrons in October 1915 to continue to smoke precisely *because* duty had been increased, 'to give smokers an opportunity of contributing' to a successful conclusion of the war.

In terms of popular spectator pastimes during the war, racing and football continued only until 1915. The (Oxford–Cambridge) University Boat Race was also abandoned that year, for the first time since its institution in 1856, and the Whitsun and August bank holidays were cancelled in 1916. Professional and, thereby, working-class sport generally was particularly affected, professionals coming under pressure to enlist in 1914 when it was noticed that they were not coming forward as much as their amateur colleagues. Football was particularly targeted, *Punch* referring to the football results in January 1915 as 'The Shirkers' War News'. Hunting also came under pressure, with packs of hounds reduced by half at an early stage. Hunt servants were initially exempted from registration for potential military service in 1915 and later from conscription in 1916, on the grounds that the army was dependent on the breeding of hunters for its cavalry chargers. This

St Anstell,

8, Derby Road,

Bournemouth.

13th March, 1916.

re Starred Men.

Dear Sir,

Many people I am acquainted with strongly object to Lord Derby's Circular to the Hunts (so reported in the "Bournemouth Directory") exempting from Military Service all grooms,&c &c., connected with hunting, so as to encourage farmers to **breed** horses <u>to help win the war</u>, on which it can have no bearing excepting to cancel a large number of recruits.

A young married man recently told me that he would not volunteer while the War Office could spare thousands (?) of unmarried men to foster hunting.

The Circular adversely affects recruiting and should be cancelled and the men un-starred.

I long ago wrote to Mr. Asquith who informed me my letter had been passed on to the War Office to be answered, but they have not replied nor noticed my further communication.

This favouritisum is causing general discontent especially among parents who have given their all to the cause. (my only son joined at the outbreak of the War).

Faithfully yours,

(Sgd) W. Long.

policy soon came under review. Horse-racing also came under scrutiny, and organized meetings ceased in May 1915, though there were occasional events, such as the Racehorse Association Steeplechase at Gatwick in March 1916, substituting for the cancelled Grand National. In any case, it was increasingly difficult for civilians to travel to these and other events, with petrol licences required for those who could afford private cars and passenger trains becoming ever fewer in number. As one London woman later recalled, 'I often came home in a taxi with six inside and three or four on the roof!'

People still managed to go on holiday. And holiday resorts in England and Wales were able to recoup losses in the autumn of 1914 by accommodating formations of the New Army under training. Blackpool, which had continued with its novel illuminations – begun only in 1912 – in the autumn of 1914, subsequently had over 10,000 troops in the town over the 1914–15 winter. Similarly, Welsh seaside resorts actively competed to attract army camps that autumn and winter. This alternative trade – which also benefited many local businesses near army camps throughout southern and eastern England – diminished as the New Army moved overseas. In April 1915, for example, the *Daily Mail* reported that although Brighton hotels were nearly full for Easter and passenger boats were still running to Ireland and to the Continent, 'and although one hears of excursions into Wales by motor char-à-bancs, the general atmosphere of the seaside resort is one of reconciliation to their lot'. The North of England and Scotland could expect few visitors that Easter, 'for on these long journeys the ordinary fares are more than double the excursion fares', and even those venturing across the Channel were mostly visiting the wounded in hospital. Yet, the holiday trade survived remarkably well throughout the war, even if holidaymakers were said to be less boisterous than in peacetime,

'CAUSING GENERAL DISCONTENT'
Mr W. Long of Bournemouth – no relation to the President of the Local Government Board – writes to the Local Government Board on 13 March 1916 to object to Lord Derby's call in December 1915 for hunts to be protected as long as possible and for the continuing exemption from conscription now implied for those responsible for the care of brood mares and stallions.

Derby's intervention had been prompted by the War Office Director of Remounts, while the Hunters Improvement and National Light Horse Breeding Society had also pointed to the need to ensure a continued supply of cavalry

chargers. Subsequently, the Atherstone Hunt in Leicestershire was to claim exemption for its remaining servants on the basis of Derby's statement.

In response to Long's letter, the War Office, to whom the matter was referred, indicated that no unmarried men were exempted on such grounds and that married men were exempted only exceptionally. Ultimately, the partial exemption was withdrawn altogether in December 1917, despite representations by the Masters of Foxhounds Association that hunts were now kept up entirely for breeding rather than sport.
(NATS 1/964)

War as comedy. Charlie Chaplin in *Shoulder Arms*, a film released just after the armistice. It cemented Chaplin's position as the war's most popular entertainer.

and the British seaside looked somewhat different from usual. There was barbed wire along beaches and some piers were cut in half as a precaution against invasion.

As indicated earlier, places of entertainment had to close at 10.30 p.m., by legislation referred to as the 'beauty sleep order'. Nevertheless, there were measurable increases in dancing, with American jazz and ragtime the basis for the development of popular new dances such as the foxtrot and the charleston, which became the rage amid fears of cultural pollution. It was the First World War that 'put Soho on the map', with over 150 night-clubs operating in that Central London area by 1915, offering the illicit sale of liquor in coffee cups. As Mrs C.S. Peel put it, nightclubs 'had always existed, but it was not until after war was declared that they were patronized by women and young girls of good reputation'. Soho also became a favoured shopping and dining area, because of the many government offices in the vicinity, and because the 'foreigners' who managed the many restaurants were able to make meals 'more or less palatable, though not very substantial'. Attendance at the infant leisure pursuit of the cinema, equally dominated by American imports, increased in Britain to around 20 million tickets sold per week, embracing both middle- and upper-class audiences for the first time. In the same way, theatres that had been frequented primarily by the middle and upper class became popular with the working class. Music halls remained immensely popular. Museum- and gallery-going also continued, to the extent that the closure of those venues in London in 1916, largely as an economy measure, was partially rescinded, though objects of major value were removed to other parts of the country as a precaution against air raids. War exhibitions of one kind or another were often mounted, including those aimed at communicating public information, such as the exhibitions on health and hygiene targeted at housewives: museums in London, Norwich, Newcastle, Bristol, Salford, and Belfast, for example, all put on 'War on Houseflies' exhibitions in 1915, though the attraction of such exhibitions may be doubted! The Scottish Zoological Park even exhibited a body louse in October 1915, to demonstrate what the troops were going through in the trenches. At a higher cultural level, the Proms classical-music concerts continued throughout the war and, while Covent Garden was closed for the duration, Sir Thomas Beecham toured extensively with the English Opera Group.

The imposition of new taxes on places of entertainment in May 1916 had its effect on leisure habits. The additional 2d on cinema tickets costing 6d to 1s.2d, and 1d on seats up to 6d, pushed the wealthier patrons into cheaper seats and priced many working-class patrons out altogether. Licensing restrictions also had an effect, probably contributing to greatly increased sales of gramophone records, which had reached 6 million per year by 1918. Escapism had much to do with the determination to maintain leisure pursuits, as evidenced in the popularity of plays like *Peter Pan*, musicals like *Chu Chin Chow and The Maid of the Mountains*, revues such as *The Bing Boys Are Here* with George Robey and the hit song 'If You Were the Only Girl in the World', and the comedy film shorts of Charlie Chaplin. Popular culture became a unifying force at home as well as in the trenches, helping to establish what has been called a more homogenized 'nationalization of taste', which, ironically, undermined many of the older local and regional loyalties from which that popular culture had originally drawn its vitality and strength. It was during the First World War, for example, that it became customary to play the national anthem at the end of all theatrical and cinema performances, a convention that endured until the 1960s.

War as song and dance. This music cover is from the long-running wartime revue *The Bing Boys are Here*, starring George Robey (depicted at right). Its most famous song was 'If You Were the Only Girl in the World'.

While many wartime pursuits such as the cinema continued in popularity after the war, church attendance declined. Superficially at least, the war increased religious observance, if not religious belief, and stimulated what can only be described as superstition; even British soldiers who were not Catholics regularly asked the nuns of Albert on the Somme for medals. Moreover, the war resulted in a rapid growth in secular spiritualism as the bereaved turned to spiritualists in order to try and communicate with the dead. Sir Arthur Conan Doyle, who lost both a son and a brother in the war, was one prominent figure seeking such solace; another was the physicist Sir Oliver Lodge, who had also lost a son. Similarly, British soldiers made reports of spiritualist phenomena, and the return of the dead was to remain a theme of art, literature and even cinema well after the war. As Mrs C.S. Peel put it, 'Palmists, crystal gazers, thought readers reaped a considerable harvest.'

On the money-go-round

Clearly, there were winners and losers in the wartime distortion of the economy and its impact on everyday lives. Obvious winners were usually those involved in war production, some businessmen and traders. The likely losers were in non-essential employment, on fixed incomes and among marginal groups such as the elderly. In the process, social and economic differences were likely to be narrowed, but older inequalities would remain alongside the newer divisions thrown up by war.

Melodrama in wartime. Mary Pickford's most famous wartime film was *The Little American*, and this film, *The Eternal Grind* (1911), was a sorry tale of industrial poverty. Like Chaplin, Pickford offscreen worked assiduously to sell war bonds.

Cutting across the existing British class structure, the war imposed a degree of equality through taxation, not least through the increase in the numbers paying income tax, from 1.5 million in 1914, when the starting point was annual income of £160, to 7.7 million by 1918, the threshold being lowered to £130 in 1916. Indirect taxation also increased dramatically, on commodities such as beer, spirits, tobacco, matches, sugar, cocoa, coffee and motor vehicles, increasing the average burden on a family from six per cent of income to ten per cent of income.

While other wartime financial changes hit many in the middle class to varying degrees, the working class benefited from increasing wages and transfer payments such as separation allowances. In the process, there was a narrowing of the gap between the working class and the middle class. This was also true within the working class, which had been highly compartmentalized, not least in the division between skilled and unskilled workers. Socially there was also a mixing of classes to some extent in the armed forces, and civilians had been exposed to soldiers from other classes through the widespread billeting of troops on them in 1914–15.

The old British landed elite suffered disproportionally. They had already been badly affected by the agricultural depression at the end of the nineteenth century and the Liberal government's pre-war taxation policies. The burden was increased by wartime taxes and death duties. Many heirs to estates were to lose their lives on active service. There had been pre-war land sales but nothing on the scale of the sale of between 6 and 8 million acres in England and Wales, including perhaps a quarter of all cultivated land in Britain, between 1918 and 1922. Much 'new money' moved into land ownership.

In terms of the middle class, the proportion of white-collar workers in the British labour force rose from 1.7 million to 2.7 million between 1911 and 1921, representing an increase from 12 per cent to 22 per cent of the population in work. Some businessmen undoubtedly did well through the expansion of industry, some traders benefited from the black market, and some retailers (such as drapers) profited from the enhanced purchasing power of the working class. On the other hand, there was rising taxation, the fall of rentals, a collapse of traditional safe investments, and the loss of purchasing power because fixed incomes declined in value.

When war ended, the intention was to continue some wartime controls in Britain, in the expectation that Germany would remain an economically powerful enemy. The sudden and unexpected collapse of the Central Powers in 1918 removed much of this justification, especially undermining the plans of the Ministry of Reconstruction, created in 1917. Moreover, the piecemeal way in which controls had been applied during the war meant there was a lack of any coherent doctrine of collectivization to justify their retention. Some of the new wartime ministries were to survive, to be joined by the new ministries of Health and Transport in 1919. Despite the reassertion of Treasury controls over departmental staffing and public expenditure in 1919–25, though, the government machinery had been overhauled and, in many cases, had become more professional in such areas as labour and health policy.

Ration coupons expired in May 1919 and food controls lapsed by 1920, although both were reintroduced amid the postwar price boom. And the lessons of the First World War in respect of food control were

The social safety net. These coupons, for coal and cheese, were issued to the borough's poor by the Local Representative Committee for the Prevention and Relief of Distress in Fulham, London.

COAL TICKET.

BOROUGH OF FULHAM.

Local Representative Committee for the Prevention and Relief of Distress due to the War.

The Holder of this Ticket is authorised to receive

ONE CWT. OF COAL

from any of the Coal Merchants named at the back of this Card

at a cost of 1/2.

Town Clerk and Hon. Sec.

TOWN HALL, FULHAM, S.W.

BOROUGH OF FULHAM.

Local Representative Committee for the Prevention and Relief of Distress.

On the production of this ticket at the TOWN HALL, FULHAM, the holder will be given a portion of the cheese so generously presented by the Government of Quebec (Canada), for the Relief of Distress due to the War.

INFLUENZA!

"If persons entering densely crowded underground lifts and cars were to keep their mouths closed — by preference upon an antiseptic lozenge . . . the spread of influenza would be much abated."—A physician writing in "The Lancet."

"Having tried all the B.P. and proprietary antiseptic lozenges, I have been reduced to one, and one only — Formamint Tablets "— A Physician writing in "The Practitioner."

Act on this hint to-day. Buy a bottle of Formamint—carry it in your pocket or handbag — and suck a tablet whenever you enter a crowded germ-laden place. This will protect you, not only against Influenza, but also against Sore Throats and Colds, etc.

But be sure you get *genuine* Formamint—sold by all chemists at 2/2 per bottle, and manufactured solely by Genatosan, Limited (British Purchasers of The Sanatogen Co.), 12, Chenies Street, London, W.C. 1. (Chairman: The Viscountess Rhondda.)

Protect yourself by taking

THE GERM KILLING THROAT TABLET

LET OXO HELP OUT YOUR MEAT RATION.

A NEW OXO DISH

Prepared by a Celebrated Chef.

WAR TIME PUDDING.
Sufficient for Six or Eight Persons.

Ingredients.—½ lb. margarine, lard, or suet ; 1 lb. flour ; 4 teaspoonfuls OXO ; 6 ozs. onions ; 6 ozs. carrots ; 6 ozs. celery ; 6 ozs. tomatoes ; 6 ozs. potatoes ; 4 ozs. pearl barley, parboiled ; or equal quantities of any other vegetable in season.

METHOD OF PREPARATION.—Cut all vegetables into dice, not too small ; season well.

Make the pastry in the usual manner ; namely, mix well the chopped suet, lard, or margarine with flour, make into a paste in exactly the same way as for a meat pudding. Line the basin and fill with the ingredients well mixed together.

Dissolve four teaspoonfuls of OXO in half a pint of water, pour into the pudding, cover and steam for three hours.

In this recipe one OXO cube is equivalent to a teaspoonful of OXO.

OXO helps to compensate for the shortage of meat when used in cooking vegetable dishes. It increases their food value considerably and supplies that appetising and nourishing meat basis which would otherwise be lacking.

A cup of hot OXO and a few biscuits makes a sustaining light lunch and can be prepared in a few minutes with a minimum consumption of fuel.

Sole Proprietors and Manufacturers : OXO Limited, Thames House, London, E.C.4.

to be reimposed during the Second World War. Moreover, government expenditure went on growing with the general acceptance of the war years' assumption that the state should take a more proactive role in the social sphere. In the process, the relationship between government and the plethora of pre-war voluntary agencies was permanently altered.

Rent controls were retained after the war and there were extensions in unemployment insurance and other health-insurance benefits, although these, and an increase in pensions, were at levels lower than the cost of living. The principle of benefit without contribution was incorporated in the Unemployment Insurance Act in 1920, which was a major advance. On the other hand, the wage controls introduced for munitions workers in 1916 and agricultural workers in 1917, outlining a minimum wage, lasted for only 18 months after the war.

Much else was curtailed by postwar economic retrenchment, not least expectations of house building. A housing programme was pushed forward under the Housing and Town Planning Act of July 1919, but, in the event, plans to build 500,000 houses on pre-war 'garden city' lines were stymied by financial difficulties in July 1921. There was postwar legislation on transport, land acquisition, forestry, electricity supply and industrial courts, but it amounted to less than had been intended. Nonetheless, there were few areas by 1918 in which the role of the state had not been greatly enhanced. Whatever ideological or other attitudes existed towards state intervention before 1914, government was compelled to take a major role in the management of industry and agriculture in an emerging war economy. In the process, it had not only changed people's views about the nature of the state but also substantially affected even people's social lives and leisure activities.

Less 'flu, more protein. A page from the popular illustrated periodical *The Sphere*, 7 December 1918, neatly encapsulates two issues at war's end – meat rationing and the onset of the Spanish 'flu pandemic.

(1)

While the East End of London was not necessarily representative of wider British conditions, it is clear that there was wartime deprivation in many areas. Sylvia Pankhurst recalls in 1932 the story of one woman for whom the war meant financial ruin.

———

MRS PAYNE *brought her up to see me, a little plain old maid, neat, spare, respectable. Her face flushed and hands trembled as she spoke. She gave her name and age, 57, with the formality acquired by painful visits to other offices. Her painful sense of indignity embarrassed me. I tried to reassure her, parrying her pride. Her tale gushed out; gentility, penury, courage. She earned her living for forty years by making men's ties and silk belts, had become a forewoman over twenty girls. Then her eyesight began to fail. 'But for my eyes, I am as well able to work as any of the younger ones, in fact better. I often had bad health when I was young – I haven't now!' This failing of the eyes compelling her, she ventured, a year before the War, to try her fortune as a small confectioner, buying the business with the whole of the savings she had accumulated in forty years – just £40. She had succeeded; her shop was opposite a pleasure garden, and some of its visitors there came to her for refreshments. She made a profit of 18s. to £1 a week on average and 30s. to 35s. in summer. It sufficed for her simple wants. She was proud of her modest achievement and the independence it had given her. 'I had a splendid business in ice cream!' she said wistfully. The War came, just as the best of the ice cream season was beginning. The gardens were closed. Seven hundred railwaymen, 'my best customers', left the district; they were told they must either enlist or be put*
on half-time. *For a week she could get no sugar. Prices rose monstrously; she was afraid to buy. Having no capital to fall back on, overwhelmed by the prospect of debt, and torn by the bitterest disappointment she decided to close her doors. She went to the library of a provident society, to which she had belonged in her youth, to search the newspaper advertisements for a situation. The clerk there advised her to apply to the Local Representative Committee. The committee could not give her work; it had only money to offer. 'I wouldn't take it at first', she said. 'I sold my tea urn and other things from the shop, and lived on that for a little while – but I had to come to it at last!' For the first month the committee allowed her 3s. a week. Then the Government scale was announced, and her dole was raised to 10s. She strove unceasingly to find work. 'It's my age that's against me, though, but for my eyes, I can do as much work as any of the younger ones. I've been to hundreds of places, and as I can't afford to ride, I've had to tramp. I would do any kind of work if I could get it.' Her voice quavered. Last week the committee cut her allowance to 5s. 'My rent is 3s 6d., so you can see what it means!' Even the 5s. would soon be stopped they told her, for they were 'closing down the Fund.' They had spoken harshly. 'As though they believed I had closed my shop to get myself on to the Fund to live in one room on 10s a week; to take relief after keeping myself for more than forty years!' She stifled a sob, assuring me that her little shop had not been the only one to shut; five others of the sort had closed in the same road. They could not help it; their trade was gone. One of them had kept open till Christmas; then the owners had closed their doors, owing £500! 'I came out of it*

without owing a penny to anyone! I wouldn't keep on and involve other people!'

I showed her the Board of Trade form of registration for War Service. 'I should be willing to work on the land if they would have me', she said wearily. 'I would train for anything they liked, but I do not think they would take anyone of my age! I suppose I shall have to sell all I have; things I have had since I was about twenty!' She tried to shroud herself in her pride; the despair in her voice told me plainly she had nothing left to sell. I would lend my efforts to find work for her, but that would not atone to her for her little business; her own achievement. It was the loveless tragedy of a little old maid.

[Sylvia Pankhurst, *The Home Front*, London: Hutchinson & Co, 1932, pp. 139–40]

(2)

Joe Hollister, a City worker living in New Cross in Southeast London, writes to his father, living at Romford in Essex, on 19 March 1917, revealing his views on the progress of the war, including the first Russian Revolution of March 1917 (February in the Old-style Julian Calendar used in Russia). That event had led to the abdication of Tsar Nicholas II, but the Provisional Government that replaced him was still committed to continuing the war against Germany. However, Hollister also describes the way women are visibly replacing men in some jobs in the City, Zeppelin raids, food shortages, and the explosion at the Silvertown munitions factory back in January 1917. The spelling, punctuation and grammar are erratic.

———

W E RECEIVED *Amy's letter & were pleased to hear you were better after been queer, the weather has been very trying & the winter seems so long & depressing, but we had quite an agreeable change on Saturday & Sunday with warm sunshine, but the wind very nippy in the shade, just the sort of weather when you want be more cautious.*

We had a line from Bert on Saturday night, just to say he had been transferred to 'HMS Erebus' No 2. Mess c/o General Post Office, London, he says she is a fine ship, clean, plenty of room, & no beastly coaling, so I suppose she is a new oil-driven Destroyer christened after the volcano or mountain of that name; I am very glad for I think it is a scandal that youngsters of 16 or 17 should be expected to coal-ship, it would not be permitted in civil life for we should soon have the Trade Unions up against it, he enquires again after Miss White & also says that if the war lasts for another twelve months he does not expect he will get any leave during that period; its to be hoped it will not last that long.

Events seem to be moving more rapidly now on the western front, get the Huns out of their trenches perhaps our cavalry will get a look in & keep them on the run, for you don't hear of Germans having much of that arm of the service, eaten them all perhaps!, everything with them seems to be mechanically propelled. The capture of Baghdad & Bapaume & the Russian revolt is a nasty smack in the face for poor Bill, he & his dupes must be feeling very uneasy at present. There seems to be a fair sprinkling of 'Hollisters' in the forces, I have seen five altogether in the casualty lists (two last enclosed) & I see there are five in the Directory, getting quite a beastly common name, have you heard anything of Dick since you wrote last?, my understudy at the office died of pneumonia in France in January afters serving in the HAC [Honourable Artillery Company –

a Territorial unit] for a year & eight months without having been up to the fighting line, yet you hear of others being out & killed four months after joining up; its extraordinary the amount of female labour employed in the City now, in the trains of a morning of ten passengers in a compartment there is generally an average of eight females, the Bank of England employ over 400, there was a flutter of excitement in Gracechurch St the other day at two girls with trouser overalls cleaning the windows of shops, the railway Companys have employed them of course for along while, tramcars, omnibuses, mail-rooms, lamplighters, latherers in barbers shops, in fact almost every sphere of activity, when 'Tommy' comes home he will be keeping house & minding the kids while the missus earns the pieces.

The Zepps made another futile attempt to pay us a visit on Friday night, but I don't think they will get as far as London again, I expect, however, they will continue to harass the coast towns where they can drop their bombs promiscuously & then scamper off, if only to keep the enthusiasm of their misguided people flickering; it is gratifying to hear of the French accounting for another of them; we only want to find means to deal effectively with their submarines to relieve the scarcity of food stuffs when all would be well, things in London in this respect are beginning to be serious, no potatoes to be had, sugar almost unobtainable, meat & cheese 1/6 butter 2/4 bread 11 [d]. I tried vegetables instead of flowers in the garden last year, not that I expected much, more from patriotic motives, beans, savoys, sprouts, lettuce, onions, carrots, but it was just a waste of money & time & so disheartening & so I think I shall just keep it tidy this year & no more.

I suppose you did not suffer any damage by the [Silvertown] *Munitions Explosion in January,* we came out allright although about a dozen houses down the road had windows broken & shop windows as far out as Brixton (*six or seven miles away*) were thrown in, the wind was blowing directly from where it happened which I expect accounted for it to some extent, it seems almost criminal that a high explosive factory should be allowed to be situated in a densely populated residential district like that when there are vacant spaces lying idle four or five miles further out.

[IWM, 98/10/1, Hollister Mss]

PEACE

The driving force behind the tentative beginnings of 'war welfare', as described in Chapter Four, was the recognition that the maintenance of national morale was a crucial component in national survival. Successful political leadership in wartime therefore required astute manipulation of public opinion, even where governments in liberal democracies like Britain entered the war with greater legitimacy in the eyes of their populations than in the more coercive political systems.

Opponents at home – imagined and real

Many socialists had anticipated prior to 1914 that a major European war could be prevented through international solidarity. It proved an illusion, as most European socialist parties were split on the issue of support for national war efforts, a majority invariably arguing that the war was one of defence and liberty in which the working class had as much interest in victory as anyone else. The Labour Party was certainly split, with Ramsay MacDonald resigning as chairman of the Parliamentary Labour Party (PLP) in opposition to the war. Most members of MacDonald's Independent Labour Party (ILP) followed a similar anti-war course. Opposition to the war, however, remained a minority activity for some time. In September 1915 only 7 out of 607 delegates to the Trades Union Congress (TUC) conference opposed a pro-war resolution. The suffrage movement was also divided, with Sylvia Pankhurst of the Women's Suffrage Federation (WSF) breaking from her mother and sister to oppose the war and seeking to send delegates to a peace congress at The Hague in April 1915.

Understandably, governments were sensitive to the possibility of anti-war opposition, and surveillance of actual and potential dissidents was common under the additional wartime powers taken by the state. The military authorities were sufficiently worried by the prospect of 'British Bolshevism' to recast home defence plans in 1917–18. By 1917, MI5 – originally established as the Secret Service Bureau in 1909 as a result of the pre-war spy fever – had 250,000 report cards and 27,000 personal files on potential dissidents, figures representing many more people than the 70,000 or so resident aliens in Britain. The head of Special Branch, Sir Basil Thomson, began a series of fortnightly reports on pacifism and revolutionary organizations in the United Kingdom and morale abroad in early 1918, though his own later assessment was that the number of revolutionaries in Britain was 'ridiculously small'.

The Irish angle

Arguably, the greatest wartime challenge to the authority of the British government was the Easter Rising in Dublin, in April 1916, though,

Conchies on parade. This conscientious objector of October 1917, in Dartmoor prison in for refusing military service, was a former Sunday school superintendent. He makes his point with the slogan on his spade, held, perhaps unwittingly, like a shouldered rifle.

whatever the longer-term consequences, it posed little real threat at the time. In 1914 there was the real possibility of civil war in Ireland over Home Rule, against which Ulster Protestants were determined to fight, with the loyalist Ulster Volunteer Force (UVF) poised to confront the nationalist Irish Volunteers. In the event, while Irish Home Rule was put on the statute book in September 1914, its operation was immediately suspended for the duration of the First World War. Moreover, in response to the calls of one nationalist leader, John Redmond, many Irish Volunteers chose to enlist in the British Army, as did large numbers

Irish Rebellion, May, 1916.

Soldiers bivouacking opposite Liberty Hall,
the Rebel Headquarters in Dublin.

Ruins of Sackville Street, Dublin.

Republicanism in action. This set of postcards shows some of the scenes of conflict wrought by the 'Irish Rebellion', in April 1916. At the same time, as in the scene in Sackville Street, people go about their normal business while buildings are in flames.

from the UVF. A rump of Irish Volunteers, now often styled the Irish National Volunteers (INV), remained irretrievably opposed to assisting the British, and, in 1915, planning for an insurrection commenced. A former diplomat, Sir Roger Casement, who had sought German assistance for the rising, was arrested after landing from a German submarine on 21 April 1916. Three days later, on Easter Monday, some 2000 members of the INV and the radical Irish Citizen Army seized prominent buildings in Dublin and proclaimed an Irish Republic. They were forced to surrender on 29 April, 15 ringleaders being subsequently executed. The rising compelled the British government to recognize the likelihood of postwar partition of Ireland as a longer-term solution to the Irish problem, while it also swayed public opinion in southern Ireland. The nationalist Sinn Fein party won a number of by-elections and, then, a total of 73 seats at the general election in 1918. Ultimately, the Anglo-Irish war of 1919–21 was to see Ireland partitioned between Northern Ireland and an Irish Free State in the south.

The alien presence

Although many precautions were taken – understandable in the circumstances – aliens, resident foreigners, posed relatively little threat to national security. However, the 35,000 or so Germans were the third-largest immigrant group in Britain after the Irish and Jewish communities, and they soon became the object of public suspicion and attack. Since the imperial struggles with the German-backed Afrikaners in southern Africa – and more recently the naval arms race and pre-war spy scares – the British public needed little tuition in anti-German sentiment. The spy scare persisted until at least 1915, with many people caught up in wild rumours and wholly false accusations. Famously, the *Daily Mail* advised its readers that if a waiter serving them appeared German but claimed to be Swiss, they should demand to see his passport. Because of a fear of spies using carrier pigeons, the Defence of the Realm Act (DORA) required owners to have a permit for homing pigeons. Pigeons of all kinds, however, were shot on sight in the autumn of 1914, in spite of the fact that it was actually illegal to shoot homing pigeons. At Great Waltham in Essex, one hapless official from the Ordnance Survey mapping agency was arrested by special constables six times in a matter of days while surveying. In reality, some 22 known German spies were earmarked to be rounded up in 1914, of whom one escaped back overseas before he could be arrested on the outbreak of war, with a further 14 suspects being arrested subsequently. In all, 11 were executed. Increasingly the public demanded the internment of aliens, and some 30,000 were interned, mostly on the Isle of Man, all aliens having been compelled to register under the Alien Restrictions Act of August 1914.

Fuelled by the many stories of German atrocities in Belgium and elsewhere, actual or supposed Germans were subjected to harassment. There were at least seven deaths in East End riots in May 1915 following the torpedoing of the liner *Lusitania* with 1198 fatalities on 15 May. Even dachshunds, the Germanically named dogs, were stoned in the streets on occasions. Air raids, of course, only increased anti-German feeling. As Sylvia Pankhurst witnessed in Hoxton, London, it mattered little how long those with German surnames had lived in the area:

> Another mob swept round the corner, hot in fury, baiting a man in flour-covered clothing, wrenched and jerked by the collar, thumped on the back, kicked from the rear. 'All right, Gov'ner; all right', he articulated between the blows, in humble and reasoning Cockney-tones fully typic as that of his assailants.

There were large-scale demonstrations against enemy aliens in a number of cities in 1918, and a petition with 1.2 million signatures was handed in to Downing Street that August. One prominent victim of hysteria was the First Sea Lord, Prince Louis of Battenberg, hounded from office in October 1914, after which the family name was changed to Mountbatten. Similarly, Lord Haldane, the Lord Chancellor, widely

Love not thy neighbour. An angry crowd attacks German-owned premises in London during one of the periodic outpourings of anti-German feeling during 1914 and 1915. The war saw a number of such ugly scenes.

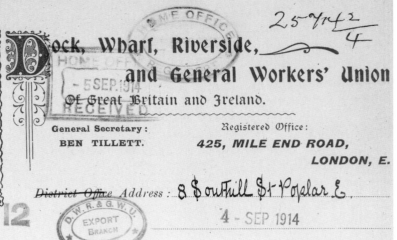

Dock, Wharf, Riverside, and General Workers' Union
Of Great Britain and Ireland.

General Secretary :
BEN TILLETT.

Registered Office :
425, MILE END ROAD,
LONDON, E.

HOME OFFICE

— 5 SEP. 1914
RECEIVED

25 9142
4

257142

A. 12

D. W. R. & G. W. U.
EXPORT
BRANCH
G. B. & I.

District Office Address : 8 Southill St Poplar E.

4 - SEP 1914

Sir

I am instructed by the Branch representing 800 Members to forward the following resolution on to you

Resolve that we the Members of the Export Branch Dock Wharfe Riverside & General Worker's Union view with regret the action taken by the Holligans and Children of Poplar in wrecking the Shops and destroying the Flour & Bread belonging to Germans and Naturalize English Bakers. We deem it necessary that these Shops should be allowed protection as far as able to prevent any destruction or Thieft, as these Shops average between 30 to 40 Sacks of ~~Flower~~ Flour at the value of 36/- per Sack which if not use for the proper purpose would be at the disadvantage of the poorer people We therefore call upon the Home Secretary to use his unflence with The Commissioner of Police to afford such protection that's necessary

Right Hon
Mr McKenna
Home Secretary

Yours faithfully
WMAdams
Secretary

D. W. R. & G. W. U.
EXPORT
BRANCH
G. B. & I.

but erroneously believed to be pro-German, was dropped from the Asquith Coalition government in May 1915 after sustained press attack. Orchestras began to avoid German composers and, absurdly, German measles became known as 'Belgian flush'.

Jews also came under physical attack in East London in 1917, in the belief that they were evading conscription. Bizarrely, Chinese premises were attacked in Liverpool after the sinking of the *Lusitania*, over £40,000 worth of damage resulting from riots in the city where most of the ship's crew had originated.

The numbers of aliens in Britain were considerably boosted by the influx of some 200,000 Belgian refugees in the autumn of 1914. As with other aliens, many Belgians were ultimately employed in war industries.

Pacifists and Bolsheviks

Pacifism had suffered something of a blow in August 1914 from the fact that the chairman of the Peace Society, J.A. Pease, chose not to resign from Asquith's Cabinet. Founded in 1816, the Peace Society was one of a number of traditional, essentially religious, groups opposed to war, to whose number was soon added the Fellowship of Reconciliation, formed by H.T. Hodgkin with mostly Quaker and other Nonconformist members. There was also the Women's International League for Peace and Freedom, in which Catherine Marshall was prominent.

New politically motivated group soon emerged. A junior minister who did resign from the government, Charles Trevelyan, formed the Union of Democratic Control (UDC) with Ramsay MacDonald, Norman Angell and Ed Morel on 5 August 1914. In theory, like MacDonald himself, the UDC was not opposed to national defence and wished to effect a negotiated peace and to assert the right of 'the people' to control policy made in its name, primarily by creating a different kind of postwar world. The UDC, which had about 10,000 members at its peak, had close links with the Independent Labour Party.

Conscription was the major issue for the British peace movement, and Fenner Brockway and Clifford Allen formed the No Conscription Fellowship (NCF) on 3 December 1914 for those of military age. The

'WRECKING THE SHOPS'
The Secretary of the local branch of the Dock, Wharf, Riverside and General Workers' Union, D.M. Adams, writes to the Home Secretary, Reginald McKenna, on 4 September 1914 to condemn attacks by 'hooligans' on the premises of bakers of German origin in Poplar, East London. Since bread represented such a staple

commodity for the working class, Adams wanted police protection extended to such premises.

The incident took place on 31 August and involved two shops, and was apparently motivated by remarks made by the bakers. The Metropolitan Police restored order quickly and there was no further trouble. (HO45/10944/257142)

JOINT REPORT AND PROPOSALS RE

BELGIANS IN "ELISABETHVILLE" BIRTLEY.

The incident which occurred on Thursday night the 21st December 1916, when a Belgian youth was shot by a Gendarme, brought to light the state of discontent which exists amongst the population of the Belgian Village.

A serious disturbance, which had every appearance of resulting in bloodshed, was averted by the intervention of the British Police and the withdrawal of the Belgian Gendarmes.

In order to avoid further disturbances, it is essential that the present control of the village be modified as early as possible. This can only be done by mutual agreement with the Belgian Government.

The alleged main causes of discontent appear to be :-

(1) Resentment of the workmen to the rigid military control in which they are classed as soldiers first and munition workers second, instead of the reverse.

(2) Unjust treatment received from the Gendarmes.

(3) Unfair punishment for minor offences and no machinery for appeal from sentences pronounced by the Officer in charge of the Gendarmes.

(4) Objection to wear uniform, which many of the men who are discharged soldiers are called upon to pay for at a high price when they are in possession of civilian clothes.

(5) Restrictions preventing the men from entering licensed houses in the district.

The output of munitions from the Factory is intimately bound up with the welfare and contentment of the men in the village. The existing control therefore must not only be modified in order to prevent disturbance of the peace, but also with a view to so improving the conditions of the men that they will put forward their energies to obtain the maximum output of shells.

The following proposals are put forward for consideration. If they are approved by the Departments of the British Government concerned, it would then remain to place them before the Belgian Government preferably at a conference to be held in London or Birtley, where, if desired, evidence could be given by a number of Belgian Officials and workmen, six of the latter to be chosen by the Belgian workmen, and six by the Belgian Government.

NCF had 61 branches by November 1915. In fact, only some 16,500 claims of conscientious objection to service were made after its introduction in January 1916. Of these, 5111 claimants were given absolute or conditional exemption by tribunals and a further 1400 by the Army Council. Others were exempted from combatant service, and only 2425 were refused exemption by tribunals. A further 1969 men exempted from combatant service declined to serve in the Non Combatant Corps and were court-martialled. In addition, 6312 men refused to appear for military service when conscripted, of whom 5790 were court-martialled. Most accepted non-combatant service or Home Office work, while others were released on medical grounds. In all, 843 so-called 'absolutists' spent two or more years in prison, with 17 given death sentences, later commuted to life imprisonment, and 142 given life sentences; 10 died while in prison custody.

Pacifism, political radicalism and opposition to conscription did yield a few high-profile and newsworthy prosecutions. One British suffragette, Alice Wheeldon, and three fellow conspirators – her two daughters and her son-in-law – received 22 years imprisonment in total for a bizarre plot to poison Lloyd George. Almost certainly, the evidence was concocted, because Wheeldon had been sheltering deserters and conscientious objectors. As already noted, the leaders of the Clyde Workers Committee were deported from the Clyde in March 1915 and one Clydeside socialist leader, John Maclean, received 8 years' imprisonment, of which he served 22 months, for incitement to sedition. The British philosopher, Bertrand Russell, was fined £100 in June 1916 for anti-conscription activities and lost his lectureship at Trinity College, Cambridge, as a result. In May 1918 he was given six months' imprisonment for 'statements likely to prejudice' relations with the United States, having alleged that American troops would be used as

'A SERIOUS DISTURBANCE'

The first page of a joint report on 27 December 1916 by Major General R.A.K. Montgomery, commanding the Tyne Garrison; William Morant, the Chief Constable of County Durham; and Maurice Gibb of the Birtley-on-Tyne North Projectile Factory, representing the Ministry of Munitions, on disturbances among Belgian refugees at the Belgian refugee village at Birtley (known as Elizabethville) on 21 December.

There had been a series of problems with the Belgians employed on munitions work, many of whom resented having to wear uniform, among other grievances.

Elizabethville was policed by Belgian gendarmerie and they had shot a Belgian worker when unrest erupted. If unrest continued then munitions production might well be jeopardized.

Among the solutions recommended by Montgomery, Morant and Gibb were the supervision of Elizabethville by British police rather than Belgian gendarmes, adequate measures to ascertain grievances, and better canteen facilities. Subsequently, they also recommended the return of all serving Belgian soldiers to the coastal sector of the Western Front held by the Belgian army.
(HO45/10738/261921)

CLAIMS OF CHARLES JOSEPH, PAUL WILLIAM AND HINMAN JOHN BAKER, HEARD
AT A MEETING OF THE LOCAL TRIBUNAL HELD AT THE COUNCIL OFFICES ON
29th FEBRUARY 1916.

The three applicants attended before the Tribunal, and stated
they objected to any kind of Military Service, whether combatant or not.
Charles Joseph and Paul William are employed in the firm of Joseph
Baker & Sons Ltd. Engineers, Willesden Junction.   They stated they were
at present engaged on exactly the same work which they were doing before
the War.   Charles Joseph was engaged on food production machinery and
Paul William was engaged in the production of machinery.   They are not
engaged on making munitions, and are continuing the business upon which
they were employed before the War.   Hinman John Baker was a student in
chemistry at the University College, and he said it would be detrimental
to him to be interrupted in his duties.

Mr. William King Baker, the father of the applicants, attended
before the Tribunal, and stated that his sons were not shirkers but
were workers.   They had given up holidays and turned holidays into
work;   work where they believed God would have them work.   These young
men simply cannot and will not take Military Service, as it would be
contrary to the views held by the Society of Friends, of which they
were Members.   Any kind of civil service they would be willing to take,
but not any Military Service.   They would object to going into the
Royal Army Medical Corps, or the Sanitary Corps.   They wish to carry
out the spirit of the Faith as their Lord did, where it does not conflict with conscience and the Law of God.   They would sooner suffer
death or imprisonment than take up Military Service.

The firm of Joseph Baker & Sons Ltd. was a Public Company and
it was not true to say they were making profits on the Government
work which they were carrying out.   On the contrary they were making
a big loss.

The younger son had offered to do relief work with the Society
of Friends in the North of France, but two of the leading men had
strongly advised him that his most important National Service was to
finish his training at the University College.   Chemists were needed
in the country.   His name, however, was still on the list, and he
might be called up at any time for that work.   The other two sons were
doing expert work for which they had been trained.

Mr. Rosslyn Earp of 96 High Street, Harrow-on-the-Hill, attended
before the Tribunal as an old member of the Friends Ambulance Unit.
He stated that the primary object of the R.A.M.C. is to keep the
maximum number of men in the firing line.   The primary object of the
Friends Ambulance Unit was to save life, and to help suffering.   He
was at Ypres for 6 months and helped to relieve the suffering of the
civil population there.   As a member of the R.A.M.C. he could not
have done that.   He also understood that when you are under Army control
there is no guarantee that you may not be called upon to take up arms.
An R.A.M.C. man at Loos told him that some of their members were called
upon to take up arms.

A motion was submitted to grant total exemption in all three
cases, but was not seconded.

The member of the Tribunal who moved that Charles Joseph and
Paul William be exempted from combatant service only, and that Hinman
John be granted conditional exemption to allow him to continue his
education or training at the University College, stated that he could
not conscientiously vote to exempt the two first-named young men who
were working in a firm who were engaged on Government work to prosecute
and help the War.

Decision of the Tribunal - That Charles Joseph and Paul William
be granted exemption from combatant service only, and Hinman John be
granted conditional exemption on the grounds that it was expedient in
the national interests that instead of being employed in Military
Service he should continue to be educated and trained as a chemist at
the University College.

'DETRIMENTAL TO HIM'

Part of the case file relating to the appeal before the Middlesex Central Tribunal of Paul William Baker, a 21-year-old mechanical engineer from Acton.

Together with his brothers, Charles and Hinman, Paul had applied for exemption from conscription on conscientious grounds. Paul and Charles worked for the family firm at Willesden while Hinman was a chemistry student at University College London. Their father, William, supported the application for exemption, indicating that both Paul and Charles were working overtime on food production machinery. He also disputed any suggestion that the firm was making a profit out of government contracts.

Hinman was allowed to continue his studies, but Paul and Charles were exempted only from combatant service. Paul launched his appeal on 2 March. On 3 May 1916 he agreed to undertake agricultural work in lieu of military service, though, in the end, he actually served in the Friends Ambulance Unit. (MH47/66)

(*right*) No escape in marriage. A leaflet of February 1916, issued by the No Conscription Fellowship, warns that the government will soon conscript married men too. They were right.

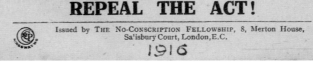

MARRIED MEN NEXT!

We have repeatedly stated that the present Military Service Act was merely required as

THE THIN END OF THE WEDGE.

As proof of this assertion we reproduce the following, which appeared in *The Pall Mall Gazette* on February 17, 1916, and in most other London papers simultaneously:—

PROBLEM OF MARRIED MEN.

WHAT WILL HAPPEN WHEN ALL SINGLE ARE CALLED?

THE UNATTESTED.

Since the calling up of all the single classes under the Military Service Act further conferences amongst the War Office authorities on two urgent matters have taken place.

Much attention, says the Central News, is now being devoted, it is understood, firstly, **as to how unattested married men are to be handled,** and, secondly, the need for a revision of local tribunals and their powers for granting exemptions.

Lord Kitchener has publicly expressed himself on the subject of exemptions in words which convey a certain significance, **but by far the most important subject under consideration now is the position of the unattested married men.** By the time the single classes are in khaki, the calling up of the groups of attested married men under the Derby scheme will be following automatically.

But here a new situation confronts the authorities, and as in the case of the single slacker **they will be called upon to deal with the young married shirker, who, with very little responsibility, and probably no family, or a small one, has failed to present himself for attestation.**

A broad hint was dropped in an authoritative quarter to-day that the War Office was considering how best to deal with the unattested married men—in the near future—up to the age of thirty, who had not voluntarily offered their services to the country. While legislative action might not be necessary, another kind of pressure, it was stated, would be brought to bear on them.

The only way to stop the onward march of Militarism is to demand that the Government

REPEAL THE ACT!

Issued by THE NO-CONSCRIPTION FELLOWSHIP, 8, Merton House, Salisbury Court, London, E.C.

1916

strikebreakers in Britain. Two other leading British pacifists were also jailed at various times, Clifford Allen being held from August 1916 to December 1917 and E.D. Morel given six months in August 1917.

Pacifism, however, made little impact. And that other perceived threat, 'British Bolshevism', was mostly concerned with the issues of 'dilution' of the workplace in favour of women and the unskilled and the erosion of pay differentials. A call to form soldiers' and workers' councils in every town – from a conference convened by the UDC, ILP, trade unions and other socialists groups, including the small British Socialist Party – was made at Leeds, in June 1917, in celebration of the Tsar's abdication. It fell on deaf ears.

The call of a former Foreign Secretary, Lord Lansdowne, for more moderate war aims and the Labour Party's own declaration of non-expansionist war aims in December 1917 did cause the government some difficulties. However, Lloyd George successfully outflanked the anti-war movement in January 1918, shifting Britain's publicly stated war aims to a vague idea of democratic peace. The fact that the Bolsheviks in Russia then signed a separate peace with Germany cut even more ground from under the peace movement, with the wide recognition that peace in the east freed German resources to pursue a decisive victory in the west. However, what was of far more concern for the government than pacifism was the Metropolitan Police pay strike on 31 August 1918, with the police demanding union recognition, an additional £1 a week and a war bonus of 12 per cent. In the event, Lloyd George managed to get the men back on the beat with what proved to be an empty promise.

Negotiated peace had become a metaphor for wider opposition to

'SWEET RELEASE'

Having received the usual condolences from King George V on the death of his daughter (who had served as a nurse with Queen Alexandra's Imperial Military Nursing Service Reserve at Salonika), James Scott Duckers appeals to the King on 22 December 1918 for clemency on behalf of his son of the same name. The son had been given three and a half years' hard labour by a court martial as a conscientious objector in May 1916.

A well-known Liberal lawyer before the war, the younger Scott Duckers, a Baptist, became prominent in the Union for Democratic Control in 1914 and the No Conscription Fellowship, and became chair of the 'Stop the War Committee'.

Called up in April 1916, Scott Duckers was arrested at his chambers for refusing to report for duty. Subsequently, on being delivered to the Rifle Brigade barracks at Winchester, he refused to undergo a preliminary medical examination or to wear uniform. A series of courts martial followed for this 'absolutist'. Regarded by the press as a 'peace crank', Scott Duckers nonetheless found a number of prominent supporters by 1918, who believed the sentence too harsh for all that he was 'an agitator type', and that he should be released as his health was deteriorating. All such appeals, including that of his father, were unsuccessful, and Scott Duckers served out his time.
(HO45/10808/311118)

HOME OFFICE
27 DEC 1918
REG. DEPT

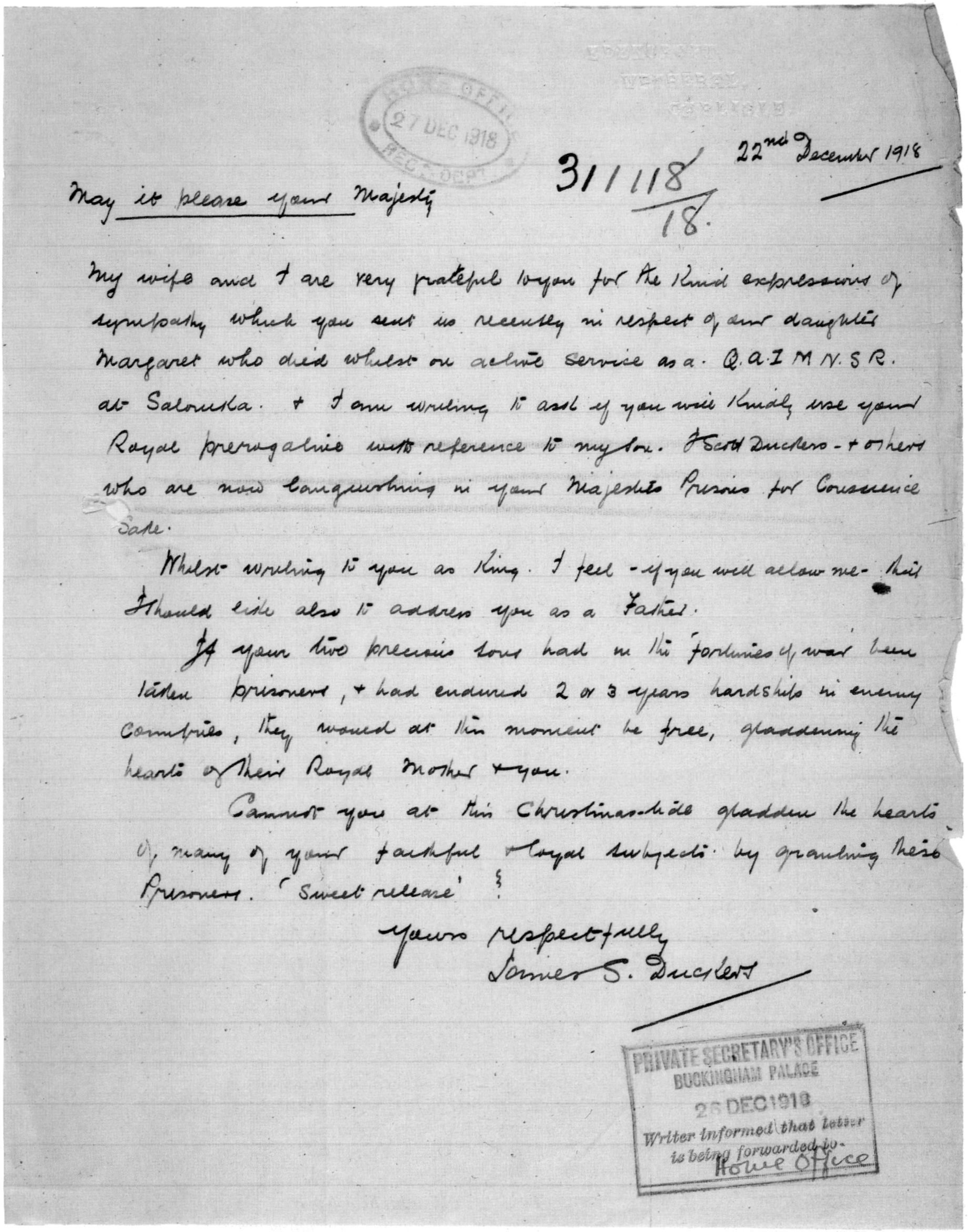

31118/18

22nd December 1918

May it please your Majesty

My wife and I are very grateful to you for the kind expressions of sympathy which you sent us recently in respect of our daughter Margaret who died whilst on active service as a Q.A.I.M.N.S.R. at Salonika. & I am writing to ask if you will kindly use your Royal prerogative with reference to my son. J Scott Duckers – & others who are now languishing in your Majesty's Prisons for Conscience Sake.

Whilst writing to you as King. I feel – if you will allow me – that I should like also to address you as a Father.

If your two precious sons had in the fortunes of war been taken prisoners, & had endured 2 or 3 years hardships in enemy countries, they would at this moment be free, gladdening the hearts of their Royal Mother & you.

Cannot you at this Christmastide gladden the hearts of many of your faithful & loyal subjects by granting these Prisoners 'Sweet release'?

Yours respectfully
James S. Duckers

PRIVATE SECRETARY'S OFFICE
BUCKINGHAM PALACE
26 DEC 1918
Writer informed that letter is being forwarded to Home Office

the war by 1917 and, alongside the growing demands for such a peace, there was something of a revival of the pre-war hopes of international socialism among the anti-war socialist minorities. In the event, however, this proved illusory, though one proposed conference at Stockholm resulted in the Labour Party voting to send a delegation in August 1917 consisting of MacDonald, George Wardle (who had succeeded MacDonald as chairman of the Parliamentary Labour Party), and Arthur Henderson, who had joined both the Asquith and Lloyd George Coalition governments. The party then changed its mind, with the majority in favour of sending the delegation falling from 1.3 million to just 3000 on a card vote. As things turned out, the War Cabinet refused to issue passports and Henderson left the government.

Message-selling

In dealing with public opinion and what might be termed 'home management', political leaders were conscious of a range of potential weapons enabling them to influence wartime public opinion. Initially, there was often more than sufficient support for the war. As a result, there was almost a process of 'self-mobilization', and attempts to manipulate the public were often indirect and even superficial. As the war continued, however, governments were increasingly concerned to maintain the national will to win. Indeed, it has been argued that, in the face of growing war weariness and the revolution in Russia, there was a concerted attempt to 'remobilize' British public opinion in 1917 as characterized by the establishment of the National War Aims Committee (NWAC). This more coordinated effort, which concentrated on the projection of war aims, targeted primarily the domestic opponents of the war, principally pacifists and socialists.

Propaganda was the most obvious tool in seeking to stimulate or revive national morale and damage that of the enemy. Propaganda, however, was not just a matter of what appeared in the press. It could also embrace the efforts of a range of official and unofficial groups and organizations, including the church, and extend into the classroom and

'AT THE DISPOSAL OF THE STATE'
Part of a pamphlet issued for the guidance of speakers for the National War Bond Campaign in November 1917, outlining arguments to be deployed against pacifists who might try to undermine the drive for investment in bonds.

The pamphlet stressed the financial costs of the war, the need for domestic economy with the benefit of a lead being given by the wealthiest, and the controls placed on excess profiteering. It also explained for the benefit of speakers the terms and conditions on offer for five-, seven- and ten-year bonds. This was the third and last war bond issue of the war.

It is estimated that 100,000 people still hold First World War war loan stock in modern Britain, although it was devalued in 1932, has no maturity date and pays only a fixed interest rate.
(NSC7/36)

A.C. 41.

BRIEF FOR SPEAKERS

in the

National War Bond Campaign.

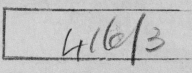

1. WAR FINANCE.

In war time the whole productive power of the nation should be placed at the disposal of the State.

All labour and material that is not placed at the disposal of the State for war purposes or used definitely to promote the health and efficiency of the individual limits our fighting strength, and helps the enemy.

Abstention from individual expenditure is essential to-day. The purchasing power of the individual must be transferred to the State.

Broadly speaking all the productive effort of the nation is required for three purposes—(a) the prosecution of the war ; (b) the production of the necessaries of life ; and (c) the manufacture of goods for export.

When we save and lend to the State we transfer our purchasing power to that extent to the Government.

By this process the purchases of the State are substituted for, instead of being added to, the purchases of the private citizen.

Thereby competition for labour and material between the State and private individuals is avoided, the rise in prices is checked and the cost of the war is reduced.

If the general body of individual consumers reduce expenditure by the same amount as that which the Government spends on the wasteful process of war, little damage occurs to the nation's economic position.

If the individual saves now and lends to the nation, the interest which he will receive from the State on the money so saved will go far to assist him in paying his share of the additional taxation which will have to be raised for interest on war debt.

Even though money earned or profits made may be the result of direct war work, we must none the less save all we can because, if we spend these wages or profits on unnecessary things, we make other people work for us instead of for the war, and so far nullify the usefulness of our own good work.

The fact of America joining the Allies is no reason for slackening our efforts to save and lend. We can only look to America to lend us a limited amount because, besides having to create her own war machine, she has to find money for other Allies. We must also remember that the more we borrow from foreign countries the more interest we have to pay them after the war, whereas if we ourselves lend to our country what she requires, the interest will be paid to us.

(14388.) Wt. 7355—2310. 2500. 11/17. D & S. G. 2.

TO THE
YOUNG WOMEN OF LONDON

Is your "Best Boy" wearing Khaki? If not don't **YOU THINK** he should be?

If he does not think that you and your country are worth fighting for—do you think he is **WORTHY** of you?

Don't pity the girl who is alone—her young man is probably a soldier—fighting for her and her country—and for **YOU**.

If your young man neglects his duty to his King and Country, the time may come when he will **NEGLECT YOU.**

Think it over—then ask him to

JOIN THE ARMY TO-DAY

Printed by David Allen & Sons Ltd., Harrow, London, etc.

Another kind of khaki fever. This typical pre-conscription effort of the Parliamentary Recruiting Committee, using women to persuade their menfolk to join up, draws an unlikely parallel between patriotism and fidelity. In fact, many women were enthusiastic recruiters, handing out the notorious white feathers to 'shirkers'.

popular leisure activities such as the cinema, listening to the gramo-phone and visiting the music hall. It could involve use of a variety of popular forms, from graphic art, such as pictorial postcards and cartoons, to souvenirs. Media for propaganda included porcelain figures of Kitchener, china plates with illustrations of other national figures, as well as the crested china busts, binoculars, artillery, shells and tanks produced by the Goss factory in Stoke-on-Trent and similar firms.

War-related jigsaw puzzles, parlour games and toy soldiers all fulfilled similar purposes for children. In December 1917, one young Liverpool girl reported to her father, serving in France, that she had visited a Christmas grotto that included a trench scene with a tank. Commercial advertisements also commonly reflected the impact of the war. Oliver Typewriters, for example, proclaimed that the War Office and other government departments had bought over 3000 of their latest machines.

Certainly, there was an eagerness to be informed in wartime. Rumours could spread quickly, such as the extraordinary story in September 1914 that Russian troops had landed at Aberdeen en route for France, still with snow on their boots! Snow was reputedly being swept from the railway carriages, and station slot machines jammed with roubles. Circulation figures for the press generally increased. The circulation of the national dailies, including illustrated newspapers, had been about 4.4 million in 1914, and Fleet Street alone produced 326 daily, weekly or monthly titles. All saw big increases in readership, but rising production costs and declining advertisement revenues led to falling profits and the demise of many smaller newspapers.

Souvenirs of war. These Toby jugs, from 1918, depict (top left to right) Woodrow Wilson, 'Old Bill', Jan Smuts, Douglas Haig, Joseph Joffre, and Ferdinand Foch; and (bottom left to right) John Jellicoe, David Beatty, George V, David Lloyd George, and Lord Kitchener.

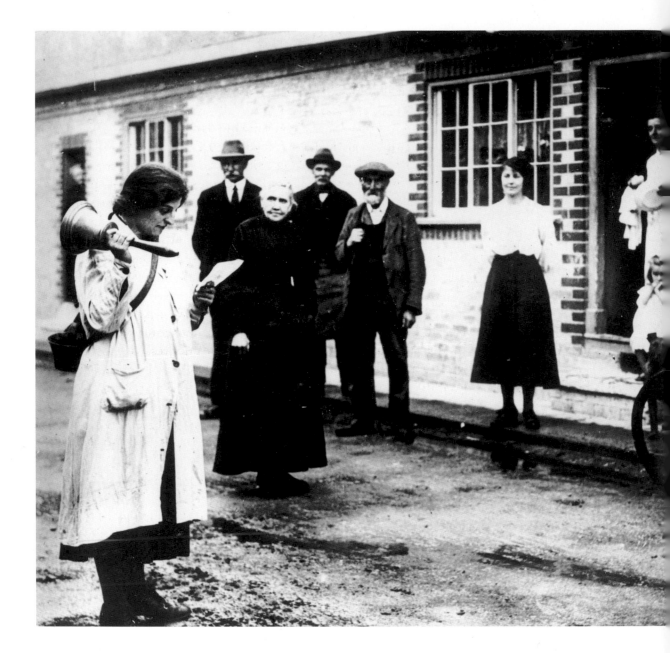

The censor's blue pen

All the wartime powers, of course, applied censorship, although this was initially military rather than political. The Defence of the Realm Act (DORA) gave the British government sweeping powers in this regard. Kitchener, who had enjoyed a poor relationship with the press in his own colonial campaigns, simply expelled British journalists from France in August 1914. To keep the press informed, Ernest Swinton became 'Eyewitness' (or 'Eyewash', as he was more popularly known) at General Headquarters (GHQ) in September 1914, to be

News, the old-fashioned way. The image is of Thetford's Official Bill Poster and Town Crier in action, the young woman having taken over the post from her father when he was called up.

succeeded in July 1915 by five official war correspondents. On the rare occasions when maverick correspondents did not observe discretion, the newspaper proprietors and editors themselves operated a self-censorship far more effective than that of the official Press Bureau. Indeed, the latter – based at the Royal United Service Institution in Whitehall – was small and concentrated largely on a few newspapers believed to have particular significance in forming opinion. The chief censor was E. T. Cook, a former editor of the *Daily News*, the *Pall Mall Gazette* and the *Westminster Gazette*. Things could be dully literal. On one occasion, the Home Secretary, Sir John Simon, had to explain in the House of Commons that the Press Bureau had directed the removal of the phrase 'and the Kings' from a military article quoting Kipling, 'The Captains and the Kings depart', because there had been no monarchs present and it was factually incorrect.

The British national and provincial press was overwhelmingly hostile to Germany, and its customary outrage at what was generally very light censorship was immediately muted when the victims were socialist or pacifist journals, a number of which were suppressed. However, one right-wing newspaper, *The Globe*, which had been prominent in the hounding of Prince Louis of Battenberg, was also briefly suppressed. Overall, censorship appears to have had little effect in changing the ways in which the press operated and it was far less significant in that respect than the reductions in advertising revenues and the increase in the price of paper.

Writers and clerics

The general tendency of the press to portray domestic news in a patriotic fashion meant that most government propaganda was targeted at opinion overseas, but a variety of patriotic private organizations supplemented government efforts on the home front. The semi-official Central Committee for National Patriotic Organisations provided some degree of direction in 1914, but it was only in August 1917 that the voluntary groups were adequately coordinated through the National War Aims Committee in an attempt to mobilize the sense of national purpose against strikers and dissenters.

Official agencies, such as Charles Masterman's War Propaganda Bureau at Wellington House in London's Buckingham Gate found little difficulty in persuading writers, artists and intellectuals to produce material for them. Among the many that Wellington House enlisted were Gilbert Murray, Rudyard Kipling, Sir Arthur Conan Doyle, Thomas Hardy, Arnold Bennett, John Galsworthy and H.G. Wells. The novelist John Buchan became head of the Department of Information, which succeeded Wellington House in December 1916.

AN "OBJECT" LESSON

FATHER BROTHER MOTHER SISTER UNCLE COUSIN

CONSCIENTIOUS OBJECTOR

Frank Holland

Principled or pampered? This none-too-subtle cartoon from the populist periodical *John Bull* contrasts a feckless, comfort-loving 'conchy' with the selfless patriotism of the rest of his family.

Universities were also pressed into service. One example was the attempt to explain the war to the British public through the University of Oxford History Faculty's *Why We Are at War: Great Britain's Case*, known as the 'Red Book'. Many institutions of higher education contributed in other ways.

Church and religion played their part, too, in reinforcing the state, and the use of religious iconography was a common propaganda device, suggesting the continuing recognition of the significance of at least a secular Christianity. The Archbishop of Canterbury would not sanction the use of the pulpit for recruiting, but Church of England clergy were active away from it, not least the Bishop of London, A.F. Winnington-Ingram, who pushed the concept of a holy war.

'FREE TRAINING OF DISABLED MEN'

A letter from the University College of Southampton, dated 4 October 1917, describing its contribution to the war effort in response to a circular sent out by Captain Basil Williams of MI7 in the War Office Directorate of Military Intelligence.

Some 41 institutions, as well as Oxbridge colleges, were circulated

between 18 September and 26 October 1917. Alex Hill, the Principal of the University, records his institution's war work. This included assisting in munitions production, training specialists, and using buildings as hospitals for war wounded.

In the case of one university, Trinity College Dublin, staff and students had actively helped to defend the university against Irish rebels during the Easter Rising in April 1916. (WO106/336)

**THE UNIVERSITY COLLEGE OF
SOUTHAMPTON.**

4th October, 1917.

Dear Sir,

In accordance with your request for information
regarding the special War Work carried out by this College:

June 1915, Engineering laboratories adapted for making
shells. Several thousand shells made by the members of
the College Staff, between that date and September, 1916.

Guages and other apparatus made for Munition Factories
in neighbourhood. Tests carried out in Engineering, Physical
and Chemical Laboratories.

April 1916, Scheme for free training of Disabled Men
in various technological and commercial subjects adopted by
the Council.

October 1916, Serbian students received for free training.

Special course of 40 Health Lectures with practical work
given for the benefit of nurses engaged in local hospitals
and others.

New College Buildings at Highfield, opened by the Lord
Chancellor in June 1914, offered in August to the War
Department as a Military Hospital rent free and accepted.

The new Hall of Residence at Highfield offered furnished
to the Red Cross as a Hospital rent free, and accepted, 114
beds.

College Buildings in the High Street lent to War Department for recruiting and other purposes, and to very numerous
agencies connected with the War, e.g., Food Economy Exhibition,
Local Food Control Committee.

Drawing office and lecture rooms placed at the service
of the Admiralty.

Yours truly,

Alex Hill

Principal.

German 'atrocities'

In many ways, the Germans themselves did much to make the work of British propagandists easier. In October 1915, for example, they executed the British nurse, Edith Cavell, for helping allied servicemen to escape from Belgium to the Netherlands. In July 1916 they executed Captain Charles Fryatt of the British steamer *Brussels*, for trying to ram a U-boat attacking his vessel. The issue, by a German firm, of a medal commemorating the sinking of the *Lusitania*, intended as a satirical statement on British hypocrisy in allegedly carrying munitions on a liner, was turned against the Germans, as the British produced replicas to demonstrate German callousness.

Of course, such German gifts to Allied propaganda did not prevent home-made fabrication, such as the photograph of three German cavalrymen seemingly loaded down with loot in Belgium, which appeared in the *Daily Mirror* on 20 August 1914; it was actually a photograph of the three winners of a cavalry competition holding their trophies, which had appeared in a Berlin newspaper in June 1914. The German factory allegedly turning the corpses of German soldiers into lubricating oils and fertilizer was another wartime fantasy. Somewhat reluctantly exploited by the British government in May 1917, this was the only atrocity story promoted by the government during the war. Its longevity, however, was shown when it resurfaced in 1925.

A new propaganda medium

An interesting development in the use of propaganda was the manipulation of a medium in its infancy: the cinema. However, films directly related to the war represented only a small proportion of the total produced in 1914–18, amounting perhaps to no more than ten per cent in Britain. A war tax imposed on cinema admissions in 1916 also reduced the potential audience and closed perhaps as many as 1000 cinemas. Nonetheless, as related earlier, the demand for information as well as for entertainment made the cinema a potent means of propaganda.

In August 1914 a number of British film companies attempted to get cameramen out to the Front. However, photographers as well as newsmen were expelled by the War Office, which even wanted to ban the export of newsreel on grounds of security, and the propaganda bureau at Wellington House became increasingly frustrated with the lack of film. The main press agencies would not cooperate with the restrictive preconditions that the War Office laid down for any relaxation of the prohibition, so Wellington House turned to the cinema newsreel firms, which in March 1915 had established a consortium known as the Topical Committee of Film Manufacturers' Association. The Topical Committee had already been in contact with the War Office, and an

We're better than them. Atrocity stories, such as the one on this billboard, were part and parcel of wartime propaganda, a campaign made all the easier by a good number of genuine German atrocities.

[*Following pages*] Caught on film. The H. Dickson company extravagantly advertises to the trade its interviews with Cabinet members of the Asquith Coalition, guaranteeing 'packed houses'. The novelty of seeing politicians filmed in this way would have been a considerable draw.

official film unit was agreed sometime between March and July 1915. A veteran of filming during the South African War (Anglo-Boer War), at the beginning of the century, Charles Urban began producing *Britain Prepared* in October 1915, a film of military and naval units at home that was widely seen in neutral countries. By 1918, over 700 films of one kind or another had been made.

Meanwhile, the Topical Committee had sent two cameramen, Geoffrey Malins and Teddy Tong, to France in November 1915 to begin

CABINET MINISTERS FILMED

MESSAGES TO THE NATION

Each member of the Cabinet shown in the Cinema Interview films is making a Statement thro' the medium of the Screen to the Nation which will stir the hearts of the people, and create unbounded enthusiasm from one end of the Country to the other.

READ WHAT THE PRESS HAS ALREADY SAID.

Truly never has such publicity been given to an idea. . . .

The
Cinema-Interview Series of Cabinet Ministers

Will be ready for the Open Market as follows:

No. 1	....	....	....	SEPTEMBER 11th.
No. 2	....	....	....	SEPTEMBER 18th.
No. 3	....	....	....	SEPTEMBER 25th.

TERMS OF HIRE ON RELEASE:

3 DAYS, per subject - - £8

1 WEEK, per subject - - £12

Each film approximately 1,000 ft. long.

By this time everybody knows that press publicity means packed houses. No series of films has had or will have the press publicity attached to these.

All Enquiries to H. DICKSON, 30 GERRARD STREET, LONDON, W.

THE LONDON COLISEUM

Proprietors,
THE COLISEUM SYNDICATE LIMITED.

Chairman & Managing Director,
OSWALD STOLL.

SECRETARY:
W. S. GORDON MICHIE.

MANAGER:
ARTHUR CROXTON.

STAGE MANAGER:
HENRY CROCKER.

St. Martin's Lane, London, W.C.

Oct. 20. 1915

NOTICES

TO ARTISTES.—Artistes engaged must Communicate Three Weeks before opening, forwarding Matter for Bill Pictorial Block, or Picture Cut from which Block can be made; and Samples and Prices of Lithographs and Posters that really Represent the Act.

IMPORTANT.—All performances must be entirely free from vulgarity.

TO AUTHORS.—The Management will not hold themselves responsible in the event of loss of or damage to any MSS., Songs, etc., Submitted for consideration.

TO SUPPLIERS.—No order or contract for goods or services must be accepted for the above Theatre except upon receipt of an Official Form, issued from the Stoll Offices, Coliseum Buildings, London, W.C., and signed by either the Managing Director or the Secretary, otherwise the Company, will not be responsible for same, and will refuse payment. In special cases where goods are required at once, suppliers must look to the individual placing the order, who will be personally liable, unless an official confirmatory order, signed as above, is received within 48 hours.

Invoices must be sent direct to the Theatre. Monthly Statements should be sent to the Stoll Offices, from which all accounts are paid.

Sir W. Graham-Greene,
Secretary of the Admiralty,
The Admiralty,
Whitehall, S.W.

M; to put with papers

Sir,

    With reference to the Cinema Films of the Fleet which have just been taken by Mr. Urban for public exhibition, will you permit me to ask on behalf of Mr. Oswald Stoll whether it would be possible for us to show the Films immediately at the London Coliseum?

    We regard the Films as of the greatest importance both from a recruiting and from a National point of view, and we are naturally anxious to show them to the Public at once.

    I am, Sir,

      Your obedient servant,

      Arthur Croxton

making a series of newsreels behind the lines. Tong fell ill and was replaced by J.B. McDowell in June 1916. In fact, it was not originally intended to produce a documentary of the Somme offensive, and Malins and McDowell were sent to the British Fourth Army merely to do some general filming. However, postponement of the Somme attack enabled them to take additional scenes of preparation. On 1 July, Malins filmed the famous sequence of the detonation of a large British mine under the German Hawthorn Redoubt. They left the front on 10 July. The first rushes were seen in London on 12 July and it was at this point that William Jury of Imperial Pictures, who was on Wellington House's cinema committee, realized that it could be made into a documentary. Jury and Urban worked quickly, and *The Battle of the Somme* was given its trade screening on 7 August, a special premiere before an invited audience on 10 August, and it opened in 34 London cinemas on 21 August 1916. Its availability in the provinces a week later in a general release of 100 prints was helped by dropping the hiring charges. Eventually, it made some £30,000 and was still being booked regularly 15 months after its premiere.

Strictly speaking, *The Battle of the Somme* was not conceived as a propaganda film, since it had been made at very short notice and was assembled from film not shot to provide a continuous narrative. Quite what its purpose was meant to be is uncertain, since it had not been decided in advance to record the offensive; but it seems there was some

'OF THE GREATEST IMPORTANCE'
Arthur Croxton of the London Coliseum writes to the secretary to the Admiralty, Sir W. Graham Greene, on 20 October 1915 asking to show the new film Britain Prepared *at his cinema.*

It was made by Charles Urban of London Cinematograph Film Producers and Kineto Ltd, who had reached agreement with the Admiralty only in September 1915, the project having first been raised with the First Lord, Arthur Balfour, by Sir Gilbert Parker and Charles Masterman in August 1915. Masterman, who ran the War Propaganda Bureau, and Parker from the Neutral Press Committee had been impressed by German film propaganda and wanted to influence neutral opinion. The first half of the film depicted the New Armies under training and the second the activities of the Fleet, with

a particular emphasis on HMS Queen Elizabeth. *Joining the fleet at Invergordon on 5 October, Urban and his three assistants, all of whom were Englishmen as the Admiralty had specified, exposed some 55 rolls of both black and white and kinema-colour film. Since it was intended for neutrals, the Admiralty was initially loath to release the film to British audiences and insisted on retaining close control of the negatives. A copy, however, was made available to the Fleet.*

The film, which ran for three hours, was eventually premiered for public audiences at the Empire Theatre in London on 27 December 1915, showing there for six weeks before being released to about 100 cinemas across the country. It was very successful in the United States, where Urban handled the distribution himself, and was even shown in Russia.
(ADM116/1447)

A DUTY YOU OWE TO
THE IMPERIAL GOVERNMENT.
SEE
The Battle of the Somme.
———
COME AND SEE
The Battle of the Somme.
The very punch of the Allies. Backed
by the hall-mark of
THE IMPERIAL GOVERNMENT.

War as documentary. Harehills Picture House in Leeds advertises the hugely popular *The Battle of the Somme*, August 1916. That the film was essentially a propaganda tool is made plain by imprimature of the 'Imperial Government'.

intent to use the example of men at the front to rally civilian support for the war. The film caused a sensation – notably some faked scenes of men falling dead and wounded – and, although no overall viewing figures are extant, it was clearly widely seen. It has been suggested that 1 million saw it in the first week and 20 million had seen it in its first six weeks. It was shown simultaneously in 20 cinemas in Birmingham, and huge queues were reported in Edinburgh, Glasgow and Swansea; crowd control had to be introduced outside the cinema in West Ealing, London.

The depiction of death, in the sense of seeing falling soldiers as opposed to dead bodies, was not repeated in other British wartime films. Moreover, the organization that had made *The Battle of the Somme* was reorganized, with a new War Office Cinema Committee being established in November 1916. After a third film, *The German Retreat and the Battle of Arras*, was produced in 1917, twice-weekly newsreels were instead produced for the rest of the war. This third film was a commercial failure and it was believed that the novelty of battle films had worn off and the public was jaded.

Propaganda – the net effect

There is considerable debate as to the effect of wartime propaganda in general, and it is wise to get the propaganda effort into perspective. Famous recruiting posters such as Alfred Leete's 'Kitchener Wants

You', an image first published in Britain on 5 September 1914, did not arrest the decline in military recruitment. While the Parliamentary Recruiting Committee (PRC) eventually printed almost 6 million posters and over 14 million leaflets at a total cost of £24,000, this was less than Rowntrees of York had spent on advertising a single brand of cocoa in 1911–12. Similarly, for every PRC leaflet produced in 1914–15, at least ten had been produced by the three main political parties during the 1910 election campaigns. Clearly, bearing in mind the limits of technological and media development in this period, military victory and not propaganda was the most significant factor in Germany's defeat.

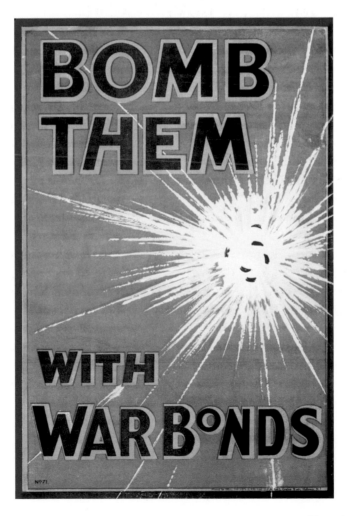

More money, more shells. This poster was issued by the National War Savings Committee to support the last of the wartime war bond issues in September 1918.

Ada McGuire of Wallasey writes to her married sister, Eva Grandison, living in Boston in the United States, on 11 May 1915. She discusses the impact on Liverpool and its surrounding districts of the sinking of the *Lusitania*, and the eruption of anti-German riots. The reference to the 'Pals' is to the Liverpool 'Pals', the city having raised four battalions – the 1st, 2nd, 3rd and 4th Battalions of the King's (Liverpool) Regiment – between August and October 1914, in response to Lord Derby's call for men to come forward to enlist in the army 'with their friends'. The Liverpool battalions were still training in local camps at this time.

———

H *ADN'T TIME to finish this for today's mail but will post it tomorrow though probably the mails will be held up. There have been dreadful riots in Liverpool & Seacombe against the Germans. The Scotland Rd women I believe were just like the women of the French Revolution so I was told by an eyewitness. They came from the seafaring quarters of the town & of course the crew of the Lusitania belonged chiefly to L'Pool. They boarded the [tram] car after a German had escaped them. I believe it would have gone badly with him if they had caught him. But it is horrible! Of course they will be punished but I think we all feel the same only we are more restrained. Miss Phythian told me she was terribly frightened last night going home from school. She lives in Liverpool & onto the boat came a gentleman (English) & a German fighting – at least they started when they got on. She said blood was flying about & they fairly flew at each other. The Englishman said the German insulted him in an hotel. 'It's a mad world, my masters'. Miss Huston who was drowned in the Lusitania belonged to Wallasey.*

She was a Wallasey High School girl & went in for teaching. I believe she gave it up & went in June on a visit to her married sister in America. When war broke out her sister would not let her come home but as her Mother was ill she finally sailed in the L. Miss Elkin met her father yesterday. She said he seemed quite dazed. He had had a telegram saying her body had been found & then had received another to say it was a mistake it was not her body. O no wonder the poor people go for the brutes. Fancy if it had been you coming home!

Well there seems no other news at present. Did mother tell you of poor Mrs Wachorst (from Vackers). She used to live in Gerrard Rd. Her mother & sister lived in Kinnaird Rd off Seaview Rd. Do you remember that big fine looking girl who was a great friend of Beattie Lloyd. She was one of the family. Mrs Wachorst was married to a German & when war broke out he lost all his money. They let their house in Gerrard Rd to Belgian refugees. Mr Wachorst was in a consumption & died 10 weeks ago. They were a devoted couple & poor thing, last week she took laudanum & died. Dr Baker was called in & under her pillow he found a photo of her husband. She was only 36.

Well I will conclude this cheerful epistle. Summer is coming in spite of war. The cuckoo woke me up yesterday morning – cuckooing like mad.

Give my love to Ralph. I expect he knows a lot of the fellows at the front. I forgot to send you the paper about the Pals. I have been so busy.
[IWM, 96/31/1, McGuire Mss.]

In one sense, the public did not need to be told of the human and material costs of war, for Britain itself was increasingly coming under attack. Unrestricted German submarine warfare – the sinking of merchant ships on the high seas without warning – was certainly an indirect means of attacking civilians by trying to starve Britain. Direct attack was also soon to feature. On 16 December 1914 the German High Seas Fleet bombarded West Hartlepool, Scarborough and Whitby, with over 1500 shells fired causing 127 deaths – the majority in Hartlepool – and forcing thousands to flee temporarily: the youngest victim was six months old and the oldest 86. The event was unprecedented for the British, and it was said that over 10,000 people subsequently went to Scarborough to see the damage, which included the destruction of the Grand Hotel. Visiting the town over Christmas, Sylvia Pankhurst reported:

> The big amusement 'palaces' on the front were scarred and battered by shell-fire, iron columns twisted and broken, brickwork crumbling, windows gone. Yawning breaches disclosed the pictures and furnishings, riddled and rent by the firing, dimmed and discoloured by blustering winds and spray.

She also found that the Germans had laid mines in the bay, leading to the loss of several minesweepers attempting to clear them. There was something of a sense of panic:

> People could not sleep now; many would not even go to bed. Everyone had a bundle made up in readiness for flight; but how little one could carry in a bundle! One could not afford to move's one's home; and one's living was here in Scarborough.

In fact, the Germans had actually opened fire on Great Yarmouth and Lowestoft on 3 November 1914, but at such a distance that few were aware of what had taken place. Naval bombardment of civilian targets was not repeated on a large scale, with only some 12 incidents taking place over the war as a whole, but technological developments meant that a new danger was posed by aerial bombardment.

Attack from the air

Technically, aerial attack was prohibited by The Hague conventions of 1899 and 1907; but since Germany had not signed them, the prohibition was not operative. In any case, the wording of the conventions was obscure with regard to air war, and most states assumed bombing was legitimate. The first air raids on civilian targets were those by Zeppelins on French and Belgian Channel ports on 21 August 1914, followed by a raid on Paris on 30 August. Great Yarmouth became the first British town attacked, on 19 January 1915, with London attacked for the first

Nowhere to hide. The flower-decked hearse contains the coffin of Postman Beal, killed during the German naval bombardment of Scarborough on 16 December 1914.

'FIVE WARSHIPS ON THE HORIZON'

[Following pages] A report by Captain A. Adams, Brigade Major at Norwich, of the bombardment of Lowestoft by German warships on 25 April 1916.

Some 40 houses had been wrecked, with a further 200 damaged, but the casualties were relatively light at 4 dead and 12 wounded. This particular raid on both Lowestoft and Great Yarmouth by the battle cruisers of the German High Seas Fleet was intended to coincide with the Easter Rising in Dublin, of which the Germans were aware through their contacts with Irish republicans.

The Royal Navy's Harwich Force came into action against the German

ships, but then broke off and headed for home. Neither the Grand Fleet at Scapa Flow nor the Battle Cruiser Fleet at Rosyth were able to get south sufficiently quickly to become engaged. The Third Battle Squadron – mostly older ships – was detached from the Grand Fleet to be stationed in the Thames estuary in May. British seaplanes then bombed German Zeppelin sheds in the hope of drawing the German Fleet out again.

*On this occasion, the Germans did not respond, but the pattern of raid and counter-raid created the climate that was to result in the largest naval battle of the war, off Jutland, between 31 May and 1 June 1916. (*AIR1/577/16/15/167*)*

BOMBARDMENT 25TH. APRIL.

Headquarters, Outpost Troops,
Northern Army, Norwich.

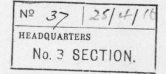

GENERAL STAFF
S309/1
26 APR. 1916
HEADQUARTERS, N. ARMY

SECRET

S. 14/1

MOUNTED DIVISION

    I beg to forward my final report on the Bombardment
which took place at Lowestoft and Yarmouth this morning.

    At 4.8 a.m. I received a message from the Naval
Base, Lowestoft, to the effect that there was a hostile
fleet off the town.   On proceeding to the front I
saw about five warships on the horizon.   At about
4.15 they began bombarding Lowestoft.   The telephone at
this Office being shelled down I sent a motor despatch
rider to your Headquarters; I considered that this
would be more certain and as quick as the telegraph
under the circumstances.   The Bombardment continued
from 4.15 a.m. to 4.35 a.m..   I am informed by the
Captain i/c, Naval Base, Lowestoft, that there were
apparently about 30 enemy warships engaged including
Battle cruisers, cruisers, destroyers and a submarine,
also two or three Zeppelins.   The latter could be
seen from the shore, they did not drop any bombs, and
were presumably scouting.   From about 4.40 A.M. till
5 a.m. the hostile warships were shelling a British
light cruiser and destroyer flotilla which appeared
off Lowestoft.   This flotilla went Southwards and the
hostile fleet then drew off towards the N.E..   Nothing
has occurred since 5 a.m..   The damage done appears
from reports received from the Police at Lowestoft
and from the Commandant, Yarmouth to be as follows:-

<u>AT YARMOUTH.</u>

No military or civilian casualties.

One Naval Aircraft rating wounded.

3 fires in warehouses.

<u>AT LOWESTOFT.</u>

About 40 houses wrecked.

200 Houses damaged.

Naval Base damaged.

4 civilians killed.

12 " wounded.

1 Naval anticraft rating killed.

1 " rating wounded.

1 man bruised foot. 68th. Prov. Battn..

Two men of 69th. Prov. Battn., slightly cut.

The enemys' targets at Lowestoft were evidently the Naval Base and the Wireless Stations.

A large number of shell passed over and fell in the country from the River WAVENEY East of BURGH ST. PETER to CARLTON COLVILLE Village.   Eight fell near the UPLANDS alone (between CARLTON COLVILLE Village and OULTON BROAD)   In the latter village a few houses were hit.   Up to the present there are 3 unexploded shell reported in Lowestoft and 3 in the country to the West.

Four bases, one nose, and some pieces are collected, from which it appears that shells of 8.4" and 12 inches, armour piercing were employed.

Some British aeroplanes were employed.   One was brought down and towed in from KESSINGLAND.

LOWESTOFT.

25. 4. 16.

C. S. Adam Capt ᵗ Bde Major
for Brigadier General.
No.3 SECTION.

time on 31 May 1915. Since the Zeppelins required dark but fine nights for their raids, these conditions became 'Zeppelin weather', with London theatres reporting audiences trailing off as the moon waned. So novel was the development of aerial bombing that there were sightseers in the East End from other parts of the capital after the first significant raids in early 1915. According to Sylvia Pankhurst:

> Impatient passengers on the tops of buses were asking before they had yet passed Bishopsgate: 'Is this the East End'. Sightseers paused at Shoreditch Church because rumour declared it had been injured, though not a sign of damage was to be seen. Crowds stood with chins uncomfortably upstretched arguing whether the thin shadow cast by the lightning conductor might really be a crack.

Rumours were rife of German night surveys of potential targets, and, on occasions, the authorities attempted to play down the risks. On 31 April 1915, for example, an explosion was heard in Greenwich and at the Royal Arsenal, Woolwich, and rumours spread of a 'terrible air attack on North London' to the extent that the lack of warning received caused workers temporarily to refuse to resume work after the 'all clear' was announced. Those responsible for air-raid precautions at Woolwich enquired whether there had been a raid: 'Not an official one' was the laconic reply. In fact, bombs had fallen on Dalston, Leyton, and Stoke Newington. The sensation of being under attack was itself an unusual experience. One worker at Woolwich, leaning out of a window, saw a Zeppelin 'hovering about overhead' and a heard a 'strange buzzing sound' followed by a crash and a 'cold blast of air' as a bomb hit a storeroom with a corrugated roof nearby, which 'rose into the air several feet and smashed down on the cobblestones'. In Liverpool in February 1916 it was reported that: 'Most people are very cool & collected over the raid – no panic at all but there is a great depression over everything and everybody.'

Two years later, on 25 May 1917, the first German air raid using conventional aircraft – Gotha G.IV bombers based at Ghent – was

'SHOULD HOSTILE AIRCRAFT BE SEEN'
An Air Raid Precautions poster issued in February 1915, showing British and German aircraft and airships for identification purposes.

If a German craft was observed then the public should take cover. German aircraft were characterized by wings that sloped back, while Zeppelins had a distinctive arrangement of their passenger cars.

Printed for the Home Office by Sir Joseph Causham & Sons, a total of 2000 posters were issued for public sites in London and 500 for police stations by 10 February 1915. It was soon found, however, that this was an inadequate number and a further 10,000 posters were ordered on 27 February, with the Admiralty issuing its own separate identification posters. Members of the public could buy the poster for themselves for 2d. (MEPO2/1621)

was
Ger-
were
were
the

out
pre-
that
long

the
en-
the

the
ched
have

ly I
He
air-
took
im-

de-
ually
the

The sky was simply a blaze of light," said an eye-witness. "It seemed as though the heavens were vomiting fire, while from the earth beneath our gunners fired incessant and deadly volleys of shells."

During the night of September 22-23 a Zeppelin flew over the Calais district. Furiously bombarded by anti-aircraft batteries it was forced to make off without dropping any projectiles.—Reuter.

"r
abou

Asl
repli
I pu
room
"T
road
saw
now,
of th

D

At
took
wher
pene
top
rescu
A s
the f
to fi
been
lay u
Th
and
dowr
strai

SHRAPNEL FROM AIR RAID STORIES.

Blown Out of Bed.

A tobacconist living close to a place where a house was wrecked was blown right out of bed.

Thirty Bombs—One Fowlhouse.

In Lincolnshire thirty bombs were dropped, and, so far as reported, only one fowlhouse was destroyed.

Defiant Householder.

"Are we downhearted? No!" was obviously the spirit of the man who, one of his windows being smashed, covered the aperture with the Union Jack.

Souvenir Hunters.

In one suburban street there was a line of children—quite 150 of them—busily digging bits of shrapnel and bombs from the wood paving with hammers, chisels, pincers, old knives and, of course, the toes of their boots.

Seen Sixty Miles Away.

The blaze from the Zeppelin which fell in flames was seen sixty miles away.

Pretty Green Flare.

A large green flare dropped by one Zeppelin made a pretty sight as it hung suspended, it seemed, midway between heaven and earth.

Cold Water Cure.

Thinking that a bomb dropped in a southeastern district contained poison gas, people drank cold water in the belief that it would nullify ill effects.

Wanted a Ladder.

The predicament of a woman in a house next to one that had been demolished struck a novel note. The staircase had been blown away, and she stood for some time at the window of an upstairs room shouting for someone to bring her a ladder.

launched, on Folkestone. The 23 aircraft involved dropped 159 bombs and succeeded in killing 71 people, a number of whom had been queuing outside a shop for food. The campaign was then extended to London by day and night. Indeed, unlike dirigibles, the Gothas could also operate on moonlit nights. One daylight raid over the capital and the Southeast of England on 13 June 1917, by 14 Gothas, caused 158 deaths, including 18 children at a school in Poplar, and led to near panic in the East End. A special constable was mesmerized by the appearance of so many aircraft: 'the sight was so magnificent that I stood in the yard spellbound. The noise of the air being churned up by this fleet of aeroplanes was very loud.' His wife had been on a bus in Knightsbridge when the raiders appeared and took cover in Hyde Park House:

The basement was packed with women clerks, some of whom were crying hysterically. One caught hold of me. 'Oh, I'm going to be killed! I'm going to be killed!' she moaned, pinching my arm so violently that what with pain and excitement I flared up and replied quite venomously, 'I hope you *will*', which so surprised her that she stood still staring at me with her mouth open, the picture of idiocy. A girl near who also had been crying, but quietly, remarked, 'You aren't very sympathetic.' 'I'm sorry', said I, beginning to recover my temper, 'but my sympathies are with the men who have to bear this kind of thing day after day and night after night.' I wasn't in the least brave, but I was excited.

Shrapnel stories. This collection of air raid stories was given to the press by the War Refugees Committee. It reports a variety of experiences in the early Zeppelin raids.

'FIRST RAID BY GOTHAS'

A page for the first half of 1917 from the personal record of air alarms and attacks kept by F. Blythe, who worked in the Section Office of Main Factory East (MFE) at the Royal Arsenal, Woolwich (see also his Personal Testimony in this chapter).

Blythe was responsible for passing alarms to the main factory floor and to other sites at Woolwich. Over 1000 men and women were employed at MFE, and hundreds of lathes were being worked in the automatic machine shop, which reputedly had the largest single glass roof span in the country and which could not be blacked out at night. 'Blacking out' remained a casual affair well into 1915 and little thought had been given to shelters.

The longest close-down in production, of 6 hours and 35 minutes, was caused by a Zeppelin raid on 31 March 1916. The 1917 record shown here covers the beginning of the Gotha raids in June 1917. The last alarm was on 21 August 1918. The Arsenal managed to escape major damage throughout the war.
(SUPP5/1052)

Night and Day Attacks

Close Down =

58

During January reports circulated at danger buildings that Stand By was being received all most every day. Certainly Action office had not received the alarm

In this month a lone plane made its first attempt to reach London. This then was the fore runner of those attacks by Taubes, Fokkers, & Gothas.

All quiet at Woolwich. not even gunfire being heard. Is it Zeppelin or Taubes.

East coast raid nothing heard here Stand By only

June 13 Wednesday morning. First raid by Gothas on London. Two machines seen over Arsenal One English fighter was seen attacking them Bombs on school at Poplar.

The first the Brain Factory knew of this was a *workman rushing in from the wharf shouting "they're here" This was the remarkable raid when something like 60 planes and bombers sailed majestically across London bombing the City and north London

In this alarm the hooter went whilst * Workman was in the office. See Commentary.

On this Sunday morning Authorities decided without notifying public to try out the new method of Warning by maroons being exploded at local fire headquarters.

Just a month since last raid also Sunday All quiet at Woolwich Thanet Raid

This raid and the appearance of 21 Gothas over London in daylight on 7 July, which resulted in riotous attacks on allegedly German-owned property in the East End, persuaded George V to change his dynastic name from Saxe-Coburg-Gotha to Windsor. It also played a decisive role in the establishment of the Smuts Committee. The South African prime minister and member of the Imperial War Cabinet, Jan Smuts, was the first to recommend a reorganization of home air defence with more and better aircraft. In a second report, on 17 August 1917, Smuts recommended retaliation directed by an authority independent of Army and Navy rivalries. Following further raids, an air ministry and air staff were established in January 1918, with the Independent Force, Royal Air Force (RAF), coming into existence on 1 April 1918 to take the war direct to German soil in retaliation for their air raids over London and the Southeast of England.

German raids – euphemistically described by the Press Bureau as 'visits' – resulted in 1413 of the 1570 wartime military and civilian deaths in Britain through enemy action. Little thought had been given to coordinating air defence prior to the war. A blackout, or rather 'dim

Shattered houses, broken lives. This destruction in Hull was the work of a single Zeppelin, L9, on the night of 6/7 June 1915.

out', was introduced for defended harbours in August 1914 and was extended to other designated areas. Zeppelin attacks on inland targets, such as Burton-on-Trent and Walsall in early 1916, necessitated a more general extension. The Gotha raids then forced the introduction of an official air-raid warning system in July 1917. Earlier warnings had not been given in the belief that false alarms would halt war production and prove counter-productive in the longer term.

The new system consisted of the firing of maroons (a type of firework) and policemen on bicycles issuing warnings. Boy Scouts on bicycles sounded the 'all clear' by bugle, while vehicles also carried 'all clear' notices. Public shelters had to be improvised, such as the caves at Dover, the London Underground and the tunnels under the Thames. Those people unable to get to shelters were advised to avoid top-floor rooms, place mattresses on the upper floors to cushion any impact, turn off electricity and gas supplies, and to make sure of escape routes from cellars in the event the house was hit. More important buildings were draped with steel nets. London was ringed with 353 searchlights, 266 anti-aircraft guns and 159 fighter-planes by day with 123 night fighters for additional protection, the system coordinated by a centralized London Air Defence Area (LADA) headquarters. Anti-aircraft balloons were also introduced in January 1918. On raid nights, the capital was a cacophony of sound and light, the cumulative effect of bombs, guns, flares, and searchlights.

The problem was that air defence proved highly ineffective. In 397 sorties the Germans lost only 24 Gothas over England, while tying up over 300 British machines – although another 37 Gothas were lost in accidents. Moreover, it was calculated that the anti-aircraft guns had needed to fire 14,540 rounds to bring down just one aircraft. It was therefore concluded that there was no effective defence against the bomber. Zeppelins, however, could be caught through their slow rate of climb. Flight Sub-Lieutenant Rex Warneford successfully dropped bombs on one on 6 June 1915 over Ghent, and Lieutenant W. Leefe Robinson shot down a similar Schütte Lanz dirigible with new Buckingham incendiary bullets over Cuffley, in Hertfordshire, in the

'A ZEPPELIN WAS PASSING OVER'
[*Following pages*] *A report by J.B. Knight, the Chief Constable of Newcastle-upon-Tyne, to the Under Secretary of State at the Home Office on 16 June 1915.*

It indicates that the blackout had been extended to the area when German Zeppelins raided Wallsend. On this occasion, only one house had been destroyed and that possibly by an anti-aircraft shell rather than by a bomb.

Windows had been broken, but there had been no casualties, though part of one fragment of bomb or shell had actually passed through a bed in which three men – presumably shift workers – were sleeping, without harming any of them.
(AIR1/552)

City & County of Newcastle upon Tyne.

Chief Constable's Office.

Newcastle upon Tyne.

16th June, 1915.

Sir,

I have the honour to report for your information that about 11.35pm on 15th instant a message was received from the Police at Bedlington, Northumberland, stating that a zeppelin was passing over that district, and proceeding in the direction of Newcastle.

At 11.41pm this message was confirmed from the Tyne Coast Defences, and intimation was immediately sent to armament works, lighting authorities, and the electric power station. (I may remark that, during the summer months, all public lighting of street lamps in Newcastle has been discontinued).

The aircraft appears to have taken an almost similar route to that taken by the zeppelin on 14th April last, and seems to have passed over a small portion of the City near the eastern boundary, travelling thence in the direction of Wallsend.

It was observed by several of the Police on duty, who report that, when close to the City boundary, it was flying at a great height, but stopped and descended to a much lower altitude, and then went off at a great rate of speed in a south easterly direction.

Immediately afterwards they observed star shells being dropped, and subsequently several loud reports, apparently from bombs, were heard, followed by other reports, as if from anti-aircraft guns.

I understand from the Military Authorities that considerable damage was done at Wallsend in the County of Northumberland, and at Jarrow in the County of Durham.

The only damage in this City was to the house of Ernest

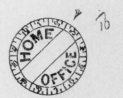

Lindley,109 Canterbury Street,and in this case the probability
is that it was due to a shell fired from the anti-aircraft gun,
a portion of which went through the roof, ceiling, and floor, of
Lindley's house,which is an upstairs flat of four rooms.

Windows were broken, the gas pipe severed and some furniture
damaged,but none of the inmates were hurt.

A portion of shell,which is now in my possession,went through
a bed in which three men were sleeping without injuring any of them.

                         I have the honour to be,
                              Sir,
                         Your obedient Servant,

                                   Chief Constable.

The/
     Under Secretary of State,
          Home Office,
               London, S.W.

No. 728.

Reference to Papers.

/

Metropolitan Police.

Limehouse STATION. K DIVISION

13th September 1917

I beg to report that
Blackwall Tunnel is closed to
vehicular and pedestrian traffic
by L.C.C. employees at 8pm daily
during the summer, and 7pm
during winter months.

On night of 4th–5th Septr.
it was closed as usual.

The main entrance, at East
India Dock Road, is closed by
means of a pole placed in the
centre of the road, a chain is
attached to the off side and
carried across that part of the
road and footway. The near
side half of the road and
footway remain open. About
800 Arsenal Workers and persons
with permits pass through after
closing time.

At Blackwall Cross, High Street,
Poplar, 250 yards farther in from
the main entrance, there are two
stairways, one each side of the
tunnel roadway, which can only
be used by pedestrians. These
stairways are closed by means
of a pole placed horizontally
about 4 feet from the ground

300000 6 16 M.P. 507

anyone can easily enter by bending under the pole.

Still farther in the tunnel, about 500 yards, is another stairway known as the spiral staircase, Prestons Road. The street entrance to this is surrounded by an iron fence 7 ft high. The gates here are locked at closing time, but on the night in question they were unlocked and thrown open at about 11.30pm to enable the public to enter.

Police are on duty continuously outside each entrance and inside the tunnel.

If persons seek the shelter of the tunnel during an air Raid they are admitted at any hour. Very few people use the stairway entrances. During recent raids it has been noticed that the crowds are increasing in numbers, especially at the main entrance. Extra police are sent to assist those already on duty. The care of the public is the first consideration.

There has never been a rush anything approaching breaking down of barriers. Police arrangements have been quite adequate to keep the crowd under control. A. Mann, SDInsp

A. Roxhall Supr.

'CLOSED AS USUAL'

A report by Superintendent A. Roxhall of the Metropolitan Police K Division in Limehouse, London, on 13 September 1917. It concerned the use of the Blackwall Tunnel under the Thames as an air raid shelter.

Roxhall denied that the barriers had been broken down by crowds in the rush to take shelter when public admittance was refused during a raid on the night of 4–5 September. However, he cautioned that additional police would be needed.

Vehicles had been banned from the Blackwall and Rotherhithe tunnels since the start of the war, though it appears that the two smaller footway tunnels at Greenwich and Woolwich had remained open. Since crowds had been flocking to the tunnels since July, and with the onset of heaver raids, the London County Council agreed to officially open the tunnels in August 1917, though it was made clear that the public used them at their own risk. On occasions it was reported that 10,000–12,000 people used the Blackwall Tunnel and up to 30,000 the Rotherhithe Tunnel, with 3000 or so in each of the footway tunnels. The crowds had been 'excited' but the police been able to maintain control.
(MEPO2/1657)

early hours of 3 September 1915. Many thousands of people came out on the streets to view the dramatic fall of the burning airship, with large crowds subsequently visiting the wreck site. Leefe Robinson was awarded the Victoria Cross; he was to die in the influenza pandemic of 1918. Other Zeppelin wrecks attracted similar crowds. Poor wireless security on the part of Zeppelin crews greatly assisted British naval and military signals intelligence. In all, Germany lost 17 airships in combat, with a further 21 lost in accidents.

Bombers operating in daylight, however, did not use wireless. But, even given forewarning, without radar (yet to be invented) or adequate

Carcass of a killing machine. This wreckage of Zeppelin L33 resembles some monstrous sculpture. It crash landed in Essex on the night of 23/24 September 1916, and was set on fire by its crew.

S.—1121. (Established—October, 1904.)
(Revised—February, 1914.)

*REPORT of the Death of an Officer, Man or Boy, in accordance with Article 575 of the King's Regulations.

H.M.S. ____"PEMBROKE"____

at ____Chatham.____

Date ____26th September 1917.____

Name (Christian Names in full)......	Frederick Upson.
Rank or Rating	Able Seaman, R.N.V.R.
Official No. (if unknown, date of first entry)	P.Z.3001
Date of Death	4th September 1917.
Place of Death..	R.N.Hospital Chatham.
Cause of Death .... (If due to accident or violence, particulars to be stated briefly.)	Injuries (Enemy Air Raid.)
Whether reported to the Registrar General on Form S.—544 (see Note 2)	————————
Nearest known Relative or Friend — Name and Relationship	Mother Annie Hall
Address	Farm Cottage, Kesgrove, Nr.Ipswich, Suffolk.
Whether informed by Ship.........	No.
Place and date of Burial (if known) ..	Gillingham New Cemetery, 6th September 1917
Religion (if known)...............	Not Known.
If borne for Discipline only, date on which man was D.S.Q. or Invalided	————————

Lieutenant,
for the Commanding Officer.
(on duty).

The Accountant General of the Navy.

* N.B.—(1) This Form is to be sent in addition to the report by telegraph required by Cl. 4, Art. 575, King's Regulations, and whether the Officer, Man or Boy, is borne for pay or, under Art. 601, for discipline only.
    (2) Whenever a death occurs on board, or amongst the members of a special active service expedition, care is to be taken that a Return on Form S. 544 is forwarded to the Registrar General of Births, Deaths and Marriages as directed by Article 1857. This is not applicable to deaths occurring on board Royal Fleet Auxiliaries ("Maine," etc.), which are reported by the Master under the Article quoted.

N.P. 2566/09.
Sta. 5/10.
Sta. 9/14.

6000/3/14—[2053] 16959/D577 6000 8/14v   G & S 5947

The legacy of the bombs. These are patients of the Llangattock School of Arts and Crafts for crippled and raid-shocked girls at Chailey, near Hayward's Heath, East Sussex.

ground to air communications, air-defence fighters were initially grop-ing for contact with the Gothas and the heavier *Riesenflugzeuge* (liter-ally 'giant planes') introduced by the Germans in late 1917. Improved range-finding and sound-location devices became available, but the fighters themselves remained technically limited. As a result, it came to be generally accepted that, to use a later phrase of Stanley Baldwin, the 'bomber would always get through'.

Mr Blythe of Chingford in Essex recalls – not always grammatically – in December 1939 his responsibilities for warning of 'intending enemy aircraft attack' while working in the Section Office at Main Factory East of the Royal Arsenal at Woolwich, between April 1915 and August 1918.

T HE SECTION OFFICE *was very small and though much overcrowded during day there were only two of us to 'Stand By' each night, our period of duty being 8 p.m. to 8 a.m. Towards the end of 1916 the night staff was doubled and later considerably increased with the enlargening of the Section Office.*

From this office we had to give warning to Bullet Factory, L.M.S. [Light Machine Shop] and 'Auto' Main Factory West, Yard Branch, Gangers Shop, Quick Firing Cartridge Factory 142, Brass Foundry, Turners Shop, Tailors Shop, Metal Box Factory, and others. These shops were scattered about and by no means easily contacted on dark nights with railway lines to trip the hurrying messenger.

There must have been several thousand employees scattered among these factories yet upon the occasion of the first alarm which was in the nature of a test call the whole area was closed down in a minute and three quarters. Nice work and we were proud to receive the congratulations of the Chief. I think it was Colonel Donaldson.

The group of factories known as the Danger Buildings that had their own Air Raid Office also were successful with four minutes.

Only those who have entered this forbidden area realise how smoothly things must go, without flurry or excitement when handling T.N.T to close down a series of scattered buildings in a few minutes.

Of course it would have been a simple matter to have installed electric indicators and by a flash of coloured light give the warning to the whole 'shop'. This was just what we wished to avoid as often a 'Stand By' might last an hour or two before further alarm was received and the danger of keeping an eye on a fast moving driller or cutter can easily be understood.

It was decided at a short conference to rely upon the human element rather than resort to phones which might easily be engaged at the vital moment, or upon light signals for the reason before stated.

It was agreed then that a series of slips of which a sample is attached to end of this book, be prepared in the official wording adopted by the authorities, they were
'Foreman Light Machine Shop'
'Stand By'
'Lights Out'
'Resume Work'
'All Clear'
Each foreman of the fifteen factories or shops that was controlled through Section received one of these slips on every occasion.

The Stand By was usually distributed rather secretively to the different foremen who would quickly make their way back to their respective cabins and would then busy themselves with a pile of papers to ward off the half suspecting fears of the workpeople. Apart then from the official notices how to quickly notify each shop of 'Lights Out'.

It could not be taken for granted that because a shop was suddenly plunged into darkness that their warning was out. Fuses had a habit of failing more than twenty years ago than they have now. It was agreed then that the system adopted by the coast guards of England who by personal contact could pass a signal along in a remarkable short time over a very long distance.

In each shop certain men, who were appointed to act as guards, worked on machines that always faced one way. A workman always stood by these machines even during mealtimes and during working hours kept an eye upon their fellow guards whilst still continuing their job on the machines.

In the Section Office we two received the 'Stand By' on the phone one of us would then see that the warning notices were passed among the foremen.

For a short time the 'Lights Out' order were also received over the phone but after a breakdown at a critical time a small type of Klaxon Horn was fitted in the office and a blast from this was immediate action for Lights Out. As the Section Office was fitted with almost sound proof doors the horn could not be heard outside

in the factory above the noise of the automatic machines etc.

One of us would stand in the gangway outside the office and extend both arms this signal would be seen by the first guard who passed it on and in a few seconds the guard at the end was warning Bullet Factory and so by means of the human element the desired quick result was achieved.

Very primitive yes but effectual, and this method of warning all factories prevailed until 1917 when a public alarm was installed that gave the warning not only to Arsenal workers but also to the townspeople who up to this period had mainly to rely on watching lights out behind the Arsenal gates. This alarm with its alternating high and low notes was popularly known as 'Screaming Lizzie'. A sense of humour has always been a magnificent asset of the English speaking race. [TNA, SUPP 5/1052]

The end of the war came unexpectedly. The Germans had been pushed back on the Western Front almost continuously since August 1918, but the front line was still intact and the expectation was that the war would continue into 1919. Germany's allies, however, began to crumble, with Bulgaria the first to seek an armistice on 26 September, Ottoman Turkey on 26 October and Austria-Hungary on 28 October 1918. Hostilities ceased on 30 October in the case of Bulgaria and Turkey and on 3 November in the case of Austria-Hungary. In Germany, too, there was talk of an armistice, and the American President, Woodrow Wilson, was contacted by Germany on 3 October to begin negotiations, though this was seen primarily as a means of securing a breathing space rather than as a cessation of hostilities. In the event, a German armistice commission met the supreme allied commander, Marshal Ferdinand Foch, on 8 November and, on the following day Kaiser Wilhelm was forced to abdicate and a German republic was proclaimed. The German delegates signed the armistice at 05:10 hours on the morning of 11 November 1918 and it came into effect at 11:00, initially for a period of 36 days; but the terms were such that the Germans would have found it all but impossible to renew the war.

In London maroons, those detonating fireworks, were set off and Boy Scouts went around on their bicycles blowing the 'all clear' on bugles. One woman recalled that 'buses had to cease running for the soldiers seized the boards from sides and front to help make a big bonfire in Trafalgar Square'. Big Ben struck noon for the first time in five years and, just as they had back in August 1914, large crowds gathered outside Buckingham Palace. Unusually for an undemonstrative woman, Queen Mary, when she came out on the balcony with the king, waved a small flag 'violently'. One young woman working in the War Office contrasted the two very different occasions of 1914 and 1918:

> It was a very different sight from that of that August night, with its deep blue sky and the beds of scarlet geraniums and brightly lighted streets and houses. Now it was a grey November morning, the roads were muddy, the lake in St James's Park drained and full of huts.

The crowd was different as well:

> … munition girls in bright overalls, who arrived in large lorries, shouting and beating tea-trays and waving flags, staff officers in cars driven by smart khaki girls, and cars from the Admiralty with their even smarter 'Wren' chauffeuses, and everywhere men in hospital blue.

As she put it, 'we should have rubbed our eyes in 1914 if we had seen some of those who mingled in the 1918 crowd'. Another woman, who was working as an assistant newspaper editor, was unable to leave her

A different way to celebrate. The people of Brackley, Northamptonshire, hang effigies of Kaiser Wilhelm and Crown Prince Wilhelm ('Little Willie') on Armistice Day, 11 November 1918.

office until 5 p.m.:

> I went through the Temple, which was deserted, and up one of those lit-
> tle streets near Charing Cross, and there under an archway were two old
> women in prehistoric-looking bonnets and capes dancing stiffly and
> slowly to a barrel organ, the kind which has one leg and which you hardly
> ever see nowadays, played by a man so ancient that he looked as if he
> should have held a scythe rather than a hurdy-gurdy. In the Mall crowds
> had come to look at the German guns, and there were still people stand-
> ing and gazing at Buckingham Palace.

Counting the costs

Victory had not come cheap. Total war expenditure may have been, in
dollar terms, about 43.8 billion (roughly £8.5 billion). The National
Debt had increased by a factor of eleven from £650 million to £7.4 billion and, in 1919, the economist John Maynard Keynes was to estimate
the damage sustained by Britain as equivalent to at least £570 million.
Precise figures of war losses are all but impossible to determine. There
are even conflicting figures for Britain's military losses. Military dead

numbered approximately 722,000, of whom almost 39 per cent were aged between 20 and 24, and over 22 per cent between 25 and 29. It has been argued that the total effect reconfigured the social make-up of Britain, in that some sectors of society had volunteered in greater proportion to others. Many working-class men had been physically unfit for military service through the level of pre-war deprivation in urban areas, while officers suffered proportionally more dead than other ranks.

The beginning of remembering. Servicemen march past along London's Whitehall on Peace Day 19 July 1919. The Cenotaph here is the original temporary wood and plaster structure built for the occasion.

There was an element of truth in the postwar concept of a 'lost genera-tion' among the potential future elite. In addition, Britain lost some 228,000 people to the visit of the 'Spanish Lady', as the influenza pan-demic of 1918–19 became known.

The losses of life seemed horrific and were unprecedented. Soon, indeed, what were to become the familiar rituals of remembrance would be established – the first observance of Armistice Day on 11 November 1919; the consecration of the Tomb of the Unknown Warrior unveiled in Westminster Abbey and the unveiling of the Cenotaph in Whitehall, both in November 1920; the first Poppy Day in November 1921; and the war cemeteries, of which 891 had been completed on the Western Front alone by 1930.

Nevertheless, the British population grew by some 2 million between 1911 and 1921 – albeit with a reduced growth rate compared to that between 1901 and 1911 – and in this sense the 'demographic gain' out-weighed the demographic loss. Other factors affecting population need to be borne in mind. Possibly 12 per cent of the British war dead would have died in the period 1914–18 anyway, without a war to increase the odds. Men over military age actually experienced improved chances of survival during the war, and, generally, there was an improvement in the life expectancy of manual workers. Female health also improved, although there was an increase in tuberculosis that went against the general trend, perhaps because of the greater migration in wartime to urban centres coupled with the deterioration in housing conditions under population pressures.

Infant mortality declined even further than would be expected from the mere fact that the British birth rate declined in wartime, from just under 24 per 1000 of population (1914) to about 19.5 per 1000 (1918). By the 1920s it had reverted to its pre-war pattern of a more gradual decline. Conversely, the mortality rate of elderly women increased by about five per cent, because of such factors as falling income, poorer diet and because there was less in the way of charitable concern for their welfare

Children tended to fare better in the war than they had done hither-to. Much of the credit for this was due to the improvement in the nutri-tion of mothers and children alike, the enhanced concerns for infant and maternal welfare – as seen in better medical care – and increases in family income, as a result of separation allowances and wages keeping pace with inflation. Generally, the working classes were better fed and clothed during the war. Even the acute wartime housing shortage, by compelling children to remain with their mothers, and thus keeping the size of households large, contributed to greater income for individual households and thus to the overall improvement in living standards.

State liquor control also had its social effect by lowering the incidence of neglect from parental alcoholism. Surprisingly, even rationing may have improved diets in some cases.

The paradoxically higher living standards were not eroded by the postwar economic depression, particularly as families remained smaller. Moreover, through the general adoption of the 8-hour working day and 48-hour week the working class had more leisure opportunities after the war than they had had before it. The social scientist A.L. Bowley concluded that in 1924, 'there was only half as much poverty in Britain as there had been in 1913.'

All change?

While the reach of the state was undoubtedly extended in 1914–18, the war had far less long-term impact than is popularly imagined. Although it is more difficult to measure changes in perceptions and attitudes as opposed to those social/economic changes detectable in official statistics, there were undoubtedly more continuities than discontinuities between the pre-war and postwar periods. Most of the wartime controls had disappeared by 1920–1 and it was already apparent that the majority of the expectations for major postwar social, economic and political change had evaporated with the onset of financial stringency. As already indicated, the majority of women who had entered wartime

Informal celebrations. A street party in full swing in London, also on Peace Day, 19 July 1919. The paucity of men in the scene is uncannily suggestive of the dislocations of wartime.

employment soon left it, and, though some now had the vote, wider gender equalities had not been achieved. In industry, too, much had reverted to the familiar. The railways, for example, returned to private ownership in 1921, albeit with the 120 or more pre-war companies amalgamated into just four large concerns. Lloyd George had hoped that, in the interests of British industrial competitiveness, wartime cooperative spirit would be continued, but employers and trade unions alike urged the restoration of pre-war practices. Indeed, the term 'reconstruction' was open to widely differing interpretations. For a few it did imply transformation, but for many it simply meant the restoration of the status quo; and the Ministry of Reconstruction itself disappeared in 1923. For many people, the usual pattern of everyday life in the 1920s would not have appeared very different from that before the war.

It may seem, therefore, as many in Britain have come to believe, that the war was largely futile. It needs to be remembered that it is defeat rather than victory that is likely to result in the greatest social, economic and political change in a society, and that victory was infinitely preferable to defeat. The loss of life, the sense of slaughter, certainly had a profound legacy. The subsequent foreign policy between the two world wars was hampered by both the sense of vulnerability from the air, derived from the experiences of the First World War, and by the desire to avoid the kind of massive military casualties the British had sustained, not least on the Western Front. And the Battle of the Somme, in particular, still casts a particularly pernicious shadow over popular modern perceptions of the First World War.

Lessons had certainly been learned, however, about how civil society must organize itself in wartime. For example, when war threatened Britain once more in 1939, proper labour policies for regulating the demands of armed forces, industry and agriculture were already in place. The waging of the war on the home front between 1939 and 1945 was also to be informed by the perception that what had been promised between 1914 and 1918 had not been delivered. In that sense, the most significant long-term effect of the Great War in Britain took place after the Second World War: the emergence of the welfare state in 1945.

Historians have often suggested that, following the assassination of Archduke Franz Ferdinand in Sarajevo on 28 June 1914, a 'Third Balkan War' was started as a result of the Austro-Hungarian declaration of war on Serbia on 28 July. It is also suggested that decisions then taken by the German leadership in Berlin transformed a localized conflict into the First World War by the end of the first week of August. Initially, the Central Powers – Germany and Austria-Hungary – were arrayed against the 'Entente', comprising Belgium, Britain, France, Montenegro, Russia and Serbia. Effectively, however, the conflict became a global affair immediately, since it automatically drew in the respective colonial empires of the great powers. In the case of Britain, some 2.8 million men from the empire fought alongside British forces. India alone contributed 1.4 million men, while the war effort also embraced a high percentage of the white male populations of the 'white dominions': Australia, Canada, Newfoundland, New Zealand and South Africa. By the end of 1914 Japan had joined the Entente and the Ottoman Empire had joined the Central Powers, as Bulgaria was also to do in 1915. Other European states subsequently joined the Entente, including Italy in 1915, Portugal and Romania in 1916, and Greece in 1917. In 1917, too, China, Liberia and Siam (modern Thailand) all joined the Entente, while the entry of the United States into the conflict as an 'associated' member of the Entente in April 1917 saw a raft of Central and Latin American states following suit. Bizarrely, even the Onondaga American Indian nation also declared war on Germany in July 1918. Ultimately, 32 Entente Powers confronted the four Central Powers.

In all, the war cost perhaps 10 million military dead; of course this is a lower figure than either the total war dead or war-related dead worldwide, figures almost impossible to calculate through such distortions as wartime and postwar refugees, the postwar redrawing of national frontiers, and continuing conflict in Russia, which had dissolved into civil war between the Bolsheviks and their opponents. Estimates of what social scientists call the 'demographic deficit' vary enormously, with the calculation of the loss of potential births because of the war dead being even more problematic. Conceivably, the demographic deficit may have exceeded 20 million, but this still excludes an estimated 1.5 million Armenian victims of the Turks in 1915. There is also the influenza pandemic of 1918–19 to consider, though it should be noted that, while often linked to notions of the effect of wartime privation, the great majority of the estimated 21 million deaths from 'Spanish 'flu' occurred in India, which was not directly affected by the war.

As earlier suggested, demographic gains almost certainly outweighed demographic losses in Britain in the ten years from 1911, and there

The Americans are coming. This music cover for 'A Battle Hymn and March' was created for US wartime propaganda purposes.

were improvements in general health. The same could not be said for all the warring states. Change tends to be greatest in states that are defeated, occupied or, indeed, newly created as a result of war. Victorious states have less inclination to change and are more likely to try to revert to the status quo of pre-war practices, as happened in Britain. Moreover, through accidents of geographical location, some states will suffer far more disruption than others. In terms of general material damage and loss of population, Serbia, Belgium and Poland probably suffered the most. Nearly all of Belgium was under German occupation throughout the war, while German and Austro-Hungarian forces finally overran Serbia in October 1915. Almost 90 per cent of Poland, partitioned among Germany, Austria-Hungary and Russia since the late eighteenth century, was fought over between 1914 and 1918. Large numbers of Belgians and Poles were deported to Germany for forced labour in industry and agriculture. Since the United States did not enter the war until April 1917, and was also distanced from any fighting front by several thousand miles of ocean, the domestic impact of the war was considerably weaker there.

Generalizations, therefore, are somewhat hazardous. Nonetheless, there are common patterns of war experience in terms of the home fronts that extend even to those states that were most distant from the fighting fronts, such as the United States or Australia. In all the belligerent powers there was the same enhancement of the power of the state through emergency legislation. If Britain had the Defence of the Realm Act (DORA), Germany had the Prussian Law of Siege, Austria the War Precautions Act, Australia the Unlawful Associations Act, and the United States the Sedition Act. In the United States, for example, there were over 2200 wartime prosecutions under emergency legislation. Moreover, all the warring powers attempted to manage and manipulate morale on the home front through propaganda. In the face of growing war-weariness and the outbreak of revolution in Russian in 1917, there were concerted efforts to reinvigorate public opinion, Britain's National War Aims Committee being echoed by similar organizations elsewhere, such as the Union of Associations against Enemy Propaganda in France, the Federated Society for Assistance and National Propaganda in Italy, and the Fatherland Party in Germany.

British moves to take railways, mines and shipyards under direct governmental control were paralleled among all belligerents, and it was not just in Britain that new ministries, departments and agencies appeared. American wartime creations included the War Industries

1. M. Dutasta (General Secretary).
2. M. Ph. Berthelot (France).
3. M. Pichon (France).
4. Col. E. M. House (United States).
5. Lieut.-Col. Hankey (Great Britain).
6. President Wilson (United States).
7. Mr. Lloyd George (Great Britain).
8. M. Clemenceau, President (France).
9. Mr. A. J. Balfour (Great Britain).
10. Mr. H. White (United States).
11. General Bliss (United States).
12. Mr. R. Lansing (United States).
13. Lord Milner (Great Britain).
14. Mr. A. Bonar Law (Great Britain).
15. Mr. G. N. Barnes (Great Britain).
16. Lord Robert Cecil (Great Britain).
17. M. A. Tardieu (France).
18. Sir Robert Borden (Canada).
19. Prince Charoon (Siam).
20. Sir J. Ward (New Zealand).
21. M. Phya Bibadh Kosha (Siam).
22. Mr. W. M. Hughes (Australia).
23. Mr. L. L. Klotz (France).
24. M. Beneš (Czecho-Slovak Republic).
25. M. Bratiano (Roumania).
26. General Botha (South Africa).
27. M. Cambon (France).
28. M. Bourgeois (France).
29. M. Vesnitch (Serbia).
30. M. Dmowski (Poland).
31. M. Paderewski (Poland).
32. Lieut.-Gen. Smuts (South Africa).
33. Mr. W. F. Massey (New Zealand).
34. M. Burgos (Panama).

A Plenary Session

Words instead of war. This print, from the *Illustrated London News*, shows a plenary session of the Allied delegations at the Paris Peace Conference. The setting is the Hall of Mirrors at the Palace of Versailles, where the treaty with Germany was signed on 28 June 1919.

THE PEACE CONFERENCE.

...ock Room at the Ministry of Foreign Affairs, in Paris: The Allied leaders in conclave during the preparation of the Peace Treaty.

FROM THE DRAWING BY J. SIMONT. COPYRIGHTED IN THE UNITED STATES AND CANADA.

35. The Maharajah of Bikanir (India).
36. Lord Sinha (India).
37. The Emir Faisul (Hedjaz).
38. M. Trumbitch (Serbia).
39. M. Pachitch (Serbia).
42. M. Haidar (Hedjaz).
41. Signor Orlando (Italy).
42. Dr. Menitz (Portugal).
43. Dr. Villela (Portugal).
44. M. Matsui (Japan).
45. Baron Makino (Japan).
46. Baron Sonnino (Italy).
47. Marquis Saionji (Japan).
48. M. Dorn y de Alsua (Ecuador).
49. Mr. C. D. B. King (Liberia).
50. M. Calderon (Peru).
51. M. Mantoux (Interpreter).
52. Marquis Salvago Raggi (Italy).

53. M. Guilbaud (Haiti).
54. M. Barzilai (Italy).
55. Marshal Foch (France).
56. M. Politis (Greece).
57. M. Blanco (Uruguay).
58. M. Venizelos (Greece).
59. M. Lou Tseng Tsiang (China).
60. M. Sao Ke Alfred Sze (China).
61. M. de Bustamante (Cuba).
62. M. Montes (Bolivia).
63. M. Mendes (Guatemala).
64. M. O. de Magalhaes (Brazil).
65. M. Vandervelde (Belgium).
66. General Weygand (France).
67. M. Hymans (Belgium).
68. President E. Pessoa (Brazil).
69. M. van den Heuvel (Belgium).

Board and the Food Administration, while Italy created an organization known as Industrial Mobilization to oversee war production. The splendidly named Imperial Potato Office emerged in Germany as one response to food-supply difficulties, the ongoing crisis subsequently producing the War Food Office, itself eventually incorporated with other agencies, such as the Weapons and Munitions Procurement

The First 'World' War 209

Office, into a Supreme War Office. It is not surprising that the attempt to establish an effective war economy became a priority for all states at war, not least in terms of the production of munitions. The Ministry of Armament and War Production in France echoed Britain's Ministry of Munitions, while Canada set up an Imperial Munitions Board to handle the orders received from the War Office in Britain. In Russia, where the Tsarist government proved unequal to the task, industry itself established the Special Council of Defence modelled on the British Ministry of Munitions. Much day-to-day administration in Russia increasingly fell into the hands of voluntary organizations such as the All Russian Union of Zemstvos (rural councils) and the Union of Municipalities, both of which subsequently combined to create Zemgor as an agency to intervene in war supply. The self-mobilizing process was further extended by the appearance of the central and local War Industries Committees. In some ways, this development mirrored the introduction of business people to government in Britain, something also seen in the organizing efforts of other businessmen, such as Walther Rathenau in Germany, Louis Loucher in France and Bernard Baruch in the United States.

In the general picture of the various home fronts – one of war production taking precedence over consumer production, direct government intervention in the labour market, increasing shortages, and rising prices – Britain had by far the highest rate of wartime industrial militancy. Yet, conversely, industrial militancy as such had far more serious repercussions in those states where governments did not enjoy the same degree of democratic legitimacy. While at various times Britain, France and the United States all held the threat of military conscription over those pursuing strike action in essential industries, food rioters were shot down in Turin in August 1917 and strikes were ruthlessly suppressed by force in Germany in early 1918. In Russia, of course, the progressive radicalization of industrial militancy contributed mightily to the collapse of the Tsarist government in March 1917.

At the root of many industrial problems were the issues of prices and food supplies in urban areas, with Britain doing far better than many continental states in maintaining adequate levels of nutrition. Rationing in Germany, whose population was, of course, subjected to economic blockade by the Entente, began as early as January 1915, and the measure was introduced in Austria-Hungary in April 1915. Italy brought in rationing in 1917, and France, a little later than Britain, in June 1918.

Another measure of the German failure to meet the challenges of the war was the haphazard extension of welfare provision compared to that in Britain or other Entente powers. Just as the Ministry of

Munitions developed housing projects in Britain, so France provided state housing for workers and encouraged employers to provide a range of facilities and leisure activities. In the United States, the Emergency Fleet Corporation similarly initiated a public housing programme.

State welfare programmes were driven in part by the increasing importance of incorporating women into the war effort, and it can be noted that the events in Petrograd in March 1917 were actually initially sparked by a riot among women textile workers, while women were also prominent in the food riots in Turin five months later. Certainly, the kind of increase in the numbers of women employed in industry witnessed in Britain was a general trend. In Germany, the female labour force rose from 1.5 million in 1914 to 2.3 million by 1918 and in

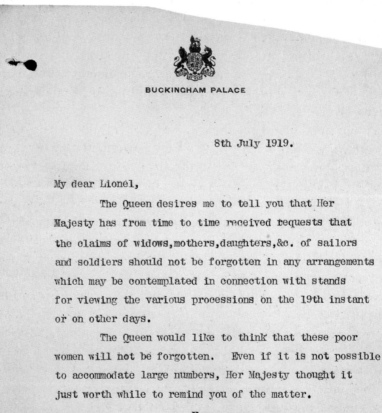

Make room for the women. This note, written on Queen Mary's behalf, requests that the Office of Works makes special arrangements for the female bereaved at the Peace Day celebrations in July 1919.

PEACE CELEBRATIONS

19th July, 1919

Not transferable

H.M. OFFICE OF WORKS

Admit Bearer to the enclosed space on the Green Park side of Constitution Hill

Austria by about 1 million. There were two and a half times more women employed in American industry in 1918 as in 1917, while the proportion of women employed in industry in France rose from almost 30 per cent in 1914 to over 37 per cent by 1917. A parallel can be drawn in the United States with the significant switch of the black population from the rural south to the urban and industrial north as war industries expanded. As in Britain, however, most women world-wide returned to domesticity either through choice or coercion once the war ended. Just as in Britain, too, it is difficult to assess how far the attitudes of individual women were changed by wartime experiences.

The question of how far women's contribution to the war effort related to the achievement of the franchise in Britain has been mentioned already in this book. Much the same question can be asked of the situation elsewhere. In Canada, Germany, the Soviet Union, the Baltic States and the new states carved from Austria-Hungary, women got the vote after the war. American women already had the vote in 11 states by 1917, and, though President Woodrow Wilson proclaimed that extending the franchise to them was vital to winning the war, the Nineteenth Amendment (introduced in January 1918) was not ratified until 1920. In France, while the Chamber of Deputies voted in favour of female suffrage in May 1919, the Senate rejected it in 1922 and the vote was not granted to French women until 1944.

In some ways, one of the most significant longer-term impacts of

Ephemera of peace. The images are of an admission ticket for one of the stands set up for the bereaved attending the Peace Day celebrations, 19 July 1919, together with a bus ticket used on the occasion.

the war was on what might be termed the 'colonial home front'. While the military response of the British and French empires to the war was immensely impressive, participation was not without opposition. Those of Irish extraction, for example, certainly opposed the extension of conscription to Australia, a course of action rejected in two wartime referenda. French Canadians were also resistant to enlistment, sympathy for France being muted by distance, and there were riots in Quebec following the introduction of conscription in 1917. Some die-hard Afrikaners staged a short-lived revolt in South Africa in 1914. Conscription, either of soldiers or of labourers, was also at the root of wartime revolts in French West Africa, the British southern African colony of Nyasaland, and Egboland in Nigeria. A degree of indigenous nationalism in the colonial empires was undoubtedly stimulated by wartime service, while a new sense of a distinctive national identity certainly emerged from the wartime performance of the soldiers of the white dominions, notably Canada and Australia. The colonial empires also derived general benefit from increased wartime demands for their raw materials and other products, the war accelerating industrialization in Australia, Canada and India.

Clearly, political events had the greatest capacity to change states and societies, and it was where there was a substantial breakdown in the functioning of the state, and in the capacity of political leaderships, that social and political collapse occurred. Russia in 1917, and Germany and Hungary in 1918, all experienced revolutions, and the empires of Tsarist Russia, Imperial Germany, Austria-Hungary and Ottoman Turkey were all swept away. Broadly defined, liberal democracy was victorious in 1918; but liberalism was also to prove a victim of the war, as the democracies seemed incapable of dealing with either the economic consequences of the war or the threat posed by extremists on both the political left and right. In Italy, for example, the failure of wartime state mobilization and the idea that wartime sacrifices had not been sufficiently rewarded in the peace settlement were to contribute to the postwar emergence of fascist ideology. Moreover, with the withdrawal of the United States into diplomatic isolation, the policing of the international settlement rested on what would prove the uncertain commitment of Britain and France – which reflected, at least in part, the psychological legacy of the First World War on the policy-makers in London and Paris. While the war was won, in the views of many the peace was lost: the 'war to end all wars' would be succeeded by an even greater conflict just 20 years later.

214   *The Home Front, 1914–1918*

The scale of the effort.
Allied contingents
march past the Victoria
Memorial in The Mall,
outside Buckingham
Palace, on Peace Day,
19 July 1919 – a testament
to the truly global nature
of the Great War.

Chronology

1914

28 JUNE Archduke Franz Ferdinand, heir to Austro-Hungarian throne, is assassinated in Sarajevo, and the Serbian government is blamed

23 JULY Austria-Hungary presents ultimatum to Serbia

28 JULY Austria-Hungary declares war on Serbia, and Russia mobilizes to protect Serbia

31 JULY Home Front: the London Stock Exchange is closed

1 AUGUST Germany, Austria-Hungary's ally, declares war on Russia and issues ultimatum to Belgium

3 AUGUST Germany declares war on France, Russia's ally, and invades Belgium

4 AUGUST Britain's Liberal government under Asquith declares war on Germany

5 AUGUST Austria-Hungary declares war on Russia

5 AUGUST Home Front: Field Marshal Lord Kitchener is appointed Secretary of State for War

5 AUGUST Home Front: The generally anti-war Union of Democratic Control is formed

6 AUGUST Home Front: the Currency and Bank Notes Act authorizes issue of the 'Bradbury' 10s and £1 notes

7 AUGUST Home Front: Kitchener calls for the 'First 100,000' volunteers for his 'New Armies'

8 AUGUST Home Front: the Defence of Realm Act (DORA) is introduced, widening government powers

12 AUGUST Britain and France declare war on Austria-Hungary

16 AUGUST The British Expeditionary Force (BEF) finishes disembarking in France

20 AUGUST Britain imposes an economic blockade on the Central Powers

23 AUGUST Battle of Mons, and the the BEF retreats

23 AUGUST Japan declares war on Germany

25 AUGUST A Royal Flying Corps aircraft become the first aeroplane to force down an opponent

26 AUGUST Battle of Le Cateau

30 AUGUST German forces inflict crushing defeat on invading Russians at Battle of Tannenberg

3 SEPTEMBER HMS *Pathfinder* becomes the first warship to be sunk in action by a submarine (U21)

5 SEPTEMBER Britain, France and Russia agree not to make a separate peace (Declaration of London)

5 SEPTEMBER The Allied counter-attack on the Marne begins

15 SEPTEMBER Home Front: the Irish Home Rule Bill and Welsh Church Bill are suspended for duration of the war

10 OCTOBER Antwerp falls to the Germans

15 OCTOBER First Battle of Ypres begins

20 OCTOBER *Glitra* becomes the first merchant ship to be sunk by submarine (U17)

29 OCTOBER Ottoman Turkey enters the war, against the Allies

1 NOVEMBER Battle of Coronel off the coast of Chile: two British cruisers are sunk

5 NOVEMBER Britain and France declare war on Ottoman Turkey

6 NOVEMBER Tsingtao falls to British and Japanese forces

17 NOVEMBER Home Front: the First British War Loan is launched

22 NOVEMBER First Battle of Ypres concludes

3 DECEMBER Home Front: the No Conscription Fellowship is formed

8 DECEMBER In the Battle of the Falkland Islands, the German cruiser *Scharnhorst* is sunk

16 DECEMBER Home Front: The German Navy bombards Scarborough, Hartlepool and Whitby

24 DECEMBER Home Front: German bombers mount their first air raid against Britain, attacking Dover.

24 DECEMBER The so-called Christmas Truce on the Western Front, as Allied and German soldiers and mix with each other, even playing some football

1915

4 JANUARY Home Front: the London Stock Exchange reopens for trading

24 JANUARY Battle of Dogger Bank

19 JANUARY Home Front: Britain experiences its first Zeppelin raid, on Great Yarmouth

18 FEBRUARY Home Front: The Germans begin a submarine blockade of Britain

19 FEBRUARY Britain and France begin Dardanelles naval operation

5 MARCH Home Front: employers, government and unions conclude the Shells and Fuses Agreement

10 MARCH Battle of Neuve Chapelle

17 MARCH Home Front: The War Service Register for Women opens

19 MARCH Home Front: Treasury Agreements with 35 unions, to ensure workers do not take excessive advantage of their increased industrial muscle

30 MARCH Home Front: George V announces abstinence from alcohol for the duration of the war

22 APRIL Second Battle of Ypres begins, in which poison gas is used for the first time (by German forces)

23 APRIL The poet Rupert Brooke dies, and his book *1914 and Other Poems* is later published

25 APRIL Allied forces land in the Dardanelles

7 MAY The passenger ship SS *Lusitania* is torpedoed and sunk off the coast of Ireland, killing about 1200, including 128 US citizens

14 MAY Home Front: *The Times* inaugurates the 'Shell Scandal' concerning the shortage of munitions

15 MAY Home Front: Lord Fisher,

Admiral of the Fleet, resigns as
First Sea Lord
19 MAY Home Front: The Asquith
Coalition government is formed
24 MAY Italy declares war on
Austria-Hungary
26 MAY Home Front: Asquith
forms Coalition government, and
Winston Churchill is forced out
as Lord of the Admiralty, after
the failures at Gallipoli and the
Dardanelles
31 MAY Home Front: Zeppelins
raid London for the first time
9 JUNE Home Front: the Ministry
of Munitions is formed
10 JUNE Home Front: the Central
Control Board (Liquor Traffic) is
created
16 JUNE Home Front: Lloyd
George becomes Minister of
Munitions
19 JUNE Home Front: the
Munitions of War Act
13 JULY Home Front: the Second
British War Loan is launched
17 JULY Home Front: women
demonstrate in London for the
'Right to Serve'
15 AUGUST Home Front: National
Registration Act introduced to
record everyone who might be
eligible for military service
3 SEPTEMBER Home Front: Leefe
Robinson shoots down German
dirigible over Cuffley
7 SEPTEMBER Home Front: The
Trades Union Congress (TUC)
votes against conscription
11 SEPTEMBER Home Front: the
first of many Women's Institutes
opens, in Anglesey, Wales
25 SEPTEMBER Battle of Loos
begins
5 OCTOBER British and French
forces land at Salonika
6 OCTOBER Bulgaria invades Serbia
12 OCTOBER Edith Cavell, a British
nurse, is executed by Germans in
Belgium for helping POWs
escape
15 OCTOBER Britain and France
declare war on Bulgaria
6 NOVEMBER Home Front: *The
Globe* newspaper is suppressed
19 NOVEMBER The British advance
on Baghdad begins
5 DECEMBER The Turkish siege of

Kut, Mesopotamia (now Iraq),
starts
15 DECEMBER Sir John French
resigns as Commander-in-Chief
of the BEF
19 DECEMBER Sir Douglas Haig is
appointed new Commander-in-
Chief of the BEF
21 DECEMBER Sir William
Robertson becomes Chief of the
Imperial General Staff

1916

4 JANUARY Home Front: Sir John
Simon resigns as Home Secretary
in opposition to conscription
8 JANUARY Allied forces are finally
evacuated from the Gallipoli
peninsula
9 FEBRUARY Home Front: the
Military Service Act introduces
conscription for unmarried men
21 FEBRUARY Battle of Verdun
begins
31 MARCH Home Front:
A Zeppelin L15 is shot down
over Suffolk
21 APRIL Home Front: Sir Roger
Casement is arrested for his
support of the Irish Republicans
24 APRIL Home Front: Easter
Rising takes place in Dublin
25 APRIL Home Front: the German
Navy bombards Great Yarmouth
and Lowestoft
29 APRIL Kut falls to Turkish
forces
2 MAY Home Front: Military
Service Act (No 2) introduces
conscription for married men.
15 MAY Home Front: Sir Roger
Casement's trial begins
21 MAY Home Front: British
Summer Time is introduced
31 MAY Battle of Jutland begins in
the North Sea
5 JUNE Home Front: Kitchener
drowns when HMS *Hampshire*
goes down off the Orkneys, after
hitting a mine
7 JUNE The Arab Revolt against the
Turks begins, encouraged by
T.E. Lawrence
29 JUNE Home Front: Sir Roger
Casement is sentenced to death
1 JULY Battle of the Somme begins,
with over 19,000 British dead in
just one day

6 JULY Home Front: Lloyd George
becomes Secretary of State for
War
21 AUGUST Home Front: The film
The Battle of the Somme opens in
London
27 AUGUST Italy declares war on
Germany, and Romania declares
war on Austria-Hungary
15 SEPTEMBER Tanks appear on
the battlefield for the first time,
at Flers-Courcellette on Somme
18 NOVEMBER Battle of the Somme
ends, the Allies having advanced
seven miles at a cost of three-
quarters of a million casualties
23 NOVEMBER The Greek
Provisional Government declares
war on Germany
28 NOVEMBER Home Front:
German aircraft bomb London
for the first time
1 DECEMBER Home Front: the
Women's Army Auxiliary Corps
is established
5 DECEMBER Home Front:
Lloyd George resigns from the
Coalition government
6 DECEMBER Home Front: Asquith
resigns as Prime Minister, to be
replaced by Lloyd George
6 DECEMBER Fall of Bucharest,
Romania, to German occupying
forces
15 DECEMBER Battle of Verdun
ends
20 DECEMBER US President
Woodrow Wilson circulates Peace
Note
22 DECEMBER Home Front: the
ministries of Food, Labour,
Pensions and Shipping are
established

1917

19 JANUARY Home Front: An
explosion rips through the
Silvertown munitions plant, East
London
1 FEBRUARY Germany declares
unrestricted submarine warfare
2 FEBRUARY Home Front: the
Corn Production Act introduces
bread rationing
8 MARCH Russian food riots begin
in Petrograd
11 MARCH Baghdad falls to the
British

14 MARCH The Russian Provisional government is formed

15 MARCH Tsar Nicholas II abdicates

26 MARCH The British advance into Palestine begins

28 MARCH Home Front: The Ministry of National Service is established

6 APRIL United States declares war on Germany

9 APRIL Battle of Arras begins

10 MAY The first, experimental convoy leaves Gibraltar for Plymouth

21 MAY Home Front: the first National Kitchen opens

25 MAY Home Front: Gotha heavy bombers strike Britain for the first time, at Folkestone

29 MAY Home Front: George V makes a proclamation to encourage voluntary bread reduction

7 JUNE British forces capture Messines Ridge

12 JUNE King Constantine of Greece abdicates

13 JUNE Home Front: Gotha heavy bombers strike London

19 JUNE Home Front: the royal family renounces the Saxe-Coburg-Gotha name in favour of the more English and patriotic 'Windsor'

27 JUNE Greece officially declares war on Austria-Hungary and Turkey

31 JULY Third Battle of Ypres (Passchendaele) begins

14 AUGUST China declares war on Germany and Austria-Hungary

24 OCTOBER Battle of Caporetto begins in the Italian Front

2 NOVEMBER Home Front: the Foreign Secretary Arthur Balfour's 'Declaration' supports a Jewish homeland in Palestine

5 NOVEMBER The Allied Supreme War Council is established at Rapallo

6 NOVEMBER Passchendaele village is captured by Canadians

8 NOVEMBER A Bolshevik coup takes place in Petrograd

11 NOVEMBER Third Battle of Ypres ends, with little progress for the Allies

20 NOVEMBER Battle of Cambrai begins, featuring the first use of massed tanks

29 NOVEMBER Home Front: Lord Lansdowne's 'Peace Letter' in the *Daily Telegraph* appeals for an end to the war

29 NOVEMBER Home Front: the Women's Royal Naval Service is established

7 DECEMBER United States declares war on Austria-Hungary

9 DECEMBER British forces capture Jerusalem

31 DECEMBER Home Front: sugar rationing is introduced

1918

5 JANUARY Home Front: Lloyd George's makes his War Aims speech to union leaders

8 JANUARY Woodrow Wilson announces his 'Fourteen Points for a Just Peace'

25 FEBRUARY Home Front: rationing of meat and fats begins in London and the Home Counties

3 MARCH Germany and the Russian Bolsheviks agree the Treaty of Brest-Litovsk

21 MARCH The German Spring Offensive begins

26 MARCH The Doullens Agreement establishes an Allied Supreme Command

1 APRIL Home Front: the Royal Air Force and Women's Royal Air Force are established

9 APRIL Home Front: the Women's Army Auxiliary Corps is renamed Queen Mary's Army Auxiliary Corps

18 APRIL Home Front: Military Service (No 2) Act increases maximum conscription age to 50 and controversially extends conscription to Ireland, though this provision is not enacted

APRIL Home Front: meat and fats rationing is extended to the country as whole

23 APRIL Allied forces attack U-boat base, in the Zeebrugge Raid

7 MAY Romania signs Treaty of Bucharest with Germany

19 MAY Home Front: the last air raid on London takes place

10 JUNE Home Front: in the Representation of the People Act women over 30 get the vote, but conscientious objectors lose it

16 JULY Tsar Nicholas and his family are murdered by Bolsheviks

3 AUGUST Home Front: British troops land at Archangel and Vladivostock to support anti-Bolshevik forces

8 AUGUST Home Front: H.A.L. Fisher's Education Bill raises the school leaving age to 14

8 AUGUST German lines are broken at Battle of Amiens ('Black Day of the German Army')

31 AUGUST Home Front: the Metropolitan Police go on strike

15 SEPTEMBER The Allied offensive at Salonika begins

27 SEPTEMBER The German fortified Hindenburg Line is broken on Canal du Nord

30 DECEMBER Damascus falls to British and Arab forces

17 OCTOBER The Czech Republic is declared

24 OCTOBER Battle of Vittorio Veneto begins

28 OCTOBER Home Front: Spanish 'flu peaks in Britain

30 OCTOBER Turkey and Bulgaria sign armistices with Allies

3 NOVEMBER Austria-Hungary signs armistice with Allies

4 NOVEMBER The war poet Wilfred Owen is killed on the Western Front

9 NOVEMBER Kaiser Wilhelm II abdicates

11 NOVEMBER Germany signs armistice with the Allies, and Emperor Karl of Austria-Hungary abdicates

14 NOVEMBER Home Front: the Labour Party leaves the Coalition government

25 NOVEMBER The last German forces surrender, in German East Africa

14 DECEMBER Home Front: in the General Election, the Conservative-Liberal coalition wins, and women vote for the first time

1919

18 JANUARY The Paris Peace
Conferences opens, which will
bring peace and establish the
League of Nations

21 JANUARY Home Front: The
republican murder of two policemen heralds the Anglo-Irish War
(Irish War of Independence)

21 JUNE The German High Seas
fleet is scuttled in the Orkneys, at
Scapa Flow

28 JUNE Germany and the Allies
sign the Treaty of Versailles

12 JULY The economic blockade of
Germany ends

19 JULY Home Front: the population celebrates Peace Day

10 SEPTEMBER The Treaty of St
Germain (with Austria) is signed

11 NOVEMBER Home Front: A two-
minute silence commemorates
the fallen of the war

27 NOVEMBER The Treaty of
Neuilly (with Bulgaria) is signed

29 NOVEMBER Lady Nancy Astor
becomes the first female MP in
the House of Commons

1920

30 APRIL Home Front: compulsory
military service ends

4 JUNE The Treaty of Trianon is
signed with Hungary

10 AUGUST The Treaty of Sèvres is
signed with Turkey

11 NOVEMBER Home Front: In
London, the Cenotaph memorial
is unveiled and the ceremonial
Burial of Unknown Warrior takes
place in Westminster Abbey

1921

31 AUGUST Home Front: the
1914–18 conflict is officially over,
as an Order in Council declares
an end to the state of war

6 DECEMBER Home Front: The
Anglo-Irish Treaty creates the
Irish Free State, but the six
northern Irish counties remain
part of the UK

Further reading

IAN F.W. BECKETT, *The First World War: The Essential Guide to Sources in the UK National Archives* (Public Record Office, 2002)

IAN F.W. BECKETT, *The Great War, 1914–1918* (Pearson Longman, 2001)

GAIL BRAYBON, *Women Workers in the First World War* (Croom Helm, 1981)

JOHN BOURNE, *Britain and the Great War, 1914–1918* (Edward Arnold, 1989)

KATHLEEN BURK (ed.), *War and the State: The Transformation of British Government, 1914–1919* (Allen & Unwin, 1982)

MARK CONNELLY, *The Great War: Memory and Ritual* (Royal Historical Society, 2002)

STEPHEN CONSTANTINE, Maurice Kirby and Mary Rose (eds), *The First World War in British History* (Edward Arnold, 1995)

CAROLINE DAKERS, *The Countryside at War, 1914–1918* (Constable, 1987)

GERARD DE GROOT, *Blighty: British Society in the Era of the Great War* (Longman, 1996)

PETER DEWEY, *British Agriculture in the First World War* (Routledge, 1989)

ADRIAN GREGORY, *The Silence of Memory: Armistice Day, 1919–1946* (Berg, 1994)

ADRIAN GREGORY and Senia Paseta (eds), *Ireland and the Great War* (Manchester University Pres, 2002)

JOHN HORNE (ed.), *State, Society and Mobilisation in Europe during the First World War* (Cambridge University Press, 1977)

ANDREW HYDE, *The First Blitz: The German Air Campaign against Britain, 1917–18* (Pen and Sword Books, 2002)

KEITH JEFFERY, *Ireland and the Great War* (Cambridge University Press, 2000)

ALEX KING, *Memorials of the Great War in Britain: The Symbolism and Politics of Remembrance* (Berg, 1998)

CATRIONA MACDONALD and E.W. MCFARLAND (eds), *Scotland and the Great War* (Tuckwell Press, 1999)

SUE MALVERN, *Modern Art, Britain and the Great War* (Yale University Press, 2004)

ARTHUR MARWICK, *The Deluge*, 2nd edition (Macmillan, 1991)

ARTHUR MARWICK, *Women at War, 1914–1918* (Fontana, 1977)

GARY MESSINGER, *British Propaganda and the State in the First World War* (Manchester University Press, 1992)

DEBORAH THOM, *Nice Girls and Rude Girls: Women Workers in World War I* (I. B. Tauris, 2000)

JOHN TURNER (ed.), *Britain and the First World War* (Unwin Hyman, 1988)

JOHN TURNER, *British Politics and the Great War* (Yale University Press, 1992)

BERNARD WAITES, *A Class Society at War* (Berg, 1987)

RICHARD WALL and JAY WINTER (eds), *The Upheaval of War: Family, Work and Welfare in Europe, 1914–1918* (Cambridge University Press, 1988)

TREVOR WILSON, *The Myriad Faces of War* (Polity Press, 1986)

JAY WINTER, *The Great War and the British People* (Macmillan, 1985)

JAY WINTER and Jean-Louis Robert (eds), *Capital Cities: London, Paris, Berlin, 1914–1918* (Cambridge University Press, 1997)

SIR LLEWELLYN WOODWARD, *Great Britain and the War of 1914–1918* (Methuen, 1972)

Index

page numbers in italics denote illustrations (photographs, letters, documents)

Active Service League 66
Adams, A. *179, 180*
Adams, D.M. *152, 153*
aeroplane manufacture 20–1, *61*, 85
aeroplane poster *182, 183*
agriculture 75, 77, 112, 141
air raid wardens 195–6
air raids 182, *183*, 184, *185*, 186, 187, *190–1, 192, 193, 194*
airships *39*, 192; *see also* Zeppelins
Albert, King of Belgium 11
alcohol 96, *97*, 98, 124, *125*, 131; *see also* liquor control *and* temperance
Alexandra, the Queen Mother *109*
alien residents 149–50, *151*, 152
Allen, Clifford 153, 155, 158
allotments 113, 117, *118*
Amalgamated Engineering Union 53
Amalgamated Society of Carpenters and Joiners 90
Amalgamated Society of Engineers 48, 50, *51*, 90, 91
Angell, Norman 153
anti-German riots 150, *151, 152*, 176
anti-war demonstrations 11
armed forces 32, 147, 149; *see also* recruitment drives
Armistice Day 198, *199*, 201
Armstrong Whitworth 83
Army Council 70, 72, 155
Askwith, Sir George 58, *59*
Asquith, Herbert 8, 11, 15, 153
Associated Equipment Co Ltd *84*
Australia 208, 213
Austria 208, 212
Austria-Hungary 8, 198, 206, 213
Avonmouth 31

Baldwin, Stanley 194
Balfour, Arthur 45, *173*
Barefoot, J.P. *125*
Barry Docks 40, *42–3*
Barstow, Mrs Montague 66
Battenberg, Prince Louis 150, 165
Battle Cruiser Fleet *179*
The Battle of the Somme 173–4
Beecham, Sir Thomas 135
Belgian munitions workers *30, 63–4, 154, 155*

Belgian refugees *10*, 153, *154, 155*
Belgium 8, 11, 15, 207
Belgravia War Hospital Supply Depot *108*
Beveridge, William 120
Billeting of Civilians Act (1917) 127
Billing, Noel Pemberton 96, 98
The Bing Boys Are Here 135, *136*
Birmingham 96, *97*
birth control 94, 96, 98
birth rate 201
Birtley munitions *30, 154*, 155
Black, Sir Frederick 40, *42*
black market 138
Blackwall Tunnel *190–1*
Blythe, F. *185*, 195–6
Board of Agriculture 75, 112
Board of Agriculture and Fisheries 36
Board of Education 100
Board of Trade 34, 40, 77, 110, 143
Boiler Makers 40, *43*
Bolshevism 158, 160, 206
bombardments 16, 178, *179*, 180–1, *194*
bombers 144, 192, 194
Bovril 119
Bowley, A.L. 203
Boy Scouts 187, *197*
Bradburn, Alfred *62–4*
bread *115*, 119–20
brewing industry *92*, 119–20
Bridgeman, W.C. 53
Britain Prepared 169
Britannia Works *90*
British Expeditionary Force 15
British Summer Time 16, 128, 130
Brockway, Fenner 153, 155
Buchan, John 165
Buckingham Palace *70*, 198, *205, 214–15*
Bulgaria 198, 206
Buxton Lime Farms Company *112, 114*

Cabinet Ministers *170–1*
Canada 210, 213
Canterbury, Archbishop of 166
Carlisle, Wilson *130*
Casement, Sir Roger 149
Causham, Joseph & Sons *182*
Cave, Sir George 50, 100, *101–2*
Cavell, Edith 168
Cenotaph *200*, 201
censorship 69, 164–5
Central Committee for National Patriotic Organisations 165

Central Committee on Women's Employment 66
Central Control Board (Liquor Traffic) 96, *97*, 131
Central Powers 138, 206
Chamberlain, Neville 96
Chaplin, Charlie 69, *134, 135*
charities 108–10
Charlton, Lieut. Colonel L.E.O. *84*
Chatham air raid *192, 193*
children: cinemas 69; custody of 93; delinquency 98–9, *103*; diseases 74; employment 100; growing food *118*; illegitimate 96, 98; infant mortality 74, 201; orphans *99*; queueing for coal *122*; street party *203*; welfare provision 126, *128*, 201
Chilwell accident 88
Chinese premises attacked 153
Chu Chin Chow and The Maid of the Mountains 135
Church Army 130
churches 136, 166
Churchill, Winston 8, 14
cinemas 69, 99, 100, *101–2*, 135–6, 168–9, *170–1, 173–4*
Cinematograph Exhibitors' Association 100, *101–2*
class, social: agricultural work 75; education 100; fitness 200; food 116; housing 127–8; living standards 110, 201, 203; solidarity 53, *54–5*; unrest 127–8; wages 138
clothing 60, *83*, 144
Clyde Bank Singer Company *128*
Clyde shipyards 40, 45, *46–7*
Clyde Workers Committee 40, 45, 155
Co-operative Societies 108
Co-operative Wholesale Society 78
coal industry *18–19*
coal miners 48, *54–5*, 56
coal ration 122–3, *139*
coke heavers *74*
colonies 206, 213
Commission of Enquiry into Working Class Unrest 127–8
conscientious objectors *145*, 147, 155, *157*, 158, *159, 166*
conscription 16, 32, 36, 153, 155, 210, 213; *see also* exemptions
Cook, E.T. 165
cooking 117–9
Corbett, Adrian 56
Corn Production Act 112–13
cotton industry 53, 56, 74

Coventry 53
Croxton, Arthur *173*

D*aily Mail* 98, 133, 150
Daily Mirror 168
Defence of the Realm Act (DORA)
   19–20, *46–7*, 50, 108, 128, 150,
   164–5, 208
Deleuvigne, Malcolm *128, 129*
Derby, Lord *132, 133*
Devon Women's War Service
   County Committee *76, 77*
Devonport, Lord 119–20
Dickson, H., Co *169*
diet 114, 117, 119, *140*, 203
divorce 93
Dock, Wharf, Riverside & General
   Workers Union 40, *42–3, 152,
   153*
dock workers 40, *42*
domestic service 73, 82, 83, 86, 91
Doyle, Sir Arthur Conan 136, 165
Dublin 146–7, *148, 166, 179*
Dundee 18

Easter Rising 146–7, *148–9, 166,
   179*
Eat Less Bread 115, 116
education 99–100
electoral reform 93
elites 138
Elizabethville *see* Birtley munitions
employment 34, 80, 83, 100, 137;
   see also labour force; women
   workers
Engineering Employers Federation
   39
engineering workers 48, 50
English Opera Group 135
Entente 206
entertainment 134, 135
The Eternal Grind 137
exemption from recruitment and
   conscription 34, *35, 36, 37, 38,
   39, 132, 133, 155, 156, 157*
explosives manufacturing 31, 32, *33*

Factory Acts 124
family life 94–6, 98
farmers *see* agriculture
Fawcett, Millicent Garrett 94
Feed the Guns Campaign 109
Fellowship of Reconciliation 153
Ferdinand, Franz 8, 206
Fernside, Mrs Elizabeth 105–6
Fiat Motor Co Ltd *84*
First Aid Nursing Yeomanry
   (FANY) 67

Fisher, H.A.L. 100, *103*
Foch, Ferdinand 198
Folkstone 184
Food, Ministry of 23, 60, 114, 116,
   119
Food Control campaign 114, *115*
food prices *50*, 110, *111*, 112
food production 77, 112–14
food supplies 112–14, 116–17,
   119–20, 139–40, 144, 210
football 131
Formamint tablets *140*
France 8, 15, 208, 210–12
French, Sir John 25
Friendly Societies 108
Friends Ambulance Unit *157*
Fryatt, Charles 168

General Federation of Trade
   Unions 110
George V 11, 15, *115, 123*, 186
German High Seas Fleet 178
German immigrants 149–50,
   152
German premises attacked *151,
   152, 153*
*The German Retreat and the Battle
   of Arras* 174
Germany 8, 11, 168, *169, 173*, 198,
   208, 209–13
Gibb, Maurice *154, 155*
Glasgow Corporation Gas
   Department *19*, 44
Glasgow rent strike 45, 126
The Globe 165
Goodwin, F.R. 100, *101–2*
Gothas 184, *185*, 186, 187, 194
Government Bread 116
Grain Supplies Committee 117
Grand Fleet *179*
Great Yarmouth 178, *179, 180*
Greene, Sir W. *173*
Greenwich 182, *190–1*
Gretna National Cordite Factory
   and related sites *28–9, 36*, 56, *57,
   83, 88*
Grey, Sir Edward *9*, 11
Grillo Oleum plant 31
Guardianship of Infants Act 93

Hague conventions 178
Haldane, Lord 150
Hamilton, Mary Agnes 96
Hammersmith Palais *20*
Hankey, Sir Maurice *121*
Harwich Force *179*
Health, Ministry of 139
health and safety provisions 124

health-insurance benefits 141
Health of Munitions Workers
   Committee 124
Henderson, Arthur 160
Henry, Sir Edward 48, *49*, 69, *128,
   129*
Hicks, Miss 69
Hill, Alex *166, 167*
Hodgkin, H.T. 153
holiday resorts 133–4
Holland and Cubitts plant 31
Hollister, Joe 143–4
Home Office memorandum 48,
   49
Home Rule 147, 149
homosexuality court cases 70
Hotchkiss works *50, 52*, 53
housekeeping guides 94
housing 60, 126–8, 141, 201, 203,
   211
Housing and Town Planning Act
   (1919) 141
hunting 131, *132*, 133

Illustrated London News 119,
   208–9
illness 32, *33*
income tax 138
Increase of Rents and Mortgages
   (Amendment) Act (1918) 126
indecency charges 70, *71–2*
Independent Labour Party 11, 146,
   158
industry 18, 19, 23, 209;
   see also strikes
infant mortality 74, 201
inflation 53, 60, 110, 112
influenza *140*, 201, 206
Inglis, Elsie 70
Institute of Hygiene *89*
Intoxicating Liquor (Temporary
   Restriction) Bill *130*
Ireland 8, 146–9
Irish Rebellion *see* Easter Rising
Iron and Steel Ship Builders
   Society 40, *43*
Iron and Steel Trades
   Confederation 51–2
Iron Moulders Union 53
Italy 206, 208, 209, 213

Japan 206
Jarrott, Captain C. *84*
Jenkins, W. St D. 40, *42*
Jews attacked 153
John Bull 166
Joint Engineering Shop Stewards'
   Committee 48

Jury, William 173
jute industry 18
Jutland *179*
juvenile delinquency 98–9, *103*

King's Cross coal depot *122*
Kirkaldy, A.W. 81
Kirkwood, David 45
Kitchener, H.H. *15*, 16, 25, *26–7*, 34, 164
Knight, J.B. *187, 188–9*
knitted comforts 66, *67*

Labour, Ministry of 23
labour conscription 36
labour force 16, 18, *19*; categories 81; dilution 56, 83; skilled/unskilled 56, 58, 60, *62*, 138; *see also* women workers
Labour Party 48, 146
labour policy 32, 34, 36
Labour Statistics Department *111*
Labour Tribunals 50
Labour Troubles Committee *51–2*
land ownership 138
Lansdowne, Lord *35*, 158
laundry trade 91, 93
Law, Andrew Bonar *121*
Leefe Robinson, W. *187*, 192
Leete, Alfred *15*, 174–5
Leslie, Dr R. Murray *89*
liberal democracy 213
Liberal government 15
licensed premises 16, 96, *97*, 130–1
Liddell, Captain John 66
life expectancy 201
liquor control 130–1, 134, 203
Liquor Traffic Board *125*
The Little American 137
Liverpool *108*, 182
living standards 60, 110, 201, 203
Llangattock School of Arts and Crafts *194*
Lloyd George, David 8; Clyde 45; economy 11, 16; liquor control 130, 131; ministries 23, 24; national pay bargaining 48; peace 158; plot against 155; post-war 204; rations *121*
Local Government Board *38*
Local Representative Committee *139*, 142
Lodge, Sir Oliver 136
London 9, 142–4, 178, 184
London, Treaty of 11, 15
London Air Defence Area 187
London Cinematograph Film Producers *173*

London Coliseum *172, 173*
London Postal Service 80
Londonderry, Lady 70
Long, W. *132, 133*
Long, Walter 39
Lowestoft *179*, 180, *180–1*
Lusitania 150, 153, 168, 176
Luxembourg 8
Lytton, Earl of *103*

MacDonald, Ramsay 146, 153, 160
McDowell, J.B. 173
McGuire, Ada 176
McKenna, Reginald *152, 153*
Maclean, John 155
Macnamara, J.T. 45
Maisie's Marriage 95
Malins, Geoffrey 169, 173
Manchester 99
Manchester Guardian 11
Manpower Distribution Board 32
margarine 116, *120*
marriage 74, 86, 91, 93, 96, *157*
Marshall, Catherine 153
Marshall, Sons & Co *90*
Mary, Queen 124, 198, *211*
Masterman, Charles 165, *173*
Maternity and Child Welfare Act (1918) 126
Mather-Jackson, Lady 78
Matrimonial Causes Act (1923) 93
Maybole and District Shoe Manufacturers 58, *59*
meat rationing 120, *121, 123*, 140
Metropolitan Police 48, *49*, 70, *71–2*, 158, *190–1*
military losses 200–1, 206
Military Service Act 36, *156, 157*
milk 126, *127*
Million Egg Week 109
Monant, William *154, 155*
Monmouthshire Women's War Agricultural Committee 78, *79*
Monro, H.C. 39
Montgomery, R.A.K. *154, 155*
morality patrols 66–7, 94
Morel, Ed 153
mortality rates 74, 201
Moulton, Lord 25
munitions 18, 104–6; Belgian workers *30*, 63–4, *154, 155*; casualties 32, *33*, 88; personal experiences *62–4*; wages 62–3, 104–5, 141; women workers 29, 32, *81*, 95–6; workforce for *38*, 86, 95–6, 104–6; *see also specific sites*

Munitions, Ministry of 23, 24, 25; casualties 32, *33*; Health of Munitions Workers Committee 124; housing 126; morality patrols 67; poster for women workers *85*; production 28–9; women's wages 89
Munitions of War Act 24, 40
Muspratt, M. 25
mustard gas 32, *33*

Napier Motor Co Ltd *84*
national anthem 135
National Council of Public Morals 69, 99
national debt 110
National Filling Factory, Barnbow 88
National Food Economy League 94
National Kitchens 124, *124*
National Organising Committee for War Savings *131*
National Propaganda 208
National Registration Act 36
National Salvage Department *113*
National Service, Department of 23, 32
National Service, Ministry of 34
National Service Committee, Ministry of 50
National Service Scheme 32, 34
National Union of Women Workers 67, *68*
National Union of Women's Suffrage Societies (NUWSS) 94
National War Aims Committee 160, 165, 208
National War Bond Campaign *160, 161*
National War Savings Committee 114, *115*, 175
naval reserves memorandum *14*
Newcastle-upon-Tyne *187, 188–9*
Newman, Sir George 96, *124, 125–6*
newspapers 98, 163, 165
Nicholas II, Tsar 143
No Conscription Fellowship 153, 155, *157, 158, 159*
Nobel Explosives Company 32
Non Combatant Corps 155
Nonconformists 153
Northcliffe, Lord 98
Notification of Births Act (1907) 126

nurses 67, *70, 89, 109*
nutrition 117, 119, 210

Oliver, F.S. 15
Oxford University 166
Orphans *99*
Oxo *140*

Pacifism 153, 155, 158, 160
Pankhurst, Christabel *81*, 94
Pankhurst, Emmeline 80, 94
Pankhurst, Sylvia *81*, 96, 110,
    142–3, 146, 150, 178, 182
paper money 110
paper shortages 110, 112
Parker, Captain R. 40, *42*
Parker, Sir Gilbert *173*
Parliamentary Recruiting
    Committee *162*, 175
pay disputes 40, *42–3*, 158
Peace Day *200, 202, 211, 212, 214–15*
Peace Society 153
Pearson, E. 56
Pease, J.A. 153
Peel, Mrs C.S. 98, 134, 137
HMS *Pembroke 192, 193*
Peter Pan 135
petrol licensing 133
Phillips, W.H. 53
Pickford, Mary *137*
Playne, Caroline 8
plumbing *91*
Poland 207–8
Poole, Mrs Dorothy 104–5
Poor Law hospitals 66
Poppy Day 201
Portugal 206
poverty 110, 123, 142–3, 203
Press Bureau 165
Prevention and Relief of Distress
    in Fulham, London *139*
price rises 60, 110, *111*, 117, 210
prisoners of war *108*
promiscuity 86, 95–6
propaganda 83, 160, 162–3, 168–9,
    172, 173–5, *207*
prostitution 95, 100, *101–2*
Prussian Law of Siege 208
public transport 133
Punch 11, 131

Quakers 153
Queen Alexandra's Imperial
    Military Nursing Service 67, *109*
Queen Alexandra's Royal Naval
    Nursing Service *109*
Queen Mary's Army Auxiliary
    Corps 73

Queen Mary's Needlework Guild 66
Queen's Work for Women Fund 66

Racing 131, 133
railway carriage companies 29
Railway Executive Committee 23
railways 23, 204
Ramsay, James 58, *59*
ration card *123*, 139
rationing 16, 119, 120, *121*, 122–3,
    139, 210
Raven, V.L. *124, 125–6*
Reconstruction, Ministry of 23,
    138, 204
recruitment drives 16, *35, 162*, 175
recruits *11–12, 15*, 206, 213
Red Cross 108–9
Redmond, John 147
Rees, Tom 48
reformatory schools *103*
Regent's Park, London *11–12*
registration of births 126
religion 136, 166
rent controls 141
rent strikes 45, 126
Rents and Mortgage Interest (Rent
    Restriction) Act (1915) 126
Representation of the People Act
    (1918) 93
Requisitioning (Carriage of
    Foodstuffs) Committee 23
reserved occupations 34, 39
restaurants 98, 135
Restoration of Pre-War Practices
    Act (1919) 91
Rhondda, Lord 119, *120, 121*
Riesenflugzeuge 194
Roberts, Field Marshal Lord *130*
Roberts, Robert 119
Robey, George 135, *136*
Rowntree, Seebohm 123
Roxhall, A. *190–1*
Royal Air Force 186
Royal Arsenal, Woolwich 48, 86,
    125, 126, 182, *185*, 195–6
Royal Commission on Sugar
    Supplies 117
Royal Commission on Wheat 117, 119
Royal Flying Corps *84*
Royal Navy *179*
Royal Ordnance Factory 25
Russell, Bertrand 15, 155, 158
Russia 8, 23, 143, 163, 206, 210, 213

St Helens 130
salvage *113*
Sanderson Brothers and Newbould
    23, 59

saw smiths *23*
Scarborough 178, *179*
Scott, C.P. 11
Scott Duckers, James *158, 159*
Scottish Women's Hospital
    Organisation *70*
Scottish Zoological Park 135
Sedition Act 208
separation allowances 95, 110, 138
Serbia 8, 206, 207
Sex Disqualification (Removal) Act
    (1919) 93
shell production 24, 25, *26–7, 32, 33*
Shells and Fuses Agreement 39–40
Shipping, Ministry of 23
shipyard workers *18*, 40
shop-closing orders 128, *129*
Shoulder Arms 134
Silvertown 32, *34*, 88, 106, 144
Simon, Sir John 165
Singer Company *128*
Sinn Fein party 149
small-arms factories 32
Smuts, Jan 186
social changes 16, 94–6, 137, 203–4
socialism 146, 160
Socialist Party 158
socks 66
Somme, Battle of the 204; *see also*
    The Battle of the Somme
South Africa 186
South African War 169
South Wales Miners Federation 11
Special Branch 146
The Sphere 140
Spicer, Sir Albert *103*
spiritualism 136–7
spy scare 150
Squire, W.H. 53
state 19, 23, 48, 108, 112, 119–20,
    131, 141
State Children's Society 99, *103*
steel workers *59*
Stop the War Committee *158, 159*
Stopes, Marie 94, *95*
strikes 40, *42–3, 46–7*, 48, *49, 50,
    51–2, 53, 54–5*, 56, *57, 90*, 117,
    210–11
suffragette movement *81*, 94
sugar 117, 120
Swan Hunter and Wigham
    Richardson yard *18, 22*
Swinton, Ernest 164

Talbot, Miss 78
taxation 131, 135, 138
teetotal organizations 96, 97
temperance *131*

Territorial Force Nursing Service 67
Thetford's Town Crier *164*
Thomson, Sir Basil 146
Tibbenham, Frederick, Ltd *60, 61*
The Times 25, 77, 116
TNT 29, 86, 126
tobacco 98, 131
Toby jugs *163*
Tomb of the Unknown Warrior 201
tombola scheme *108*
Tong, Teddy 169, 173
Topical Committee of Film Manu-
    facturers' Association 168–9
Trade Card scheme 40, 48
trade unions 39, 48, 50–1, 53, 90
Trades Union Congress 51, 146
Transport, Ministry of 139
Transport and General Workers
    Union 53
transport workers 81, *85*, 86, *87*, 89
Treasury 23–4
Trevelyan, Charles 153
Trinity College, Dublin *166*
Triple Entente 8, 14
Turkey 198, 206, 213

Ulster Volunteer Force (UVF)
    147–9
unemployment 66, 80, 91
Unemployment Insurance Act
    (1920) 141
uniforms 67, 77, *78*
Union of Associations against
    Enemy Propaganda 208
Union of Democratic Control 153,
    158, 159
United Alkali Company 25, *26–7*
United States of America 206,
    208–9, 211, 212, 213
universities 166, *167*
University Boat Race 131
University College of Southampton
    166, *167*
Unlawful Associations Act 208
Upson, Frederick 192
Urban, Charles 169, 173, *173*

Vegetable growing 113, *118*
venereal disease 95
Versailles Treaty *208–9*
Victoria League 66
Victoria Memorial *214–15*
Voluntary Aid Detachments
    (VADs) 67, *82*

Wages 53; agricultural work 77,
    141; class 138; differentials 56,
    58, 89; gender *74, 84*, 89, 90, 105;

living costs 60; minimum 141;
    munitions 56, *57, 62–3*, 104–5,
    141; war bonuses 58, *59*; women
    74, 84
Wales 48, 133
war bonds *108*, 109, *137*, 160,
    161, 175
war bonuses 58, *59*
War Book 16
War Cabinet Committee on
    Manpower 34, 36
war cemeteries 201
war exhibitions 135
War Food Office 209
war industries 29, 56, 137, 208–9
War Office 24, 25, 28, 32
war orphans *99*
War Precautions Act 208
War Propaganda Bureau 165, *173*
War Refugees Committee *184*
War Service 143
war welfare 110, 123–4, 146
Wardle, George 160
Warneford, Rex 187
Weighall, Mrs *118, 119*
welfare provision 108, 123–4, 126,
    128, 139, 210–11
welfare state 110, 204, 211
Westminster, Archbishop of 110
wheat 112–13, *116*
Wheeldon, Alice 155
White City explosion 106
white feather campaign 66, 94, *162*
White Ribbon Band 96, *97*
Wilhelm, Kaiser 198
Williams, Basil *166, 167*
Wilson, Woodrow 198, 212
Winnington-Ingram, A.F. 166
women: changes in role 66–7, 70,
    73–4; votes 93–4, 212
women workers 65, 81, 83, 87,
    211–12; aeroplanes *61, 84*;
    agriculture 75, *75, 77*; Army
    Council 70, 72; brewing industry
    92; Britannia Works *90*; class 73,
    86; clothes *83*, 144; coal wagons
    18–19; economic independence
    88–9; marriage 86, 91; munitions
    29, 32, *81, 88*, 95–6; plumbing
    91; post-war 204; poster *85*;
    professions 93; road mending
    41; trade unions 90; transport
    86, *87*; US 212; wages 56, *74, 84*,
    89, 90, 105
Women's Army Auxiliary Corps
    (WAAC) 73, 86, 95–6, 98
Women's County Committees 78
Women's Defence Relief Corps 75

Women's Emergency Corps 67
Women's Farm and Garden Union
    75
Women's Forest Corps 75, 77
Women's Institute 77
Women's International League for
    Peace and Freedom 153
Women's Land Army 75, 77, *77, 78,
    80*
Women's Legion 73, 75
women's movement 93–4
Women's National Land Service
    Corps 75
Women's Patrols Committee 67, 68
Women's Police Service 67, 70,
    71–2
Women's Right to Serve demonstra-
    tion 80
Women's Royal Auxiliary Air Force
    (WRAAF) 73
Women's Royal Naval Service
    (WRNS) *72, 73*
Women's Social and Political Union
    (WSPU) 94
Women's Suffrage Federation 146
Women's Volunteer Reserve 67
Women's War Agricultural
    Committee 75
Workers' Union journal 50
working conditions 19, 29, 32, *62*,
    86, 88–9, 104–6
working hours 53, 56, 104, *124*, 203
World War I: British involvement
    8, 11, 14, 18; causes 206; costs
    178, 199–201, 203; end of 198,
    204; military losses 200–1, 206;
    outbreak of 14, 15; public sup-
    port 160

Zeppelins *183*; air raids 178, 182,
    184, 185–6, 187, 188–9, 192;
    crashed 192

CVs AND INTERVIEWS MADE EASY

LAWPACK

About the author

Jill Dodds is a freelance writer on career and health issues, living in Northumberland with her husband and two sons. She previously worked for ten years at De Montfort University, Leicester, as a university careers adviser. There she worked with students and graduates from a range of courses and backgrounds, specialising in Law, Science, IT and Finance.

She has extensive experience of advising clients on CV creation and development and interview skills, in one-to-one advisory sessions and interactive groups. She is also a qualified and experienced user of psychometric tests.

Jill would like to mention that the example CVs in this book are based on the careers of real people, although all names, and personal and employment details have been changed. She also would like to thank all the friends and clients who generously shared their experiences with her, and so enabled her to make these example CVs realistic and to reflect a wide variety of occupations.

CVs and Interviews Made Easy
by Jill Dodds

© 2002 Law Pack Publishing Limited

LAW**PACK**

76-89 Alscot Road
London SE1 3AW
www.lawpack.co.uk
All rights reserved.

ISBN 1 902646 81 9

Exclusion of Liability and Disclaimer

Whilst every effort has been made to ensure that this book provides accurate and expert guidance, it is impossible to predict all the circumstances in which it may be used. Accordingly, the publisher, author, distributor and retailer shall not be liable to any person or entity with respect to any loss or damage caused or alleged to be caused directly or indirectly by what is contained in or omitted from this book.